Technological Change and Environmental Policy

NEW HORIZONS IN ENVIRONMENTAL ECONOMICS

Series Editors: Wallace E. Oates, *Professor of Economics, University of Maryland, College Park and University Fellow, Resources for the Future, USA and* Henk Folmer, *Professor of Research Methodology, Groningen University and Professor of General Economics, Wageningen University, The Netherlands*

This important series is designed to make a significant contribution to the development of the principles and practices of environmental economics. It includes both theoretical and empirical work. International in scope, it addresses issues of current and future concern in both East and West and in developed and developing countries.

The main purpose of the series is to create a forum for the publication of high quality work and to show how economic analysis can make a contribution to understanding and resolving the environmental problems confronting the world in the twenty-first century.

Recent titles in the series include:

The Impact of Climate Change on Regional Systems
A Comprehensive Analysis of California
Edited by Joel Smith and Robert Mendelsohn

Explorations in Environmental and Natural Resource Economics
Essays in Honor of Gardner M. Brown, Jr.
Edited by Robert Halvorsen and David Layton

Using Experimental Methods in Environmental and Resource Economics
Edited by John A. List

Economic Modelling of Climate Change and Energy Policies
Carlos de Miguel, Xavier Labandeira and Baltasar Manzano

The Economics of Global Environmental Change
International Cooperation for Sustainability
Edited by Mario Cogoy and Karl W. Steininger

Redesigning Environmental Valuation
Mixing Methods within Stated Preference Techniques
Neil A. Powe

Economic Valuation of River Systems
Edited by Fred J. Hitzhusen

Scarcity, Entitlements and the Economics of Water in Developing Countries
P.B. Anand

Technological Change and Environmental Policy
A Study of Depletion in the Oil and Gas Industry
Shunsuke Managi

Environmental Governance and Decentralisation
Edited by Albert Breton, Giorgio Brosio, Silvana Dalmazzone and Giovanna Garrone

Choice Experiments Informing Environmental Policy
Edited by Phoebe Koundouri and Ekin Birol

Technological Change and Environmental Policy

A Study of Depletion in the Oil and Gas Industry

Shunsuke Managi

Associate Professor, Faculty of Business Administration, Yokohama National University, Japan

NEW HORIZONS IN ENVIRONMENTAL ECONOMICS

Edward Elgar
Cheltenham, UK • Northampton, MA, USA

Published by
Edward Elgar Publishing Limited
Glensanda House
Montpellier Parade
Cheltenham
Glos GL50 1UA
UK

Edward Elgar Publishing, Inc.
William Pratt House
9 Dewey Court
Northampton
Massachusetts 01060
USA

A catalogue record for this book
is available from the British Library

Library of Congress Cataloguing in Publication Data

Managi, Shunsuke.
  Technological change and environmental policy : a study of depletion in the oil and gas industry / by Shunsuke Managi.
      p. cm. -- (New horizons in environmental economics series)
   Includes bibliographical references and indexes.
   1. Technological innovations--Environmental aspects. 2. Environmental policy--Economic aspects. 3. Petroleum industry and trade--Government policy. I. Title.
   HC79.T4M3473 2007
   333.8'2311--dc22

                                         2007012776

ISBN 978 1 84720 471 4

Printed and bound in Great Britain by MPG Books Ltd, Bodmin, Cornwall

To Keiko and my parents

Contents

Acknowledgements

I am extremely grateful to James Opaluch for his patience and his dedication to supporting my academic progress. I am indebted to him for his guidance and his sound advice. I thank Tomas Grigalunas, Di Jin, Hossein Farzin, Josef Görres, Kristiaan Kerstens, Akira Hibiki, Kozo Mayumi and Timothy Tyrell, who all provided insightful comments and invested themselves in my scholarly development.

It has been my pleasure to work with James Opaluch, Di Jin and Tomas Grigalunas. Chapters 2, 3, 4, 8 and 9 are a result in part from joint work with them. Appreciation is also due to participants in conferences, workshops and seminars: Advanced Workshop in Regulation and Competition, 22nd Annual Eastern Conference; American Petroleum Institute; International Association for Energy Economics North American Conference; North American Productivity Workshop; Institute of Operations Research and Management Science Annual Meeting; United States Environmental Protection Agency National Center for Environmental Research National Science Foundation Decision, Risk and Management Science Program Decision-Making and Valuation for Environmental Policy Workshop; World Congress of Environmental & Resource Economists; National Economic Research Associates; University of Arizona; University of New Mexico; and University of Rhode Island. This research was funded by the United States Environmental Protection Agency STAR grant program (Grant Number Grant Number R826610-01). The results and conclusions of this research do not necessary represent the views of the funding agencies.

Finally, gratitude and enormous thanks go to my wife, Keiko, and to my parents for their encouragement and support.

This monograph contains some revised versions of previously published papers. Permission to reproduce the materials published in the following papers was granted by Elsevier, Taylor & Francis Group, The MRE Foundation and The University of Wisconsin Press.

1. Managi, S., D. Jin. J.J, Opaluch and T.A. Grigalunas. 2004. 'Technological Change and Depletion in Offshore Oil and Gas.' *Journal of Environmental Economics and Management* 47 (2): 388–409.

2. Managi, S., D. Jin, J.J. Opaluch and T.A. Grigalunas. 2006. 'Stochastic Frontier Analysis of Total Factor Productivity in the Offshore Oil and Gas Industry.' *Ecological Economics* 60 (1): 204–15.

3. Managi, S., D. Jin, J.J. Opaluch and T.A. Grigalunas. 2005. 'Technological Change and Petroleum Exploration in the Gulf of Mexico.' *Energy Policy* 33 (5): 619–32.

4. Managi, S., D. Jin, J.J. Opaluch and T.A. Grigalunas. 2005. 'Environmental Regulations and Technological Change in the Offshore Oil and Gas Industry.' *Land Economics* 81 (2): 303–19.

5. Managi, S., D. Jin, J.J. Opaluch and T.A. Grigalunas. 2006. 'Alternative Innovation Indexes in the Offshore Oil and Gas Industry.' *Applied Economics Letters* 13 (10): 659–63.

6. Managi, S., D. Jin, J.J. Opaluch and T.A. Grigalunas. 2004. 'Forecasting Energy Supply and Pollution from the Offshore Oil and Gas Industry.' *Marine Resource Economics* 19 (3): 307–32.

1. Introduction

Economic growth has long been a central issue in economics. Adam Smith, for instance, attempted to determine the factors that led to the wealth of nations and concluded that low taxes, peace and a workable system of justice would lead to economic growth (Smith, 1776). Clearly, economic growth remains a central issue in modern economics. For example, as Lucas (1988) points out, 'once one starts to think about them [economic growth], it is hard to think about anything else'. However, little attention was given to the relationship between economic growth and the environment until recent decades. Rapid economic growth tends to be detrimental to the environment due to the greater use of natural resources and the higher level of emission of pollutants. Hence, the issue arises of a potential conflict between economic policies and environmental quality.

Economists are interested in technology for analyzing the cause of long-run economic growth over time. In the recent literature on economic growth and the environment, the environment's ability to absorb pollution has been added to the analysis (Brock and Taylor, 2006). However, the literature on economic growth and the environment mainly focuses on technological improvements on the production side. Thus, we may conclude that economic growth could continue without bound if the increase in productive capacity allowed for both consumption growth and improved environmental quality (Aghion and Howitt, 1998; Stokey, 1998).

The Brundtland report on *Our Common Future* (WCED, 1987) defines sustainable development as 'development that meets the needs of the present without compromising the ability of future generations to meet their own needs'. This definition is ambiguous and raises more questions than it answers (Heal, 2001). A more precise definition would, for example, require utility levels, resource stocks or total capital stocks including natural capital and human capital to be non-decreasing over time (Pezzey, 1992; Smulders, 2000; Asheim et al., 2001). Thus, sustainable paths would confront standard optimal solutions as formalized in the traditional theory of economic growth (Pezzey, 1997).

Endogenous growth theory has been used to analyse economic growth and the environment (for example, Aghion and Howitt, 1998; Stokey, 1998; Andreoni and Levinson, 2001; Xepapadeas, 2003; Brock and Taylor, 2006).

Stokey (1998) and Aghion and Howitt (1998, Chapter 5) obtain a set of necessary conditions under which it is optimal to sustain both economic growth and environment conservation. One of their conditions is that the engine of economic growth should be an industrial sector that does not cause environmental degradation.[1] An intuitive explanation is as follows. Along a sustainable growth path, optimal pollution regulations become stricter. This increases the environmental expenditure of the regulated industry, and thus lowers its net marginal productivity of capital. Economic growth ceases when this marginal productivity declines to the level of the discount rate of a representative household. However, if the economy is supported by a clean industry that is a growth engine, the regulated industry can maintain productivity at a higher rate than the discount rate by increasing input from the clean industry. As a result, the economy sustains growth on an optimal path accompanied by environmental conservation.

It is plausible to believe that long-term economic growth can be made sustainable by the accumulation of human capital and knowledge: factors that generally do not damage the environment. This scenario is very appealing to those who desire sustainable development. However, empirical analyses of findings concerning technological improvements are missing from the literature. For the study of growth and the environment, this book analyses the oil and gas industry by considering not only the importance of environmental pollution abatements, but also the importance of resource depletion.

Resource depletion is of critical importance for the maintenance of the world economy. Early studies from Malthus (1826) to the so-called Club of Rome report (Meadows et al., 1972) have argued that limited resources will, of necessity, constrain economic growth. Typically, the conclusions of these studies have been pessimistic with respect to the potential for continued growth, even in the near term, and have called for a reorientation of policy towards the development of a 'spaceship' economy (Boulding, 1966; Daly, 1991). More recent studies have concluded that the world production of critical resources such as petroleum will peak in the near future, followed by an inevitable decline (for example, Deffeyes, 2001).

However, these studies have been sharply criticized for understating the potential for technological change to offset resource depletion (for example, Cole et al., 1975). These critiques have argued that, at least in principle, the exponential growth of knowledge could provide a basis for continued technological innovation that offsets resource depletion and thereby fuels continued growth for an indefinite period (for example, Stiglitz, 1974; Barbier, 1999). Proponents of this perspective have argued that the potential for technological progress to ameliorate resource scarcity is then an empirical issue.

There has been a long-standing debate concerning the direction of future oil and gas production. In a sense, we are always 'running out' of oil and gas. Because oil and gas are non-renewable resources within the relevant time horizon, each barrel produced brings us one step closer to ultimate resource depletion. As low-cost resources are depleted, new production must move to more remote, less productive, and hence more expensive, sources. Simultaneously, new technologies allow us to capitalize on reserves that were previously uneconomic to discover and extract. Thus, productivity with respect to nonrenewable resources is the net result of two opposing forces: the cumulative depletion of existing resource stocks[2] and technological change, providing access to new oil and gas resources, thereby augmenting the stock of economic resources.

Empirical evidence regarding resource scarcity must not only consider simple physical resource availability, but must also consider the net effects of resource depletion and technological change. Hence, thorough conceptual and empirical analyses of technological change are essential for identifying appropriate policy actions to be undertaken to mitigate the potentially negative effect of resource depletion.

This study models and measures technological change in offshore oil and gas production, and tests the hypothesis that technological change has succeeded in offsetting the depletion effects in offshore petroleum production which occurred between 1947 and 2002. In recent years, conceptual models and empirical measures of productivity change have progressed from 'confessions of ignorance' (for example, Arrow, 1962), where time plays the role of the principal explanatory variable of technological progress, to increasingly refined structural models (for example, Romer, 1990; Aghion and Howitt, 1992; Barro and Sala-i-Martin, 1995) and empirical methods (for example, Griliches, 1984; Färe et al., 1994b).

This book is organized as follows. Chapter 2 measures total factor productivity (TFP) in offshore oil and gas, including all categories of productivity change. In turn, these can be decomposed into technological change, or shifts in the production frontier, and efficiency change, or movement of inefficient production units relative to the frontier (for example, Färe et al., 1994a). The analysis decomposes TFP into its various constituents, thereby providing a more detailed understanding of the nature of productivity change using data envelopment analysis (DEA). These include innovations that focus on the creation of distinct new technologies, 'learning-by-doing' that considers incremental improvements with existing technologies, and diffusion that examines the adoption of new technologies.[3] I compare the relative impacts of these technology indicators on TFP in the industry. The relative sizes of these components can be important for the design of effective policy.

This study employs unique and extensive field-level data for offshore oil and gas production in the Gulf of Mexico and focuses on overall productivity in petroleum. The Gulf of Mexico was one of the first areas in the world to begin large-scale offshore oil and gas production. Since then, offshore operations in the Gulf of Mexico have played an important role in the production and stabilization of the energy supply in the US. In 2001, federal offshore oil and gas production accounted for 26 and 25 per cent of total US production, respectively (US Department of the Interior, 2001). The proportion of offshore domestic production has also been increasing over time. By 2005, oil and gas production in the Gulf of Mexico accounted for 95 and 99 per cent of total US offshore oil and gas production, respectively (US Department of the Interior, 2006).

Chapter 3 examines the impact of technological change on oil and gas exploration in the Gulf of Mexico from 1947 to 2002 using a unique micro-level data set. An index variable for technological change is constructed to capture both the number and significance of technological innovations in the offshore industry over the study period. Empirical models of exploration–discovery and drilling cost are used to assess the effect of technological change at both the field and the regional level. I then analyse the impact of technological change on the production frontier using stochastic frontier analysis.

Society faces important trade-offs between economic production and environmental quality in the design and implementation of environmental controls. In carrying out this task on behalf of the public, government agencies must evaluate the technical feasibility, economic viability and, in a broad sense, the social desirability of new regulations that define implicit or explicit trade-offs between environmental quality and production. Technological progress can then play a key role in resolving environmental problems. However, the extent of its contribution depends on how well environmental policies are designed and implemented. In other words, successful environmental policies can be judged by the extent to which they induce environmental technological innovation and diffusion (Kneese and Schultze, 1978; Jaffe et al., 2003).

Conventional wisdom suggests that environmental regulations impose significant costs on industry and impact adversely upon productivity (Palmer et al., 1995). Recently, studies have proposed an alternative hypothesis that environmental regulation can encourage innovation, potentially resulting in increased productivity with ultimately higher profits. This is the well-known Porter hypothesis (Porter, 1991; Porter and van der Linde, 1995). Some work has confirmed that, in principle, market failure associated with technological innovation (for example, Romer, 1990) can imply circumstances under which environmental regulations can benefit industry (Bovenberg and Smulders, 1996; Simpson and Bradford, 1996; Ulph, 1996; Xepapadeas and de Zeeuw,

1999; Mohr, 2002). Where these circumstances hold, carefully crafted environmental regulations can lead to solutions whereby efficiency is increased for both market and non-market outputs. However, there is a much broader class of problems where environmental regulations can potentially result in increased social efficiency in the joint production of market and non-market products. Here, any measured decrease in efficiency in only considering market outputs is made up for by the increased production of non-market environmental outputs.

Chapter 4 explores this more general class of problems using a unique micro-level data set for offshore oil production in the Gulf of Mexico. I recast the Porter hypothesis to calculate the productivity change in a joint production model using a vector of market and non-market outputs. I test for the causal relationships between technological change and environmental regulations and find weak support for the Porter hypothesis.

An important challenge faced in empirical tests of the Porter hypothesis is identifying the direction of causality between technological innovation and environmental regulations. New, tougher environmental regulations may spur R&D efforts, leading to innovation. However, at the same time, innovations in pollution control technologies will lead to federal agencies developing tougher environmental regulations that capitalize on these new technologies. For example, the US Environmental Protection Agency's (EPA) technology-based standards are based on concepts such as best conventional technology (BCT) or best available technology (BAT). These standards change over time as new technologies are developed and implemented. Because the causal relationships between regulation and innovation may go in either (or both) directions, it is important to identify the direction of causality between regulations and any advances in environmental technologies.

Although there is a significant contribution made by technologies to the offshore oil and gas industry, the extent to which each new exploration, development and production technology contributes to production and environmental efficiency (or productivity) increase is not known. Chapter 5 uses detailed data to explore the effects of new innovations by comparing their effects on the exploration, development, and production sectors.

Chapter 6 tests the hypothesis that there are increasing returns to the abatement of pollution using the environmental efficiency approach. This chapter analyses the resulting environmental efficiency and estimates regressions at the oil and gas field level with first-difference models.

There are two possible sources for the reduction of pollution and therefore the technological options available to reduce pollution. Emissions can be reduced by lowering output and/or by means of end-of-pipe treatments. The earlier term implies pollution-saving technological progress in the production process itself, which shifts downwards the emission coefficient. The innovations developed or discovered to reduce the amount of pollution generated per unit of output without changing production costs are included in this term. The latter term implies cost-saving technological progress in end-of-pipe treatments that shift the cost function downwards. Chapter 7 measures and compares the effectiveness of the two different factors.

Developing and assessing R&D policies plays an important role in developing technologies. Technologies and productivity play a critical role in determining long-term economic progress and are therefore an important policy concern. The objective of Chapter 8 is to test the alternative innovation indexes to understand better the appropriate proxy for innovation measurement.

Reliable baseline forecasts and responses to different policy actions of oil and gas production and pollution are critical for the formation of sound technology and environmental policy. The improved understanding of the role of technology and environmental policy in productivity changes will lead to improvements in decision making and the design of environmental regulations. Forecasts of production and pollution until 2050 are generated in Chapter 9 from a disaggregated model. In addition, the results of the disaggregated model are compared with an aggregated model. A detailed policy scenario study provides a quantitative assessment of the potential benefits, indicating the significance of the potential benefits of environmental policy that encourage innovation. Finally, all of the chapters' conclusions are presented as a summary of results.

NOTES

1. The engine for economic growth is an industrial sector whose product grows rapidly enough to support sustainable final goods production along an optimal path. Research and development (R&D) is a sector that causes Schumpeter's 'creative destruction' in Aghion and Howitt's (1998) models, referred to as 'exogenous technological progress' in Stokey (1998).
2. We define resource depletion broadly to include changes in resource quality (for example, field size and porosity) and location (for example, water depth).
3. To date, there is no empirical evidence that identifies the portion of technological change that can be attributed to innovation as against learning-by-doing.

2. Technological change and resource depletion

2.1 Introduction

The long-run path of production of a non-renewable resource is the net result of depletion and technological change. Offshore oil and gas operations take place in a much more difficult natural environment than onshore operations. In offshore oil and gas production depletion leads to a decline in resource availability, resulting in moving operations to more remote, deeper and smaller fields. Simultaneously, new technologies reduce the costs of discovering new fields, extracting more from existing fields and of extracting resources from previously uneconomic fields.

Thus, empirical assessments regarding resource scarcity need to consider more than physical resource availability. The effects of technological change must also be considered. Thorough conceptual and empirical analyses of technological change are essential in order to identify appropriate policy actions to mitigate potential negative effects of resource depletion.

From the late 1940s, offshore operations in the Gulf of Mexico expanded first along the coast in shallow waters, and then extended into deep waters. The continued development and production in the region has depended heavily on technological innovation. The principal focus of this chapter is to measure technological change and depletion effects in the US offshore oil and gas industry in the Gulf of Mexico using data from nearly 30 000 wells over the period from 1947 to 2002. I extend the past literature by focusing on micro-level data for measuring productivity change in outer continental shelf oil and gas production. Traditional aggregate approaches to modelling the supply of oil and gas have been criticized because aggregate data may obscure the effects of economic and policy variables on the pattern of exploratory and development activities (for example, Pindyck, 1978a). In contrast, modelling exploration and drilling at the micro level allows one to capture not only the petroleum engineering and geological characteristics of the petroleum supply process, but also the economic and policy incentives motivating producers to search for and develop petroleum resources.

This chapter introduces both aggregate and disaggregated measurements of total factor productivity (TFP). First, I develop an estimate of the growth in TFP in the industry at the regional level. Then I use a vintage model to examine the historical rate of technological change to see whether the technological progress has offset depletion over the study period. A mathematical programming technique called data envelopment analysis (DEA) is applied for computation (see, for example, Charnes et al., 1978; Färe et al., 1994a). DEA estimates the relative efficiency of production units, identifies best practice frontiers, and provides various measures of changes in productivity over time. My hybrid model decomposes net productivity change into separate effects associated with technological change and depletion. I further decompose technological change and depletion into various factors. This provides a better understanding of the relative roles of the different reinforcing and competing influences in productivity change. The decompositions may also help contribute to the design of policies that induce investment, information sharing, industry training and perhaps the timing and location of lease sales.

2.2   Background

Resource Depletion

Resource depletion is a critically important issue in maintaining the world economy. Early studies from Malthus (1826) to the so-called Club of Rome report (Meadows et al., 1972), have argued that limited resources will of necessity constrain economic growth. Typically, the conclusions of these studies have been pessimistic with respect to the potential for continued growth, even in the near term, and have called for a reorientation of economic policies towards development of a 'spaceship' economy (see Boulding, 1966; Daly, 1991).

However, these studies have been sharply criticized for understating the potential for technological change to offset resource depletion (for example, Cole, et al., 1975). Authors of these critiques have argued that, at least in principle, an exponential growth in knowledge could provide a basis for continued technological innovation that offsets resource depletion. This could fuel continued growth for an indefinite period (for example, Stiglitz, 1974; Barbier, 1999). Proponents of this latter perspective have also argued that the potential for technological progress to offset resource scarcity is an important, yet difficult, empirical issue. Related empirical studies using prices as indicators of resource scarcity have found mixed results. Some studies support diminishing resource scarcity (for example, Barnet and Morse, 1963), while others have found the evidence to be mixed or inconclusive (Slade, 1982; Berck and Roberts, 1996).

This research provides a focused analysis of issues related to the interaction of technological change and depletion by analysing production of offshore oil and gas in the Gulf of Mexico, the dominant United States area for offshore oil and gas production. This allows the analysis of micro-level data on production from individual wells, avoiding aggregation problems known to afflict traditional studies of technology–depletion interactions (for example, see the critique by Pindyck, 1978a). Of course, focusing on production of one energy resource within a single region involves trade-offs. In doing so, I necessarily ignore broader factors which can be important in determining whether technological change has overcome resource depletion at the macro level. For example, this study of offshore oil and gas production in the Gulf of Mexico cannot identify the extent to which new technologies allow industry to expand production to other regions (for example, the North Sea), or to create substitute energy supplies (for example, fuel cells). Thus, the micro level results are likely to understate the substitution possibilities in the larger world economy.

Overview of Gulf of Mexico Offshore Oil Development

The offshore oil and gas industry has played a significant role in energy supply in the United States. The Gulf of Mexico (GOM) was one of the first areas in the world to begin large-scale offshore oil and gas production. Since then, offshore operations in the GOM have played an important role in production and the stabilization of energy supply in the United States. In 2005, federal offshore oil and gas production accounted for 26 and 25 per cent of total US production, respectively (US Department of the Interior, 2006). Oil and gas production in the Gulf accounted for 95 and 99 per cent of the total US offshore production in 2005, respectively (US Department of the Interior, 2006).

A long-standing debate concerns the direction of future oil and gas production. In a sense, we are always 'running out' of oil and gas. Because oil and gas are non-renewable resources, each barrel produced brings us one step closer to ultimate resource depletion. As low-cost resources are depleted, new production must move to more expensive sources.[1] Simultaneously, new technologies allow us to capitalize on reserves which were previously uneconomic to discover and extract.[2] Thus, productivity with respect to non-renewable resources is the net result of two opposing forces: the cumulative depletion of existing resource stocks and technological change, which provides access to new oil and gas resources, thereby augmenting the stock of economic reserves.[3]

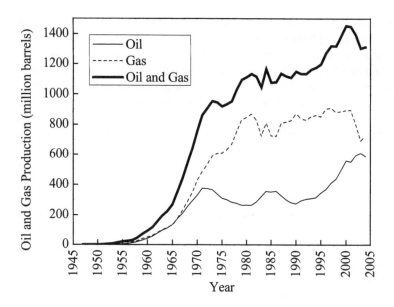

Figure 2.1   Historic production of offshore oil and gas in the Gulf of Mexico

The interplay between depletion and technological advance is well illustrated in the history of offshore operations in the Gulf of Mexico. Average field size of new discoveries declined almost monotonically from 1946 to 1999 from an average of about 240 million barrels per discovery to an average of less than 20 million barrels by 1999 (US Department of the Interior, 2006). Over the same period, average water depth for new discoveries increased almost monotonically from an average of less than 50 feet to an average of over 1000 feet in 1999 (Mineral Management Service, 2006). Taken alone, these statistics would suggest declining productivity, as production moves to smaller and more distant fields in deeper waters.

However, production in the Gulf of Mexico tells a different story, as shown in Figure 2.1 (US Department of Energy, 2006). Oil production increased rapidly from inception to about 1970. Production then generally declined from 1970 to 1990, except for a short peak in response to the oil shock years of the late 1970s to the early 1980s. By the late 1980s, the Gulf of Mexico was derided by some as 'the Dead Sea' as production declined, and extraction moved to fields that were more remote, deeper and smaller, and hence more costly to recover.

However, contrary to earlier predictions of declining production (for example, Walls, 1994), annual oil production has increased since 1990, reaching its highest historic levels in the year 2003.[4] These historic time trends reflect the interplay of depletion and technological change. But they provide limited insights into the various underlying factors because of a host of confounding factors and because of data aggregation. The DEA approach, described below, allows us to shed light on these issues by using micro-level data to construct productivity indexes for the time period from 1947 to 2002. The approach also enables us to decompose measures of productivity change into various constituents to understand better the nature and relative significance of technological advance and resource depletion in our application.

Technology in Offshore Oil and Gas Industry

Introductions to offshore technologies can be found in many studies (for example, Massachusetts Institute of Technology, 1973; Giuliano, 1981; Farrow et al., 1990; Bohi, 1997). A time line for major technological advancements in the offshore industry is shown in Table 2.1. Several recent technological innovations have had significant impacts on the offshore industry. Three-dimensional (3D) seismic technology became available in the mid-1980s and has been widely used since 1992 (US Department of the Interior, 1996). The higher-quality images from 3D seismology greatly improved the ability to locate new hydrocarbon deposits, to determine the characteristics of reservoirs for optimal development and to help determine the best approach for production from a reservoir. The new technology has substantially increased the success rate of both exploratory and development wells, which has led to reductions in the number of wells drilled for a deposit as well as in exploration and development cost.

Horizontal drilling technology has developed rapidly since the late 1980s. The technology involves a steerable downhole motor assembly and a 'measurement while drilling' package. With horizontal drilling technology, drillers are capable of guiding a drillstring that can deviate at all angles from the vertical. Thus, the wellbore intersects the reservoir from the side rather than from above (Lohrenz, 1991; US Department of Energy, 1993). Horizontal drilling has been widely used offshore to reach deposits far away from fixed platforms, thereby increasing access to distant reserves and lowering the cost of production. The time profile of horizontal drilling is shown in Figure 2.2 and reveals a marked increase in horizontal and directional drilling since 1973.[5]

Deep-water technology encompasses two production systems: tension leg platforms (TLPs) and subsea completions. TLPs float above the offshore field and are anchored to the sea floor by hollow steel tubes. TLPs have been used

Table 2.1   Time line for major technological achievements in the offshore industry

Technologies	Year
First offshore well drilled in Gulf of Mexico	1938
First OCS exploratory well drilled in Gulf of Mexico	1946
First offshore lease sale	1954
Production from water depths exceeding 100 feet	1955
First drill ship	1956
First subsea well drilled	1961
First offshore concrete gravity base structure (Beryl platform)	1975
First fixed platform installed beyond 1000 feet water depth	1979
First compliant guyed-tower platform in Gulf of Mexico	1983
Production from water depths of 2000 feet	1984
Deepest well drilled	1986
First horizontal wells drilled offshore	1991
3D seismic data acquisition widely used	1992
First sub-salt discoveries in Gulf of Mexico	1993
Producing well in GOM's deepest water	1996
GOM water-depth drilling record	1998
World's deepest water drilling and production platform located in the GOM	2000
World deepwater drilling record set at 9687 feet in the GOM	2001
World record water depth free-floating dry tree system	2002
New GOM gas flow rate record	2003

Source: US Department of the Interior, Minerals Management Service.

In several deep-water fields in the Gulf of Mexico. Although deep-water technologies are mostly used for offshore development and production, they provide a driving force for explorations in deep waters. Figure 2.3 depicts the average water depth of all exploration and development wells in each year over the study period. A dramatic rise in water depth started in 1985, resulting from innovations in deep-water technologies.

2.3   Measurements of Productivity Change

Conceptual Models

In recent decades, considerable progress has been made in advancing conceptual models and empirical measures of productivity change. The early models (for example, Solow, 1957), in which time plays the role of the principal 'explanatory' variable of technological progress, have been characterized as 'confessions of ignorance' (for example, Arrow, 1962). More recently, economists have developed increasingly refined structural models (for example, Romer, 1990; Aghion and Howitt, 1992; Barro and Sala-i-Martin, 1995) and empirical methods (for example, Griliches, 1984; Färe et al., 1994b). These advances have contributed greatly to our understanding of technological change. At the same time, the literature on resource scarcity has evolved from the use of broad aggregate measures towards increasingly structural models focusing on more specific issues (for example, Fagan, 1997; Cleveland and Kaufmann, 1997; Jin et al., 1998; Cuddington and Moss, 2001). This movement toward more micro-level research allows researchers to gain a more thorough understanding of the constituents of productivity change.

There has been a growing literature on technological change and petroleum exploration and development. In a study of natural gas exploration and discovery in the US's 48 states, Cleveland and Kaufmann (1997) found that depletion effects had outweighed technological improvements from 1943 to 1991. By contrast, Fagan (1997) found that technological change had offset resource depletion in her analysis of onshore and offshore oil discovery costs from 27 large US oil producers over the 1977–94 period. Cuddington and Moss (2001) have reached the same conclusion from their analysis of the cost of finding additional petroleum reserves (cost of exploration and development) from 1967 to 1990.

Jin et al. (1998) developed a framework for the estimation of total factor productivity (TFP) in the offshore oil and gas industry. Their model extends conventional TFP measurement by accounting for the effects of increasing water depth and declining field size. They applied the model using regional data in the Gulf of Mexico and developed preliminary estimates for TFP change from 1976 to 1995. The results suggest that productivity change in the offshore industry has been remarkable.

I also consider the effect of environmental regulations on regional-level productivity measurement (Barbera and McConnell, 1990). Detailed analysis using field-level data is provided in Chapter 4. Several studies have examined how the oil and gas industry responds to changes in environmental regulations. Kunce et al. (2004), for example, examine how the oil and gas

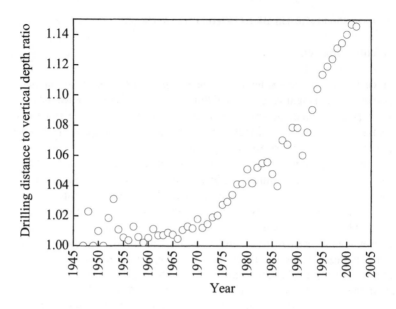

Figure 2.2　Horizontal and directional drilling

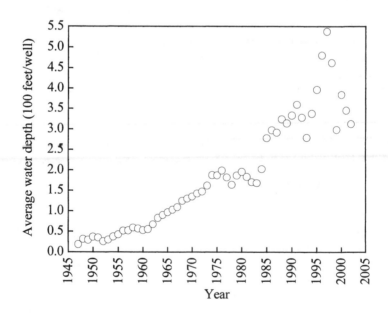

Figure 2.3　Average water depth of wells drilled in the Gulf of Mexico

industry responds to changes in environmental and land use regulations pertaining to drilling. A simulation model for Wyoming shows that drilling and future production are sensitive to changes in costs associated with environmental and land use regulations.

Since the 1970s, the offshore oil and gas industry has been subject to multiple environmental regulations. Under the Clean Water Act of 1972, the Environmental Protection Agency (EPA) first limited the disposal of free oil in drilling muds and issued effluent discharge standards based on existing technologies in 1975. Standards for toxic and non-conventional pollutants in effluent discharges and drilling muds were added in 1986, along with limits on oil and grease in produced water. In 1993, discharge standards were revised and expanded to cover: drilling fluids and cuttings; produced water; deck drainage; treatment, completion and workover fluids; and domestic and sanitary wastes for most of the OCS (outer continental shelf). These standards were extended to the Western Gulf of Mexico portion of the OCS in 1998–99.[6] In addition, under the Clean Air Act, the national ambient air quality standards first became applicable to most of the OCS in 1990. The standards became applicable to the Western Gulf of Mexico in 1993.

In the endogenous growth theory framework, technological change is decomposed into two categories: innovation and learning-by-doing (for example, Young, 1993).[7] Initially in the innovation literature, data on R&D were used as a proxy for innovation. R&D expenditure indicates the effort expended in the search for new technology, and so provides a measure of inputs to innovation, but R&D expenditure is not a good proxy for innovation (for example, Griliches, 1984). Many firms conduct R&D fruitlessly for years, and some innovative firms create major breakthroughs with little officially recorded R&D. The measurement issues are especially troublesome for analyses that capitalize on long time series of data, as the relationship between R&D expenditure and innovation may vary systematically over time. New innovations may take advantage of knowledge created in the past (Romer, 1990), implying an accelerating productivity of R&D expenditure over time. On the other hand, there may be an ultimate depletion of technological advances over time (Griliches, 1984), implying an S-shaped relationship between R&D expenditure and innovation. Either of these effects will impart a bias in R&D expenditure as a measure of technological change within a long time series of data.

As patent statistics became more rapidly available, patent counts were used as a closer approximation to innovation (for example, Schmookler, 1954; Griliches, 1984). However, patent statistics can be misleading, since many patents never see commercial application. Other innovations are not patented, and some are subdivided into multiple patents, each covering one or more aspects of the innovation. In response to these issues, refinements of patent counts use citations as a weight to the patent (see Hall et al., 2001). But changes in patent policies over time may again make patent counts a misleading measure of innovation, particularly over long time periods.

Moss (1993) and Cuddington and Moss (2001) construct a technology diffusion index that counts technology diffusion as it is reported in industry trade journals. The use of an innovation count represents a significant advance over R&D expenditure and patents. But a simple innovation count treats all innovations as having an equivalent impact on productivity. In fact, various new technologies have different levels of significance, and it is important that these differences are reflected in the computation of the technology index. A small number of major breakthroughs may have larger productivity effects than a larger number of incremental innovations. For example, during the 1990s, technologies such as the 3D seismic modelling have had some of the largest impacts on productivity and profitability (for example, Bohi, 1998).

I extend the innovation literature by capitalizing on the relative importance of specific innovations, as expressed by industry experts. An industry survey by the National Petroleum Council (NPC) analysed specific advances in each technology category and the expected level of impact of specific technological innovations, in both the short term and the long term (National Petroleum Council, 1995). The 89 companies who responded to the survey account for about 50 per cent of total US reserves. The survey identified and addressed nearly 250 individual technologies. Until 2006, the literature on technological change has not utilized these kinds of expert surveys. Further details regarding my methodology for incorporating the results of the NPC analysis are provided below.

Measures of Productivity Change: Aggregated Model

In the aggregate model, the cost function is examined to estimate the change in TFP in the offshore industry at the regional level following Denny et al. (1981) and Jin et al. (1998). Assuming that firms in the industry minimize cost, duality theory suggests that for any well-behaved production function, there exists a cost function that provides an equivalent description of the technology (for example, Fuss and McFadden, 1978). The conditional cost function is written as:

$$C = g(w_1, ..., w_n, Y_o, Y_g, D, S, E, Q, t) \tag{2.1}$$

where w_i ($i = 1,..., n$) is the price of factor input i, Y_o and Y_g are output quantities of oil and gas, D is the water depth, S is the field size, E is the effect of environmental regulation following Gollop and Roberts (1983), Q is pollution discharge (for example, produced water and oil spills) and t is time. The term 'conditional' is used to indicate that the cost is conditioned on a fixed set of attributes (for example, field size).

Generally, for a given technology, production cost is related inversely to stock size (Pindyck, 1978b) and positively to cumulative discovery (Livernois and Uhler, 1987). The average field size in a region decreases as cumulative discovery rises and it generally implies a decline in the stock size. In this study, we use the average field size (S) in the region to represent the stock factor and $\partial C/\partial S < 0$.

The offshore industry must develop new production technologies to accommodate increasing water depth as shallow water resources are depleted. Offshore oil and gas production at any given time is conditioned on certain marine geophysical and technical factors. We use average water depth (D) of all active fields at t in the region to represent the physical and technical factors of the industry. For a given technology, cost increases with water depth and therefore $\partial C/\partial D > 0$.

Offshore oil and gas exploration and production are subject to environmental regulations (Jin and Grigalunas, 1993a, 1993b; American Petroleum Institute, 1995). As noted, these regulations have been designed to control the discharge of drilling wastes and produced water. I use variable E to denote regulatory intensity (Gollop and Roberts, 1983) and, all else being equal, the cost increases with more stringent regulation, that is, $\partial C/\partial E > 0$.

Productivity measures should account for external effects (Barbera and McConnell, 1990). For example, a reduction in pollution from offshore oil could result in an increase in productivity of commercial fisheries. Thus, with all other inputs and outputs held fixed, a reduction (increase) in water pollution represents an increase (decrease) in productivity. I follow the usual convention in environmental economics of treating pollution emissions (Q) as an input to production (for example, Baumol and Oates, 1988; Cropper and Oates, 1992). Generally, $\partial C/\partial Q > 0$.

Following Jin et al. (1998), I define TFP as the shift in the cost function (g) in the study. Differentiating Equation (2.1) with respect to time (t) I obtain:

$$
\frac{\partial C}{\partial t} = \sum_i \frac{\partial g}{\partial w_i} \frac{dw_i}{dt} + \sum_j \frac{\partial g}{\partial Y_j} \frac{dY_j}{dt} + \frac{\partial g}{\partial D} \frac{dD}{dt} \\
+ \frac{\partial g}{\partial S} \frac{dS}{dt} + \frac{\partial g}{\partial E} \frac{dE}{dt} + \frac{\partial g}{\partial Q} \frac{dQ}{dt} + \frac{\partial g}{\partial t}
\tag{2.2}
$$

where $j = (o, g)$. Dividing through by C and applying Shephard's lemma ($\partial g/\partial w_i = X_i$) yields:

$$\frac{\dot{C}}{C} = \sum_i \frac{w_i X_i}{C} \frac{\dot{w}_i}{w_i} + \sum_j \varepsilon_{CY_j} \frac{\dot{Y}_j}{Y_j} + \varepsilon_{CD} \frac{\dot{D}}{D} + \varepsilon_{CS} \frac{\dot{S}}{S}$$
$$+ \varepsilon_{CE} \frac{\dot{E}}{E} - \varepsilon_{CQ} \frac{\dot{Q}}{Q} + \frac{1}{C} \frac{\partial g}{\partial t} \tag{2.3}$$

where ε is the cost (C) elasticity with respect to relevant explanatory variables. In deriving equation (2.3), I treat water depth (D), field size (S) and environmental regulation (E) as exogenous. However, pollution discharge (Q) is considered endogenous like other factor inputs.[8] Thus, there is a negative sign for the last term in equation (2.3).

Since $C = \sum_i w_i X_i$:

$$\sum_i \frac{w_i X_i}{C} \frac{\dot{w}_i}{w_i} - \frac{\dot{C}}{C} = -\sum_i \frac{w_i X_i}{C} \frac{\dot{X}_i}{X_i} \tag{2.4}$$

In the study, I define TFP as the shift in the cost function (g). Substituting Equation (2.4) into Equation (2.3) and rearranging, we gives an expression for the proportional rate of shift in the cost function $(1/C)(\partial g/\partial t)$:

$$-\frac{1}{C} \frac{\partial g}{\partial t} = \sum_j \varepsilon_{CY_j} \frac{\dot{Y}_j}{Y_j} - \sum_i \frac{w_i X_i}{C} \frac{\dot{X}_i}{X_i} + \varepsilon_{CD} \frac{\dot{D}}{D}$$
$$+ \varepsilon_{CS} \frac{\dot{S}}{S} + \varepsilon_{CE} \frac{\dot{E}}{E} - \varepsilon_{CQ} \frac{\dot{Q}}{Q} \tag{2.5}$$

Assuming that the firms in the offshore industry engage in marginal cost pricing ($\partial C/\partial Y_j = p_j$) and denoting $R = \sum_j p_j Y_j$, equation (2.5) becomes:

$$-\frac{1}{C} \frac{\partial g}{\partial t} = \sum_j \varepsilon_{CY_j} \sum_j \frac{p_j Y_j}{R} \frac{\dot{Y}_j}{Y_j} - \sum_i \frac{w_i X_i}{C} \frac{\dot{X}_i}{X_i} + \varepsilon_{CD} \frac{\dot{D}}{D}$$
$$+ \varepsilon_{CS} \frac{\dot{S}}{S} + \varepsilon_{CE} \frac{\dot{E}}{E} - \varepsilon_{CQ} \frac{\dot{Q}}{Q} \tag{2.6}$$

The conventional definition of proportional change in TFP (Jorgenson and Griliches, 1967) is:

$$\frac{\dot{A}}{A} = \sum_{j} \frac{p_j Y_j}{R} \frac{\dot{Y}_j}{Y_j} - \sum_{i} \frac{w_i X_i}{C} \frac{\dot{X}_i}{X_i} \qquad (2.7)$$

where $\dot{A}/A$ is the conventional definition of proportional change in TFP (Jorgenson and Griliches, 1967). Thus, if the cost function exhibits constant returns to scale ($\sum_j \varepsilon_{CY_j} = 1$) with respect to factor inputs, equation (2.8) can be rewritten as:

$$-\frac{1}{C} \frac{\partial g}{\partial t} = \frac{\dot{A}}{A} + \varepsilon_{CD} \frac{\dot{D}}{D} + \varepsilon_{CS} \frac{\dot{S}}{S} + \varepsilon_{CE} \frac{\dot{E}}{E} - \varepsilon_{CQ} \frac{\dot{Q}}{Q}. \qquad (2.8)$$

We know that the average water depth and the stringency of environmental regulations have been increasing while average field size has been decreasing over time. Since $\varepsilon_{CD} > 0$, $\varepsilon_{CS} < 0$, $\varepsilon_{CE} > 0$, and $\varepsilon_{CQ} > 0$, the second, third and fourth terms on the right-hand side of (2.8) are positive. If environmental discharge decreases over time, the last term is also positive. Equation (2.8) suggests that in the case of offshore oil and gas, the conventional measure of TFP change ($\dot{A}/A$) will underestimate the level of technological change by excluding the effects of water depth, field size and environmental regulations.

For empirical estimation, the Tornqvist approximation for $\dot{A}/A$ is:

$$\ln\left[\frac{A(t)}{A(t-1)}\right] = \frac{1}{2}\sum_{j}[s_{Y_j}(t) + s_{Y_j}(t-1)]\ln\left[\frac{Y_j(t)}{Y_j(t-1)}\right]$$

$$-\frac{1}{2}\sum_{i}[s_{X_i}(t) + s_{X_i}(t-1)]\ln\left[\frac{X_i(t)}{X_i(t-1)}\right]$$

with

$$s_{Y_j} = \frac{p_j Y_j}{\sum_j p_j Y_j}, \quad s_{X_i} = \frac{w_i X_i}{\sum_i w_i X_i} \qquad (2.9)$$

where t is discrete time (year), X_i is the quantity of factor input i (that is, wells and platforms), Y_j (j = oil or gas) is the quantity of output j, p_j is the output price of Y_j, and s_{X_i} and s_{Y_j} are cost and revenue shares. A general discussion of the standard method for growth accounting in its continuous time (Divisia index) form and in discrete time (Tornqvist) approximations can be found in Jorgenson and Griliches (1967), Christensen and Jorgenson (1995) and

Hulten (1986). A more detailed discussion of Tornqvist and other index numbers can be found in Diewert (1976, 1978, 1992) and Fisher (1922).

I develop estimates of TFP change at the regional level using equations (2.8) and (2.9). The approach has two major advantages. First, it captures the full effect in TFP change from offshore exploration, development and production in the entire region over a long period of time. Also, it involves only relatively simple computation.[9] However, the approach has its limitations. Most importantly, it is not possible to develop precise empirical TFP estimates using equation (2.9), since the elasticities (ε) cannot be accurately measured due to lack of relevant data. I will use sensitivity analysis to partially solve this problem.

Measures of Productivity Change: Disaggregated Model

Productivity analysis is well established. A properly constructed measure of productivity improvement is a useful indicator of how productivity gains contribute to improved economic welfare. However, traditional approaches, such as econometrics, growth accounting and index number methods, should be treated with caution since they have major limitations. For example: (1) all decision-making units are assumed to be efficient; (2) data on costs, input prices and output prices are required; (3) there is no distinction between technological change and changes in technical efficiency.

Following Caves et al. (1982a, 1982b), inefficiency in input usage or output production became crucial in measuring productivity change. I use the mathematical programming technique, DEA, to compute changes in productivity over time. A key advantage of this approach is that it provides a convenient way of describing multi-input, multi-output production technology without having to specify functional forms.

Malmquist indexes (for example, Malmquist, 1953; Caves et al., 1982a, 1982b) are commonly used to quantify productivity change, and can be decomposed into various constituents, as described below. Total factor productivity (TFP) includes all categories of productivity change. TFP can be decomposed into technological change, or shifts in the production frontier, and efficiency change, or movement of inefficient production units relative to the frontier (for example, Färe et al., 1994a). Malmquist total factor productivity is a specific output-based measure of TFP. It measures the TFP change between two data points by calculating the ratio of two associated output-oriented distance functions (for example, Caves et al., 1982a, 1982b; Fuss and McFadden, 1978). A key advantage of the distance function approach is that it provides a convenient way to describe a multi-input, multi-output production technology without the need to specify functional forms or behavioural objectives, such as cost minimization or profit maximization.

Thus, this approach allows for a very flexible characterization of productivity changes.

Malmquist's productivity index is widely used in many fields (for example, Färe et al., 1994b). However, the limitation of this productivity index is that one must choose to adopt either an output- or input-oriented approach in Shephardian distance functions. The choice depends on whether one assumes revenue maximization or cost minimization to represent the sample since the input-oriented measure has a dual in the cost-efficiency measure and the output-oriented measure has its dual in the revenue measure of efficiency (Färe and Primont, 1995).

The recently developed Luenberger productivity indicator was introduced by Chambers (1996) and Chambers and Pope (1996). The term 'indicator' is used for measures defined in terms of differences (Diewert, 2005). This indicator employs more general characterization technology, called proportional distance function, that is a dual to the profit function, and a generalization of Shephardian distance functions (Chambers et al., 1998). Thus, the methodology of using a Luenberger productivity indicator is more in line with the profit function framework. Note that it is also possible to define specialized input-oriented and output-oriented versions of the Luenberger productivity indicator compatible with the behavioural objectives of either cost minimization or revenue maximization, since the underlying proportional distance function can specialize to an input-oriented and output-oriented version.

The Luenberger productivity indicator, which is a non-parametric frontier technology approach to measure productivity, does not require that a choice be made between input and output orientations (Chambers, 1996). Since the Luenberger productivity indicator is consistent with both output- and input-oriented perspectives, it is a generalization of, and superior to, the Malmquist productivity index (Luenberger, 1992a, 1992b; Chambers et al., 1998; Boussemart et al., 2003).

I apply the Luenberger productivity indicator that employs a proportional distance function and allows for inefficiency in each decision-making unit. Using the proportional distance function specification, the problem can be formulated as follows. Let $\mathbf{x} = (x_1,...,x_M) \in \mathbf{R}^M_+$, $\mathbf{a} = (a_1,...,a_G) \in \mathbf{R}^G_+$, and $\mathbf{y} = (y_1,...,y_N) \in \mathbf{R}^N_+$ be the vectors of inputs, attributes and output, respectively. Then define the production possibilities set, $\mathbf{P}^t$, by:

$$\mathbf{P}^t \equiv \{(\mathbf{x}^t, \mathbf{a}^t, \mathbf{y}^t): (\mathbf{x}^t, \mathbf{a}^t) \text{ can produce } \mathbf{y}^t\}, \tag{2.10}$$

which is the set of all feasible production vectors. I assume that $\mathbf{P}^t$ satisfies standard axioms, which suffice to define meaningful output distance functions (see Shephard, 1970; Fuss and McFadden, 1978). The estimation of efficiency relative to production frontiers relies on the theory of distance or gauge functions. In economics, distance functions are related to the notion of the coefficient of resource utilization (Debreu, 1951) and to efficiency measures (Farrell, 1957). Luenberger (1992a, 1992b) generalizes the previous notion of distance functions as a shortage function and provides a flexible tool capable of taking account of both input contractions and output improvements when measuring efficiency. This shortage function, also known as a directional distance function, is the dual to the profit function (Luenberger, 1992b; Chambers et al., 1998).

I define the proportional distance function, which is a special case of the shortage function. Let ϕ be the scalar valued index that measures efficiency at time t, and the proportional distance function, $d^t(\mathbf{x}^t, \mathbf{a}^t, \mathbf{y}^t)$, is defined at t as:

$$d_o^t(\mathbf{x}^t, \mathbf{a}^t, \mathbf{y}^t) = (\max\{\phi : \left[(1-\phi)\mathbf{x}^t, (1-\phi)\mathbf{a}^t, (1+\phi)\ \mathbf{y}^t\right] \in \mathbf{P}^t\}) \quad (2.11)$$

where ϕ is the maximal proportional amount that the output vector, $\mathbf{y}^t$, can be expanded while remaining technologically feasible given the production set $\mathbf{P}^t$, the input vector $\mathbf{x}^t$, and the attribute vector $\mathbf{a}^t$. Note that $d_o^t(\mathbf{x}^t, \mathbf{a}^t, \mathbf{y}^t) \leq 0$ if and only if $(\mathbf{x}^t, \mathbf{a}^t, \mathbf{y}^t) \in \mathbf{P}^t$, and $d_o^t(\mathbf{x}^t, \mathbf{a}^t, \mathbf{y}^t) = 0$ if and only if $(\mathbf{x}^t, \mathbf{a}^t, \mathbf{y}^t)$ is on the boundary of the production frontier.

I use DEA to calculate output distance functions and to construct various productivity measures described below. DEA is a set of non-parametric mathematical programming techniques for estimating the relative efficiency of production units, and for identifying best practice frontiers.[10] DEA is a data-driven technique that constructs the production frontier by fitting piecewise linear segments to efficient observations. Efficiency of all units is measured relative to this best practice frontier. By applying this method over time, DEA measures shifts in the best practice frontiers (technological change) and changes in efficiency of units relative to the frontier (efficiency change).

Like the distance function, DEA can describe a multi-input, multi-output production technology without imposing any particular functional form, and DEA is not conditioned on the assumptions of optimizing behaviour on the part of each individual observation.[11] Avoiding these maintained hypotheses may be an advantage, particularly for micro-level analyses that extend over a long time series with significant uncertainty, irreversibility and fixed (and/or sunk) costs. In such cases, assumptions of static efficiency of every production unit in all time periods would likely be suspect.

When analysing productive efficiency for extraction of non-renewable resources such as in the petroleum industry, one faces challenges not met in typical applications to the single-period production of goods and services. For example, production from an oil field at some point in time depends upon cumulative past production from the field due to depletion effects, in addition to the technology employed and the attributes of the field (for example, field size, porosity, water depth).[12] Holding inputs constant, output from a given field follows a well-known pattern of an initially increasing output rate, obtaining a peak after some years of production, then following a long path of declining output (for example, Pindyck, 1978b). This implies that, for purposes of measuring changes in total factor productivity, it is inappropriate to compare contemporaneous levels of output from a newly producing field to a field that has been producing for ten years and to a field that has been producing for 55 years. Rather, comparisons across fields should be done holding constant the number of years the fields have been in operation.

Thus, productivity change is measured by looking at relative productivity across fields of different vintages. By doing so, I separate productivity effects associated with ageing of the field from effects due to differences in the state of technology. The DEA formulation with the vintage model differs from the conventional DEA formulation, such as that described in Färe et al. (1985). My DEA formulation calculates the distance function by solving the following optimization problem:

$$[d^i(\mathbf{x}^i_{k'j'}, \mathbf{a}^i_{k'j'}, \mathbf{y}^i_{k'j'} \mid VRS)]^{-1} = \max_{\phi^{k'j'}, \lambda} \phi^{k'j'}$$

subject to:

$$-(1+\phi^{k'j'})\ \mathbf{y}^i_{k'j'n} + \sum_{k \in K(i)} \sum_{j=0}^{J(k)} \lambda_{kj} \mathbf{y}^i_{kjn} \geq 0, \qquad n = 1,...,N,$$

$$(1-\phi^{k'j'})\ \mathbf{x}^i_{k'j'm} - \sum_{k \in K(i)} \sum_{j=0}^{J(k)} \lambda_{kj} \mathbf{x}^i_{kjm} \geq 0, \qquad m = 1,...,M,$$

$$(1-\phi^{k'j'})\ \mathbf{a}^i_{k'j'g} - \sum_{k \in K(i)} \sum_{j=0}^{J(k)} \lambda_{kj} \mathbf{a}^i_{kjg} \geq 0, \qquad g = 1,...,G, \qquad (2.12)$$

$$\sum_{k \in K(i)} \sum_{j=0}^{J(k)} \lambda_{kj} = 1,$$

$$\lambda_{kj} \geq 0, \quad k \in K(i), \quad j = 1,...,J(k).$$

where j is the field year, k is the field number, $K(i)$ includes all fields of vintage i (that is, discovered in year i), $J(k)$ is the final year of production for field k, λ_{kj} is the weight for field k at field year j, $\phi^{k'j'}$ is the efficiency index for field k' at field year j' and VRS stands for the variable returns to scale model.

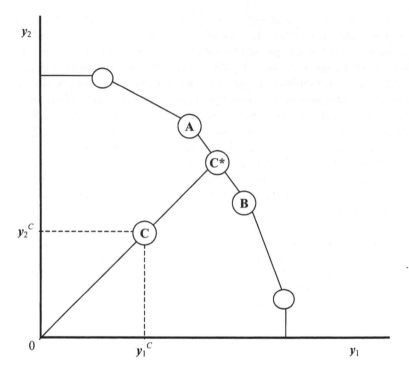

Figure 2.4   DEA efficiency frontier and inefficiency score

Figure 2.4 illustrates a two-output example of DEA.[13] The output vectors represented by points **A** and **B** are on the efficient frontier, so the associated distance functions equal 1. The feasible output vector **C** is not on the efficient frontier, and thus the distance function associated with observation **C** is less than 1. The value of the distance function for **C** is calculated by extending both outputs (y_1^C, y_2^C) by the scalar ϕ, which is increased until the associated projection reaches the efficiency frontier, illustrated by point **C***. Using the first set of constraints in equation (2.12), DEA determines **C*** as maximum radial expansion of **C** that does not exceed the linear combination of the adjacent efficient output vectors. Thus:

$$\mathbf{C^*} = \max_{\phi, \lambda_A \lambda_A} \phi\, \mathbf{C}$$

$$\text{s.t. } \phi\, \mathbf{C} \le \lambda_A \mathbf{A} + \lambda_B \mathbf{B}$$

which determines the maximum feasible value for ϕ. The final constraints in equation (2.12) require $\lambda_A, \lambda_B \le 1$ and $\lambda_A + \lambda_B = 1$, so that $\mathbf{C^*} = \phi\mathbf{C}$ is restricted to not exceed a linear combination of the adjacent efficient points. The distance function for **C** is calculated as $d(x^C, a^C, y^C) = 1/\phi = \overline{OC}/\overline{OC}* < 1$, where $\overline{OC}$ and $\overline{OC}*$ are the distances from the origin to the associated points in Figure 2.4. Note that value of 1 indicates an efficient frontier in this simple example. As the number of observations gets large, the piecewise linear production frontier approaches a smooth curve defined by the set of efficient observations. Thus, DEA does not specify a parametric form for the production technology.

My vintage model differs from the conventional DEA formulation, in that the mixed period distance functions compare fields of different vintages for a given field year. Thus, the model compares outputs and inputs for fields that have been operating for an equal number of years. In this study, t and $i \in$ [1947, 1995], and the output (**y**), input (**x**) and attribute (**a**) variables are listed in Table 2.2. Aside from the two depletion variables, attributes (for example, water depth) are constant across time for a given field. I use cumulative values for inputs (**x**) and outputs (**y**), because for the above technology definition, it is more appropriate to express the production relationship in cumulative terms for this non-renewable industry. For example, the production from a field at time t is determined by total number of wells drilled and cumulative stock depletion up to $t - 1$.

As for Luenberger productivity indicators, several proportional distance functions are needed to estimate the change in productivity over time. The Luenberger productivity indicator, TFP(L), defined by Chambers (1996), Chambers et al. (1996) and Chambers (2002), can be decomposed into two components as follows:

$$
\begin{aligned}
TFP = &\left[d^i(\mathbf{x}_{k'j'}^i, \mathbf{a}_{k'j'}^i, \mathbf{y}_{k'j'}^i \mid VRS) - d^{i+1}(\mathbf{x}_{k'j'}^{i+1}, \mathbf{a}_{k'j'}^{i+1}, \mathbf{y}_{k'j'}^{i+1} \mid VRS) \right] \\
&\frac{1}{2}\left\{ \begin{array}{l} \left(d^{i+1}(\mathbf{x}_{k'j'}^{i+1}, \mathbf{a}_{k'j'}^{i+1}, \mathbf{y}_{k'j'}^{i+1} \mid VRS) - d^i(\mathbf{x}_{k'j'}^{i+1}, \mathbf{a}_{k'j'}^{i+1}, \mathbf{y}_{k'j'}^{i+1} \mid VRS) \right) \\ + \left(d^{i+1}(\mathbf{x}_{k'j'}^i, \mathbf{a}_{k'j'}^i, \mathbf{y}_{k'j'}^i \mid VRS) - d^i(\mathbf{x}_{k'j'}^i, \mathbf{a}_{k'j'}^i, \mathbf{y}_{k'j'}^i \mid VRS) \right) \end{array} \right\}
\end{aligned}
$$

where the first difference represents efficiency change (EC) and the second term, which is an arithmetic mean two differences, represents technological change (TC).

Decomposition of Productivity Indexes in Disaggregated Model

This section discusses decompositions undertaken in order to improve our understanding of various constituents of technological change and depletion. I use the more general variable returns to scale (VRS) model, except in calculating the input and output biases in technological change, which

Table 2.2   Model specifications

Index calculated	Model 1 Base Model: Net TFP	Model 2 Gross TFP	Model 3 Innovation LBD & Diffusion	Model 4 Depletion: Field Size	Model 5 Depletion: Water Depth
Output variables					
Oil production (bbl)	X	X	X	X	X
Gas production (Mcf)	X	X	X	X	X
Input variables					
Number of platforms	X	X	X	X	X
Ave. platform size (#slot / #platform)	X	X	X	X	X
Number of exploration wells	X	X	X	X	X
Number of development wells	X	X	X	X	X
Average drilling distance for exploratory wells	X	X	X	X	X
Average drilling distance for development wells	X	X	X	X	X
Produced water	X	X	X	X	X
Weighted innovation index			X		
Horizontal & directional drilling (exploratory)			X		
Horizontal & directional drilling (development)			X		
Attribute variables					
Water depth		X	X	X	
Depletion effects (oil)		X	X	X	X
Depletion effects (gas)		X	X	X	X
Oil reserves in the field		X	X		X
Gas reserves in the field		X	X		X
Porosity (field type)		X	X	X	X

Table 2.3   Decompositions of the indexes

Index	Decomposition	Definition	Model number (Technology)
Net TFP	TFP_{Gross}	Gross TFP	1, 2
	Depletion (or $TFP_{Depletion}$)	Depletion Effect	(VRS)
TFP	TC	Technological change	2
	EC	Efficiency change	(VRS)
	SC	Scale change	
TC	IBTC	Input-biased TC	2
	OBTC	Output-biased TC	(CRS)
	MC	Magnitude component	
TC	TC_{Innov}	Innovation	2, 3
	TC_{LBD}	Learning-by-doing	(VRS)
EC	EC_{DIFF}	Diffusion	2, 3
	EC_{Resid}	Residual efficiency change	(VRS)
Depletion	Field size	Field size depletion	1, 2, 4, 5
	Water depth	Water depth depletion	(VRS)
	Residual	Residual depletion	

Note: VRS stands for variable returns to scale and CRS stands for constant returns to scale.

requires the constant returns to scale (CRS) assumption (see Table 2.3 for the summary of the decomposition and model used). Under VRS following the concept of Ray and Desli (1997), the Luenberger productivity indicator defined above is decomposed into measures associated with technological change, efficiency change and scale change:[14]

$$TFP_{VRS} = TC_{VRS} + EC_{VRS} + SC_{VRS} \qquad (2.13)$$

where TC_{VRS} is technological change under VRS, EC_{VRS} is efficiency change under VRS, and SC_{VRS} is scale change. Each of these measures is illustrated in Figure 2.5 for a simple one input, one output case. As discussed above, technological change measures shifts in the production frontier, and efficiency change measures changes in the position of a production unit relative to the frontier – so-called 'catching up' (Färe et al., 1994b). Scale change measures shifts in productivity due to changes in the scale of operations relative to the optimal scale.

As shown in Figure 2.5, the move from point *a* to *b* represents a change in efficiency, as a production unit moves from an inefficient point, to a point

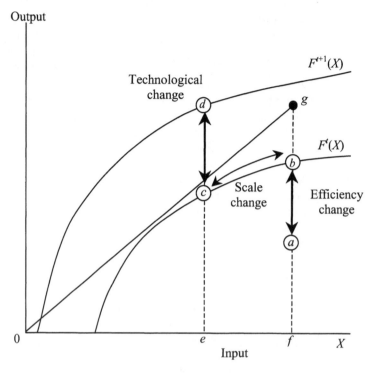

*Figure 2.5   Components of productivity change with variable returns to
          scale*

along the production frontier at time t, $F^t(X_t)$. The associated measure of
efficiency change is the ratio of the distances $\overline{fb}/\overline{fa}$, as illustrated in Figure
2.5. The movement from point b to point c represents scale change. A given
level of aggregate production can be produced most efficiently if all firms
produce at the optimal scale, where all scale economies are realized but
decreasing returns have not yet set in. This is the point where the line for CRS,
depicted by $\overline{0g}$ in Figure 2.5, is tangential to the VRS production function.
The associated measure of scale efficiency is the ratio of distances $\overline{fg}/\overline{fb}$.
Finally, technological change measures shifts in the production frontier. The
measure of technological change associated with a move from point c to point
d is the ratio of the distances, $\overline{ed}/\overline{ec}$.

The CRS measure of technological change can be further decomposed into
measures of input-biased technological change, output-biased technological
change and magnitude change.[15]

$$TC_{CRS} = IBTC_{CRS} + OBTC_{CRS} + MC_{CRS} \qquad (2.14)$$

where TC_{CRS} is technological change under CRS, $IBTC_{CRS}$ is input-biased technological change under CRS, $OBTC_{CRS}$ is output-biased technological change under CRS and MC_{CRS} is magnitude component under CRS, which is the measure of Hicks neutral technological change.[16] Thus, if the output- and input-biased measures of technological change are both equal to 1, then technological change is Hicks-neutral.

While DEA allows one to quantitatively measure technological change, its application does not directly alleviate the 'confession of ignorance' regarding the factors that constitute and shape technological change. One goal of the study is to measure various components of technological change, thereby illuminating the roles of various influences. For example, I provide the first empirical decomposition of productivity effects into those associated with specifically identifiable new technologies, as compared to less structural productivity effects, such as such as learning obtained through experience. Following the endogenous growth literature, I use the term 'learning-by-doing' as a general term encompassing these less structural productivity effects (for example, Young, 1993).

In order to identify the portion of technological change associated with innovation versus 'learning-by-doing', I construct an index of identifiable technological discoveries for our industry. In most empirical analyses, the effect of technological level is usually examined by including a time-trend or dummy variables in regression models.[17] I extend the Cuddington and Moss (2001) technology count using a measure of importance of the associated technologies. Moss (1993) and Cuddington and Moss (2001) construct a technology index based on counting specific technological diffusions in the exploration–development sector of the oil and gas industry (that is, the number of technological innovations adopted by the industry) from 1947 to 1990. For their index, Cuddington and Moss treat all innovations the same and do not differentiate technological innovations in terms of their impacts on productivity improvements in the industry. In this study, I construct an alternative technology index as follows. First, I extend the Moss (1993) index from 1991 to 2002. Specifically, we collect information from *Oil and Gas Journal* and *Hart's Petroleum Engineer International* (formerly *Petroleum Engineer International*) to construct my technology index following the methodology described by Moss (1993).[18] Examples of major innovations in the 1990s include 3D seismic data acquisition, and horizontal drilling. I apply this measure within a DEA framework to measure the impact of identifiable new technologies on productivity change, thereby contributing to a better understanding of nature of technological change for our application.

I use the results of the National Petroleum Council (NPC) industry survey used to identify the importance of various technological advances.[19] The NPC survey found the most important categories of technological advance were:

(1) more precise characterization of the resource; (2) better characterization of the reservoir, such as 3D geologic computer modelling for development; (3) well productivity and advanced fracturing techniques for drilling and completion; (4) simulation technologies for production; (5) multiphase pumps and workers for deep water offshore; (6) advances in improving the scientific basis for risk-based environmental assessment for environment.

I use the NPC survey as measure of the significance of different categories of technologies. To do so NPC technologies are allocated to 17 categories of innovations. Technology weights of short- and long-term significance from the NPC survey are then used to construct a weighted technology index. The cumulative weighted technology innovation index at time t is calculated as:

$$\text{technology}_t^W = \sum_{t=t_0}^{t} \sum_{i=1}^{I} w_{i,t} \times \text{technology}_{i,t}^{NW} \qquad (2.15)$$

where *technology*$_t^W$ is the cumulative weighted technology innovation index at time t; $w_{i,t}$ is the weight for technology in category i at time t; *technology*$_{i,t}^{NW}$ is the non-weighted technology innovation count adapted from Moss in category i at time t. As noted, N covers all exploration–development stage innovations. Figure 2.6 depicts annual growth (that is, Δ *technology*$_t^W$) in the weighted innovation index in the study period. The yearly growth in innovation reveals a rising trend, with marked increases in 1971, 1995 and 1996.

In constructing her index, Moss (1993) presumes that one can identify a specific year when an innovation takes place. Her approach has been questioned by Forbes and Zampelli (2002) for potentially serious misrepresentation of a technology's contribution. For example, there is probably not a single year when 3D seismic can be considered to have been innovated.[20] Our weighted index is an improvement over the original Moss index, since our weighting scheme allows the impact of each innovation to change over time. For example, our methodology provides a cumulative technology index, so that the weight for 3D seismic can increase over time to reflect factors such as continuing refinements or broader adoption, as reflected by expert judgement through the National Petroleum Council industry survey. The weighting scheme provides not only a better measure for technological diffusion but also a description of interactions among innovations.

Another important innovation of the recent decades is the extent of horizontal and directional drilling. This allows the well to intersect the reservoir from the side, rather from above, which can result in much more efficient extraction of resources from thin or partly depleted formations. Horizontal drilling is also advantagous for formations with certain types of

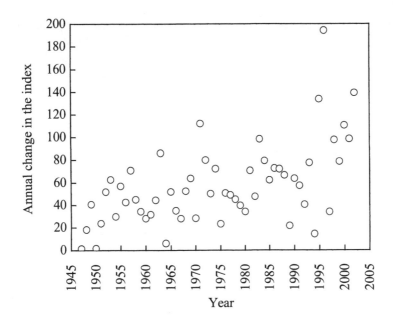

Figure 2.6   *Weighted technological innovation index for the offshore industry*

natural fractures, low permiability, a gap cap, bottom water, and for some layered formations (for details, see Selley, 1998). A measure of horizontal and directional drilling and the weighted innovation variable are used in the DEA framework to partition impacts of technological change.

I use several different versions of the model to decompose productivity changes (see Table 2.2 for a summary of the models, and Table 2.3 for a summary of the index decompositions). First, a base model, Model 1, is used to calculate net productivity change, which measures the net effect of increases in productivity due to improvements in production technology and declines in productivity due to depletion. A net technological change index greater than 1 implies that technological change offsets the depletion effects, while a net technological change index less than 1 implies that depletion dominates technological change.

Next I decompose net TFP change into decreases in productivity associated with resource depletion and increases in productivity after accounting for depletion effects:

$$TFP_{Net} = TFP_{Gross} + TFP_{Depletion}, \tag{2.16}$$

where TFP_{Net} is the measure of the net effect of increases in productivity (TFP_{Gross}) and decreases in productivity due to depletion ($TFP_{Depletion}$). To carry out this decomposition, the second model includes variables that measure resource depletion: measures of historic resource extraction from the Gulf of Mexico, water depth, porosity and field size. When these variables are treated as field attributes, DEA calculates productivity change after accounting for changes in productivity that can be 'explained' by these depletion variables. The DEA results with this model provide a gross measure of TFP change, which measures increases in productivity after accounting for depletion effects. The depletion effect is then calculated as:

$$TFP_{Depletion} = TFP_{Net} - TFP_{Gross}. \qquad (2.17)$$

Thus, subtracting the net measure of technological change from Model 1 by the gross measure of technological change from Model 2 provides the measure of the decline in productivity due to depletion.

Next I decompose the gross measure of technological change into indexes that represent specific technological innovations and a residual, which I generally term 'learning-by-doing'. Thus, the gross index of technological change is decomposed as:

$$TC_{Gross} = TC_{Innov} + TC_{LBD} \qquad (2.18)$$

where TC_{Gross} is the gross index of technological change; TC_{Innov} is the technological change associated with identifiable new technologies (the weighted innovation index and the measures of horizontal drilling); and TC_{LBD} is the index of residual technological change that cannot be explained by specifically identifiable new technologies.

This is accomplished by using the standard DEA decomposition of TFP change into technological change (TC), or shifts in the production frontier, and efficiency change (EC), or movements towards (or away from) the frontier. The TC component incorporates all forms of technological change. This is subtracted by TC calculated in Model 3, which includes the weighted technological innovation index discussed above and the measure of horizontal drilling treated as 'inputs'. Thus, applying DEA to Model 3 calculates an index of technological change after accounting for the effects that can be 'explained' by specific measurable technological innovations. So Model 3 measures shifts in the production frontier that cannot be accounted for by specific new innovations. This method permits an explanation of a portion of technological change associated with specific innovations, and narrows the 'confession of ignorance' to the residual effect. Thus, the fraction of TC associated with specific innovations is:

$$TC_{Innov} = TC_{Gross} - TC_{LBD} \tag{2.19}$$

In the same way, I calculate two efficiency change measures: efficiency change associated with identifiable new technological innovations (EC_{Innov}) and a residual efficiency change affect.

Next, I construct separate measures of the impacts on TFP over time due to reductions in field size and increases in water depth. Again following the methodology outlined above, including variable(s) associated with each effect in the DEA model calculates the residual productivity effects after accounting for changes in the variable(s). The effect of the relevant variable(s) is calculated by dividing the total TFP results by the residual TFP, from the model that includes the variable(s). Model 4 excludes variables that measure field size (initial oil and gas reserves in the field). So the effect of changes in field size over time is calculated by dividing the results of the Model 4 by the results of Model 2. Similarly, Model 5 excludes a variable measuring water depth of the field. So the effect on productivity of changes in water depth over time is calculated by dividing the results of the Model 5 by the results of Model 2.

2.4 Application of the Model

Data

The study region is the Gulf of Mexico. Offshore exploration–development–production data used in the analysis are obtained from the US Department of the Interior, Minerals Management Service (MMS), Gulf of Mexico OCS Regional Office. I measure and decompose productivity change over time in the offshore Gulf of Mexico oil and gas industry. Specifically, I develop my project database using five MMS data files:

1. Production data, including monthly oil, gas and produced water outputs from every well in the Gulf of Mexico over the period from 1947 to 2002. The monthly data include a total of 57 344 663 observations for 30 353 production wells.
2. Data describing drilling activity of each of 39 634 wells drilled from 1947 to 2002.
3. Platform data with information on each of 6412 platforms, including substructures, from 1947 to 2002.
4. Field reserve data including oil and gas reserve sizes and discovery year of each of 1043 fields from 1947 to 2002.

5. Reservoir-level porosity information from 1974 to 2002. This data
    includes a total of 17 021 porosity measurements from 421 fields.

Thus, the project database is comprised of well-level data for oil output,
gas output, produced water output and the quantity of fluid injected. The
database also has data on the number of exploration wells drilled, total
drilling distance for each exploration well, vertical depth of each exploration
well, number of development wells drilled, total drilling distance of each
development well, vertical distance of each development well, number of
platforms, total number of slots, total number of slots drilled, water depth, oil
reserves, gas reserves, original proved oil and gas combined reserves in BOE,
discovery year and porosity.[21]

Despite having well-level production data, the well level is not a good unit
for measuring technological efficiency due to spillover effects across wells
within a given field. Rather, the field level is a more appropriate unit for
measuring efficiency. For this reason, the relevant variables were extracted
from the MMS data files and merged by year and field, so that the final data
set was comprised of annual data from 1076 fields over a 55-year time
horizon. On average there are 370 fields operating in any particular year, and
a total of 20 836 observations.

Output variables in the model are annual oil production and gas production
from each field, while input variables include number of platforms, platform
size, number of development wells, number of exploration wells, average
distance drilled for exploratory wells, average distance drilled for
development wells and untreated produced water.[22] Field attributes are water
depth, initial oil reserves, initial gas reserves, field porosity and an aggregate
measure of resource depletion in the Gulf of Mexico.

To construct the Tornqvist input indexes (see equation (2.14)), I compile
costs associated with drilling and platforms (w_i). Offshore drilling cost data
from 1955 to 1996 were collected from various issues of the *Joint
Association Survey on Drilling Costs* (JAS) published by the American
Petroleum Institute. The JAS data were grouped into nine depth intervals in
each of the offshore areas in the Gulf of Mexico (for example, offshore
Louisiana and offshore Texas). My drilling data set has a total of 2221
observations. I used the *Engineering News Record* (ENR, 2000) Construction
Cost Index to covert costs in different years into 2000 dollars. The operating
costs for platforms in the Gulf are from the US Department of Energy's *Costs
and Indices for Domestic Oil and Gas Field Equipment and Production
Operations* (various issues from 1977 to 1996).

To improve precision, the regional-level input index is based on
disaggregate data. For drilling activities, I first calculate the regional total
number of wells by seven different drilling depth intervals, and then use the

corresponding average depth in each interval group to calculate the drilling cost per well for each group using a cost function estimated using the above drilling cost data. For platforms, I process the data in 12 groups by platform size (that is, slots) and water depth. The water depth (D) and field size (S) index are calculated as the weighted average water depth and field size across all producing fields for each year, and the weight for a field is the revenue share of that field.

Results: Aggregated Model

First, I attempt to measure the magnitude of the technological change in the offshore industry. As noted in equation (2.14), the computation of the Tornqvist indexes involves the costs (w_i) of relevant factor inputs (X_i). I have relatively complete cost data for drilling and platforms from 1976 to 1995. Thus, the TFP assessment is carried out for this period. Also, I include two factor input variables: the total number of exploratory and development wells, and the number of platforms. These two variables capture the bulk of exploration, development and production efforts. Costs associated with drilling and platforms are the two most significant cost components in the offshore industry.[23]

I first calculate the conventional TFP using equation (2.13). The results indicate that from 1976 to 1995, the average annual growth in output (that is, oil and gas) was 1.30 per cent, while the average growth in inputs (that is, wells and platforms) was 1.75 per cent. Thus, the conventional TFP, or net result of depletion and technological change, decreased on average 0.45 per cent per year in the study period. The result suggests that, at the aggregate regional level and in the entire exploration–development–production process, the effect of technological change was unable to offset completely the effect of resource depletion from 1976 to 1995.

Since the offshore oil and gas industry is a resource industry, it is necessary to make adjustments to the conventional TFP estimates (see equation (2.13)) with respect to resource conditions (for example, field size and water depth). I develop the adjustments as in equation (2.13). I first estimate the adjusted TFP change by accounting for the depletion effects. Over the 1976–95 study period and across all active fields in each year, average field size (S) declined at an average rate of 14.62 per cent per year, and average water depth (D) rose, on average, 0.62 per cent per year. As shown in equation (2.6), the impacts of these two indexes on TFP estimate depend on the corresponding cost elasticities (ε_{CS} and ε_{CD}). However, I am unable to develop estimates of these elasticities in the study for lack of relevant data. Instead, sensitivity analysis is used to explore the range of the adjusted TFP. In the sensitivity analysis, I vary both ε_{CS} and ε_{CD} from 0.4 to 1.2 (see the discussion in Jin et

Table 2.4   Average annual TFP growth (%), adjusted for water depth and field size

ε_{CD}					
0.4	5.64	8.56	11.48	14.41	17.33
0.6	5.76	8.68	11.61	14.53	17.45
0.8	5.88	8.81	11.73	14.65	17.58
1.0	6.01	8.93	11.85	14.78	17.70
1.2	6.13	9.05	11.98	14.90	17.82
ε_{CS}	0.4	0.6	0.8	1.0	1.2

Note: ε_{CS} is the cost elasticity with respect to field size, and ε_{CD} is the cost elasticity with respect to water depth.

al., 1998). The results of average annual TFP growth adjusted for field size and water depth are presented in Table 2.4.

The adjusted average annual TFP growth ranges from 5.64 per cent to 17.82 per cent, depending on the values of the cost elasticities. Generally, if the cost elasticities are larger, the corresponding TFP growth estimates will be higher. Although I cannot develop a point estimate, the results clearly show that true TFP growth in the offshore industry is significantly higher, when the effects of field size and water depth are accounted for (using equation (2.13)), than conventional measurement.

During the study period, the environmental regulatory intensity index (E) rose, on average, 6.27 per cent per year and the pollution discharge index (Q) declined at an average rate of 11.56 per cent per year. Again, since I do not have the necessary data to estimate relevant cost elasticities (ε_{CE} and ε_{CQ}), I employ sensitivity analysis to examine a wide range of possible values (0.01 – 0.1). Table 2.5 summarizes the resulting estimates of average annual TFP growth, adjusted for water depth, field size, stringency of environmental regulations and pollution discharges (oil spills and produced waters). In the calculation, I set the cost elasticities for both water depth (ε_{CD}) and field size (ε_{CS}) at 0.8 (for example, Fagan, 1997; Jin et al., 1998).

As shown in Table 2.5, accounting for stringency of environmental regulations and pollution discharge leads to even greater adjusted TFP growth estimates. In the base case, the adjusted TFP growth is 11.73 per cent (see Table 2.4 with $\varepsilon_{CD} = \varepsilon_{CS} = 0.8$) and the fully adjusted TFP growth ranges from 16.03 per cent to 54.70 per cent as the value of the cost elasticities (ε_{CE} and ε_{CQ}) vary from 0.01 to 0.1. The results further enhance my findings and clearly show that the true TFP growth, accounting for water depth, field size, environmental regulation and pollution discharge, is well above the conventional measure. The pace of productivity improvement in the offshore

Table 2.5   *Average annual TFP percentage growth, adjusted for water*
depth, field size, environmental regulation, and pollution
discharge

ε_{CE} ε_{CQ}	0.01	0.02	0.03	0.04	0.05	0.06	0.07	0.08	0.09	0.10
0.01	16.03	16.09	16.16	16.23	16.30	16.37	16.44	16.50	16.57	16.64
0.02	20.25	20.32	20.39	20.46	20.53	20.60	20.66	20.73	20.80	20.87
0.03	24.48	24.55	24.62	24.69	24.76	24.82	24.89	24.96	25.03	25.10
0.04	28.71	28.78	28.85	28.92	28.98	29.05	29.12	29.19	29.26	29.32
0.05	32.94	33.01	33.08	33.14	33.21	33.28	33.35	33.42	33.49	33.55
0.06	37.17	37.24	37.30	37.37	37.44	37.51	37.58	37.65	37.71	37.78
0.07	41.40	41.47	41.53	41.60	41.67	41.74	41.81	41.87	41.94	42.01
0.08	45.63	45.69	45.76	45.83	45.90	45.97	46.03	46.10	46.17	46.24
0.09	49.85	49.92	49.99	50.06	50.13	50.19	50.26	50.33	50.40	50.47
0.10	54.08	54.15	54.22	54.29	54.35	54.42	54.49	54.56	54.63	54.70

Note: ε_{CE} is the cost elasticity with respect to environmental regulatory intensity, and ε_{CQ} is the cost elasticity with respect to pollution discharge

oil and gas industry has been truly remarkable compared to standard productivity measurement.

Results: Disaggregated Model

The results for net TFP, gross TFP and depletion effects are presented in Figure 2.7. Net TFP declines by about 8.9 per cent from 1947 to 1970, or an arithmetic rate of about 0.41 per cent per year. Net TFP then remains approximately constant from 1970 to about 1982, decreasing by a total of about 0.5 per cent over the period, or about –0.03 per cent per year. Net TFP then increases by a total of over 17.4 per cent during the remainder of the time horizon, or an arithmetic average of about 0.79 per cent increase in net TFP per year for the last 22 years of the study period.

Overall, net TFP increases by about 7.99 per cent over the 55-year study period, with an arithmetic mean of about 0.15 per cent per year. To put this estimate into perspective, Färe et al. (1994b) use DEA to analyse the Malmquist output-oriented measure of productivity change in 17 OECD countries over the period 1979–88. They report an average annual growth rate of 0.85 per cent for the US and an overall average of 0.70 per cent for 17 countries. In comparison, I find productivity for offshore oil and gas (net TFP) increases at an average rate of 0.15 per cent per year. Since I estimate the Luenberger productivity indicator, I need to approximate my estimates to

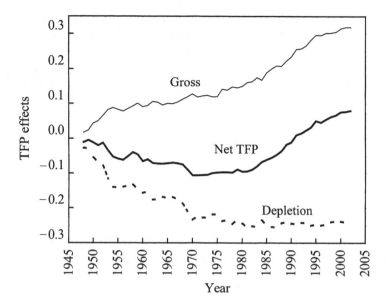

Figure 2.7   Net TFP, gross TFP and depletion

the Malmquist output-oriented measure of productivity following Boussemart et al. (2003). The approximate value is 0.30 in the oil and gas industry. Productivity growth in a non-renewable industry is expected to be lower than that for the economy as a whole due to the productivity-inhibiting effects of depletion. Correcting for the depletion effect, I find that gross productivity in offshore oil and gas (gross TFP) grows at a rate of 0.58 per cent per year. This is higher than the Färe et al. estimate for the economy as a whole, as expected, due to the fact that service industries tend to have low rates of productivity change (for example, van Biema, 1995), thereby reducing the productivity growth rate for the economy as a whole.

The pattern that I estimate for net TFP change is not monotonic. Rather, depletion effects initially outweigh the productivity-enhancing effects of new technology, but later in the study period technological advance overcomes depletion effects. This appears contrary to the commonly held notions of unidirectional (increasing or decreasing) changes in net productivity, or inverted U-shaped productivity curves (for example, Slade 1982), whereby technology temporarily prevails, eventually to be overwhelmed by physical depletion. However, the results are consistent with common reports of Gulf of Mexico production, as discussed above, with the Gulf of Mexico referred to as the 'Dead Sea' in the 1980s, and recent reports of technologies that have led to a rapid pace of productivity enhancement (for example, Bohi, 1998).

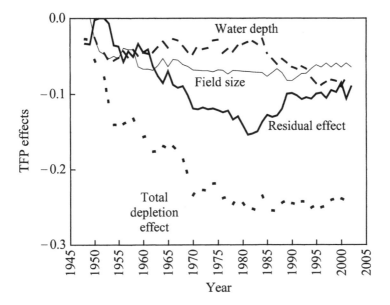

Figure 2.8   Decomposition of depletion effects

This should not, however, be taken as an indication that productivity will necessarily continue to follow this U-shaped curve of increasing productivity.Recent years have seen dramatic improvements in technology that have, to 2002, offset increasing physical resource scarcity. It remains to be seen, however, whether we can maintain this pace of increasing productivity in the near future, or whether recent productivity gains will subsequently be lost to depletion, as reserves in deep waters are depleted. Forecasting future trends is always dangerous, but it may not be realistic to expect to maintain indefinitely the current accelerating rate of technological change in offshore production technology.

Next I decompose depletion effects into those associated with field 'quality' measures, including field size, water depth, porosity and residual depletion effects (see Figure 2.8). Field size and water depth appear to have roughly comparable effects on productivity over the study period, but initially moving to smaller field size appears to have the larger effect, while water depth has a larger effect on productivity by the end of the study period. This has probably resulted because production has moved to very great water depths in recent years, with production occurring at over a mile deep by 1997 and exploratory wells being drilled in nearly 10 000 feet of water by 2001. Deep-water production has allowed the discovery of larger fields, with recent deep-water fields producing at higher rates than has ever been previously

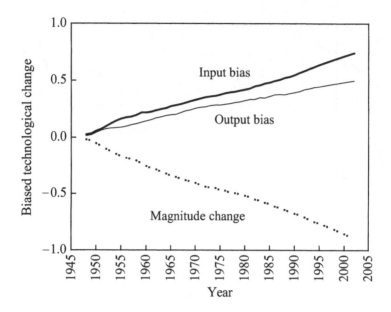

Figure 2.9   Biased technological change effects

achieved in the Gulf of Mexico. Indeed, by late 1999, more oil was produced by Gulf of Mexico deep-water fields, those in greater than 1000 feet of water, than by fields in less than 1000 feet (US Minerals Management Service, 2000a). Thus, moving production to large fields in ever-increasing depths has at least temporarily alleviated depletion effects associated with field size.

The results of technological change decomposition into output-biased technological change (OBTC), input-biased technological change (IBTC) and magnitude change (MC) are presented in Figure 2.9. The magnitude component equals the technological change under joint Hicks neutrality, when the input-biased and output-biased components are simultaneously equal to 1 (Färe and Grosskopf, 1996). My results show that input-biased technological change increases 49.9 and output-biased technological change increases 74.5 per cent, respectively. Therefore, the biased technological change index, which is the product of IBTC and OBTC, increases 124.4 per cent. This bias index is far from 1, which is not consistent with Hicks-neutral technological change. Therefore, we reject the assumption of Hicks-neutrality, and technological change is biased on both the input and output sides. The IBTC is somewhat larger than OBTC, reflecting more input-efficient use.[24] In contrast to the parametric measurement of bias (for example, Antle and Capalbo, 1988), DEA does not provide relative measures of bias, such as

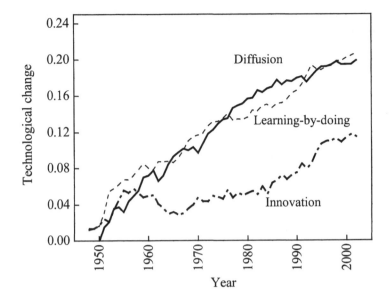

Figure 2.10   Innovation, learning-by-doing and diffusion

input using or saving with respect to each individual input. Instead DEA measures the overall extent of input and output biases.

Finally, TFP change in Gulf of Mexico OCS production is decomposed into innovation, learning-by-doing and diffusion using the weighted innovation index discussed above. Recall that I constructed a weighted technology index by extending the Moss innovation-count index using the NPC survey of importance of technological innovations. In addition, I incorporate a measure of the use of horizontal drilling technology, as discussed above. Using these innovation indexes as attributes accounts for the effects of specifically identifiable new technologies. The residual component of technological change is then interpreted as a measure of the non-structural component of technological change, which is generally termed 'learning-by-doing' effects.

Figure 2.10 shows the trends for innovation, learning-by-doing and diffusion over the period from 1947 to 2002. It shows that the learning-by-doing effect is approximately twice as large as the effect associated with specific new technological innovations. Over the 55-year study period, TFP change can be partitioned into 11.5 per cent due to innovations, 20.8 per cent due to learning-by-doing and 19.8 per cent due to diffusion. This implies that the contributions to TFP of learning-by-doing and diffusion are each approximately double the contribution of innovation. This in turn implies that although technological innovation is crucial for improving TFP, there are far more productivity gains from learning-by-doing and diffusion. This shows the importance of policies that focus on allowing flexibility in operations and that are not overly restrictive on the diffusion or adaptation of new technologies to other companies.

2.5 Conclusions

Over time, economists have greatly improved our understanding of the role of technological change in economic growth and of the constituents of technological change. We have progressed from 'confessions of ignorance' based on mere observations that productivity increases over time, to an increasingly sophisticated conceptual understanding of the mechanisms that drive technological change, and a vastly improved capability to measure various components of technological change.

This chapter contributes to this literature in several ways. First, I use a unique and extensive micro-level data set to provide a detailed analysis of productivity change at the production stage of offshore oil and gas. This contributes to our understanding of the extent to which technological progress has offset resource depletion in this important industry, and thereby the potential for technological change to fuel continued economic growth in the face of fixed stocks of non-renewable resources. The unique data set used also allows me to decompose productivity change into various constituents, which provides a more detailed understanding of the interplay of various factors that together comprise productivity change in this important industry.

My results show that increases in productivity have offset depletion effects in the Gulf of Mexico offshore oil and gas industry over the 55-year period from 1947 to 2002. However, the nature of the effect differs significantly from what is typically assumed for non-renewable resource industries. During the first 30 years of the time horizon, I found productivity declines in offshore oil and gas production. But in more recent years, productivity increased rapidly, offsetting depletion effects. Productivity change has been highest in the past ten years, indicating that we may still be along the increasing portion of a hypothetical S-shaped technological time path. I am mindful, however, that extrapolating trends into the future is risky, especially over longer time periods. It could well be that the pace of technological advance could slow in the near future, and depletion effects could lead to declines in productivity in this important non-renewable resource industry.

I decomposed depletion effects into effects associated with changes in field size, water depth, porosity and a residual that measures aggregate resource extraction in the Gulf of Mexico. I found that each of these effects is roughly similar in magnitude, and that interesting shifts occur over time. For example, initially field size appeared to be more important than water depth in explaining depletion. However, as new technologies allowed us to find larger fields by moving to ever deeper waters, water depth tended to have a stronger effect on reducing total factor productivity (TFP) than did field size. Again, it remains to be seen whether this trend will continue, or whether we will quickly deplete the stock of large, deep water fields.

I also analysed the contribution of technological change and efficiency change in sector TFP. I developed an index for decomposing technological change into that associated with specifically identifiable new technologies and a residual. The former is called 'technological innovation', and the latter 'learning-by-doing'. Similarly, I isolated technology diffusion from the residual factors that impact on efficiency change. I then compared the relative importance of technological innovation, learning-by-doing and technology diffusion on TFP in the industry.

The results indicate that both learning-by-doing and diffusion of technology had a significantly larger impact on TFP than technological innovation. This implies that although technological innovation is crucial for improving TFP, there is a larger productivity gain associated with learning-by-doing (for example, experience of engineers and mangers) and the diffusion of technology through the industry. This suggests the importance of developing policies that provide flexibility in implementing and adapting existing technologies.

Appendix: Missing Data Estimation

Complete data for porosity is available for only 390 fields out of 933 fields, with more data available in more recent years. I use a two-step estimation procedure to correct for censoring of observations (Heckman, 1979; Greene, 1981). Tables 2.A1 and 2.A2 contain estimation results from these regression models. In the first-stage results, probit is applied to determine the likelihood that a porosity measure is missing, and discovery year is the explanatory variable. Porosity is the dependent variable in the second stage, and the explanatory variables are oil reserves in the field, gas reserves in the field, water depth and the number of exploratory wells drilled in the first five years following discovery of the field. Results for the second stage indicate that higher porosity values tend to be found in larger reservoirs, in reservoirs in which more drilling occurs and in deeper-water fields (Table 2.A2).

Table 2.A1   Stage I probit estimates

Independent variable	Estimated coefficient	Standard error
Intercept	812.534 ***	65.744
Discovery year	–107.534 ***	8.574
Log likelihood	–564.56453	

Note: Dependent variable = 1 if porosity observed; 0 otherwise. *** Significant at the 1% level.

Table 2.A2   Stage II estimates

Dependent variable	Porosity	
Independent variable	Estimated coefficient	Standard error
Intercept	–134.66 *	68.865
ln(*oil reserve*)	0.55 *	0.354
ln(*gas reserve*)	2.41 ***	0.415
ln(*water depth*)	15.15 *	7.914
ln(*5Yr exp drill*)	1.05 ***	0.228
IMR	5.43 **	1.753
R^2	0.223	
Adj. R^2	0.212	

Notes:
The variable *5Yr exp drill* is cumulative drilling feet of exploration wells in the field for the first five years following discovery. 50% of total drilling is completed on average in 5.2 years, therefore I choose 5 years, based on the assumption that MMS has data for large fields.
IMR stands for Inverse Mills Ratio.
*** Significant at 1% level;** Significant at 5% level;* Significant at 10% level.

NOTES

1. When cost conditions are particularly simple, it is well known that it is optimal to extract the least-cost deposit first (see, for example, Schulze, 1974). Slade (1988) shows, however, that there are circumstances in which it is optimal to extract the least-cost deposit last in a partial equilibrium context. Her model analyses the case where marginal extraction cost rises with the rate of extraction from a given deposit. The effect of technological change is ignored in her model, and including technology may alter her results. This point is especially important since offshore oil is a technology-intensive industry, as described in the text.

2. Principal new technologies include deepwater technologies, three-dimensional (3D) seismology, advances in computer processing power, horizontal drilling methods and steerable drill head techniques. The increasing trend in production in recent years is primarily a consequence of these new technologies (US Department of the Interior, 2006). See Giuliano (1981) and Bohi (1998) for excellent reviews of technological advances in the industry.

3. Economic reserves are the proved mineral reserves in place and probable mineral reserves that can be profitably produced at a given price path over time. We define resource depletion broadly to include changes in field attributes that affect production costs (for example, field size, water depth and distance from existing infrastructure).

4. Note that Walls's analysis uses data from 1970 to 1988, with production predicted to decline monotonically over the forecast period from 1989 to 2000. In fact, oil production from federal OCS waters increased over that entire period, and oil production in federal OCS waters in the year 2000 was approximately two-thirds higher than in 1988.

5. In the figure, the level of horizontal drilling is measured as the ratio of total drilling distance to the corresponding vertical depth in each field. A higher ratio reflects a greater degree of horizontal and directional drilling.

6. Typically, EPA regulations have taken effect several years later in the Western Gulf of Mexico, where most US offshore oil and gas installations are concentrated, than in other areas of the OCS.

7. Young (1993) uses the term 'invention' rather than innovation. But his definition of invention is the same as the definition of innovation used here. This decomposition relates to the two models of technological change: innovation (for example, Romer, 1990), that focuses on the creation of distinct new technologies; and learning-by-doing (for example, Arrow, 1962; Alchain, 1963), that looks at incremental improvements with existing technologies. I provide a first empirical measure of the portion of technological change attributed to innovation versus learning-by-doing.

8. Similarly, Q may be viewed as an output with negative shadow price (that is, environmental damage).

9. By contrast, other methods such as DEA require much more intensive computation.

10. Note that parametric distance function could also be used. For example, Fuentes et al. (2001) apply a translog form specification for the estimation of distance functions.

11. Like all techniques, DEA has strengths and weakness. Since DEA is a data-driven technique, measurement error, missing variables and unmeasured quality differences can cause problems. Analogous problems exist for econometrics and other empirical techniques. Statistical hypothesis tests and confidence intervals are difficult to implement within DEA, and are the focus of ongoing research (see Simar and Wilson, 2000 for a review of recent developments). And large problems can be computationally intensive with DEA, since DEA creates a separate linear program for each decision-making unit.

12. Porosity is the percentage of the volume of the geologic structure that is made up of space between the individual granules. Thus, porosity determines the amount of oil that can be held by a fixed volume of rock, and a field with higher porosity will produce more efficiently, all else being equal. Complete data for porosity is available for only 390 fields out of 933 fields, with more data available in more recent years. I use a two-step estimation procedure to correct for censoring of observations (Heckman, 1979; Greene, 1981).

13. Note that for expository purposes, this simplified illustration considers two outputs, and ignores inputs and attributes. An actual application involves multiple outputs, inputs and attributes.

14. Ray and Desli (1997) argue that the TFP index is equivalent to the ratio of the CRS distance function even if the technology is not characterized by CRS. Productivity is a long-run problem, thus it is measured relative to the CRS technology. In other words, the TFP index under CRS equals the TFP index under VRS.

15. Standard measures of input and output biases of technological change can only be applied under constant returns for scale. Therefore, these calculations depart from the variable returns to scale measures used elsewhere in this chapter.

16. Hicks-neutral technological change can be represented as a parallel shift in isoquants, so that no inputs or outputs are favoured over others (for example, Hicks, 1932; Barro and Sala-i-Martin, 1995). The parameter measuring Hicks-neutral technological change is weakly separable from all inputs and outputs in the multi-product production function. In contrast, factor-biased technological change shifts the slopes of the isoquants and/or production frontiers, thereby affecting the relative marginal products of the inputs and/or outputs.
17. See Fagan (1997) for example.
18. This rule consists of four steps: (1) gathering information on relevant technologies; (2) sorting collected materials by category of technology; (3) compiling a chronology of technological developments for each category of technology; and (4) dating the technological innovations.
19. For example, innovation in horizontal drilling is considered more significant than innovation in depth mapping. Thus, horizontal drilling gets a higher weight than depth mapping. The weights are normalized to sum to 1.
20. In the Moss index, she considers 3D to have been innovated in the early 1980s when in fact only a small percentage of wells employed the technology at that time.
21. Oil and gas are combined using field-level thermal conversion factors when it is required. Description of these data files can be found at http://www.gomr.mms.gov.
22. I follow the usual convention in environmental economics of treating pollution emissions as an input to production (for example, Baumol and Oates 1988; Cropper and Oates 1992). Thus, a reduction (increase) in untreated produced water, with all other inputs and outputs held fixed, represents an increase (decrease) in productivity.
23. For example, for a large field (280 million barrels oil equivalent), drilling cost and production operating cost account for over 75 per cent of the total cost associated with the entire exploration, development and production process (Lewin and Associates, 1985).
24. This is consistent with the observation that fewer wells are drilled from a smaller number of large platforms, resulting from technological innovations such as 3D seismology, horizontal drilling and large deep-water platforms.

3. Econometric analysis of production and exploration

3.1 Introduction

Oil and gas production from a region is constrained by its economically producible reserves. As current reserves are depleted through production, new resource stocks must be located through exploration to replenish reserves. The amount of new resources discovered is affected by exploration effort, geological conditions, technology and cumulative discoveries in the region through the depletion effect. Despite the important role that technological change has played in the offshore exploration–discovery process after 1997, little research has been done on the long-term interaction of technological change and resource depletion in the offshore oil and gas industry. This is an important issue in that energy has an important role in the economy and estimates of future availability affect policy on leasing of public resources and also potentially affect international relations with energy-rich countries.

The purpose of this chapter is to examine the impact of technological change on petroleum production and exploration, using the Gulf of Mexico as a case-study. To maintain output over time, the industry depends heavily on technological improvements for exploration in deep waters and for significant cost reductions. Recent examples of major technological innovations include three-dimensional (3D) seismology, horizontal drilling and deep-water platforms (Bohi, 1997). These technologies have enabled firms in the offshore oil and gas industry to add economic reserves, to reduce discovery cost and to increase production as compared to a hypothetical constant-technology situation (as my later results demonstrate).

Since the pioneering work of Fisher (1964), a substantial literature on oil and gas exploration has emerged. In the 1970s, empirical analyses were mostly based on aggregate national or broad regional data.[1] Since the mid-1980s, a growing number of studies have used state-, regional- or firm-level data.[2] There are clear advantages to using micro-level data, since aggregation of data across distinctive geologic provinces may obscure the effects of economic and policy variables on the pattern of exploratory activities (for example, Pindyck, 1978a). Although the lack of data at the field level has been viewed as a major obstacle to carrying out disaggregated analysis, field-level behaviour has been considered too erratic to model successfully in empirical studies (Attanasi, 1979).

Geologic-engineering based techniques have been used to examine the exploration–discovery process (Arps and Roberts, 1958; Drew et al., 1982). A widely utilized approach involves the analysis of the quantity of oil and gas reserves discovered resulting from one unit of exploratory effort, or yield per unit of effort (YPE) (see Hubbert, 1967; Cleveland, 1992). The basic premise of YPE models is that the rate of discovery in an oil and gas region tends to decline as drilling proceeds. Cleveland and Kaufmann (1991) include economic factors in the geologic-engineering framework. They argue that the long-run path of YPE is the net result of two opposing forces: those that reduce costs, such as technological innovation, and those that increase costs, such as depletion. In their 1997 study, Cleveland and Kaufmann utilized cumulative drilling to capture the net effect of technological change and depletion, but they stressed the importance of including, in future research, separate variables to differentiate the two effects. With separate variables, the dynamic interactions between technological change and depletion in different years can be examined. By contrast, a single variable (for example, cumulative drilling) captures only the general trend of the net effect on YPE over the entire study period, obscuring the relative effects of technological advances and depletion.

Several recent studies have documented the significant effect of technological change on resource depletion in the offshore oil and gas industry. Using data from 27 large US oil producers between 1977 and 1994,[3] Fagan (1997) analysed the finding cost for crude oil in the offshore industry. She found that the cost increase associated with depletion was 12 per cent per annum, while the cost decrease associated with technological change was 18 per cent. Thus, the effect of technological change outweighed that of depletion over that period. Forbes and Zampelli (2000) examine the success rate in exploration in the Gulf of Mexico from 1978 to 1995 using data from 13 large producers.[4] They find that the small increase in the success rate from the early 1980s to 1995 was largely due to a substantial decline in price, as lower prices tend to discourage firms from pursuing less promising prospects. Before 1985, the net effect of technological change on depletion was very small. However, after 1985 technological progress resulted in an annual rate of 8.3 per cent growth in the success rate (Forbes and Zampelli, 2000).

Walls (1992) presents a comprehensive survey of studies on modelling and forecasting of petroleum supply. Her survey covers various geologic-engineering models and econometric models that describe the relationship between exploratory drilling and discovery. However, none of these models includes an explicit treatment of technological change. As a result, forecasts of future oil and gas supply from a region usually show a declining trend, which reflects only the effect of resource depletion (Walls, 1994).

In empirical analyses, a time trend has been widely used as a proxy for technological progress, since it is usually difficult to construct variables capturing the dynamics of technological change. In this chapter, I utilize the extended method of Cuddington and Moss (2001) by developing a weighted index for the technology diffusion index as explained in the previous chapter. Compared with Chapter 2, Chapter 1 focuses more on the development–production side and thus further analysis of the exploration–discovery side is required. Furthermore, in Chapter 2 it was found that the effect of technological progress dominated that of resource depletion in production from fields. Statistical relevance of results, however, is not provided. I examine different issues using alternative techniques.

In this chapter, I present the methodology, data and results of an analysis of the exploration–discovery–production process in the Gulf of Mexico, utilizing both field-level and regional-level data. Specifically, I examine the impact of technological change on exploration, discovery and production at the field level, on yield-per-effort at the regional level, and on drilling cost per well, using the technological change index and other relevant variables.

The study is important for several reasons. First, both the discovery function and the drilling cost function are key components in non-renewable resource exploration–extraction models (Pindyck, 1978b; Livernois and Uhler, 1987). Hence, improvements in the understanding of technological change in exploration and discovery will lead to improved modelling and forecasting of oil and gas supply. Since discoveries may be made at both the intensive margin (that is, within existing fields) and the extensive margin (that is, new fields), I test both field-level and regional-level models to understand the impacts of technological change on discovery. In addition, since technological change affects the discovery of additional reserves, the economically producable portion of existing reserves, and the resource rent, this study is important for the assessment of mineral reserves in the national income accounts (Adelman et al., 1991). I also examine the role that technological change in conjunction with environmental regulation has played in the offshore industry by analysing the effect of technological change on the production frontier. Finally, using data from 1947 to 2002, I provide what I believe to be the first statistical analysis of long-term interactions between technological change and resource depletion in the offshore industry.

The chapter is organized as follows. The offshore industry data used in the study are described in section 3.2. Then in section 3.3, production, discovery, drilling cost models and relevant discussions are presented. Section 3.4 contains a summary of my conclusions.

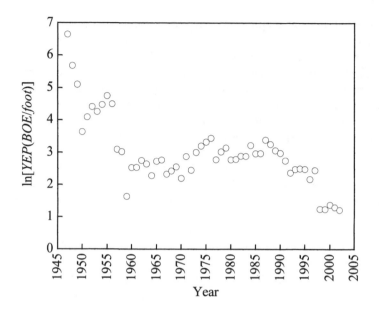

Figure 3.1   Yield-per-effort (YPE) in the Gulf of Mexico

3.2   Data

Field Exploration and Discovery

Data used in this analysis are obtained from the US Department of the Interior, Minerals Management Service (MMS), Gulf of Mexico OCS Regional Office. From the yearly reserve estimates, I calculate the quantities of original and subsequent discoveries in each field. In addition, merging relevant field-level data, annual oil and gas discoveries as well as resource stock depletion at the Gulf of Mexico regional level are constructed for regional-level analysis.

I calculated the amount of reserves discovered per unit of exploratory drilling effort (that is, yield-per-effort – YPE) in the region. The yield includes both oil and gas reserves in BOE. Figure 3.1 illustrates the time profile of YPE based on conservative field reserve growth estimates (that is, using half of the MMS growth factor value) from 1947 to 2002. Over the entire period, YPE exhibits a U-shaped trend, showing the net effect of resource depletion and technological change.

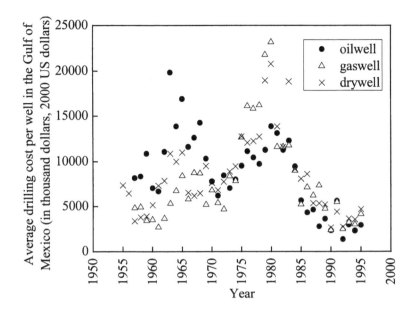

Figure 3.2   Average drilling cost per well in the Gulf of Mexico (2000 dollars)

Drilling Cost

Offshore drilling cost data from 1955 to 1996 are collected from various issues of the *Joint Association Survey on Drilling Costs* (JAS) published by the American Petroleum Institute. The JAS data are grouped into nine depth intervals in each of the offshore areas in the Gulf of Mexico (for example, offshore Louisiana and offshore Texas). The cost data set has a total of 1943 observations. I use the *Engineering News Record* (ENR, 2000) Construction Cost Index to convert costs in different years into 2000 dollars. I calculated the drilling cost per well and the average drilling distance in feet per well, including both exploratory and development wells. Figure 3.2 illustrates the average drilling cost per well for oil, gas and dry wells from 1955 to 1996. The cost declined from the early 1980s to mid 1990s.[5]

3.3   Models

Using the field-level data set, three sets of empirical models are developed to examine the impact of technological change on petroleum exploration in the Gulf of Mexico. The theory of non-renewable resources (see Pindyck, 1978b;

Livernois and Uhler, 1987) suggests that discovery of new reserves is affected by exploration effort (for example, drilling) which is in turn influenced by economic and technical factors, such as exploration cost (that is, drilling cost). Since resource discoveries may be made at both the intensive margin (that is, within existing fields) and the extensive margin (that is, new fields), I start with a field-level discovery model that describes how the initial and subsequent discoveries are affected by drilling effort and other factors within an individual field. I then analyse the long-term interaction between technological change and resource depletion at the regional level using a yield-per-effort (YPE) model. Finally, a drilling cost model for the Gulf of Mexico region is developed using the JAS data.

Field-Level Discovery Model

A number of regional-level discovery models have been developed in both theoretical and empirical analyses (Pindyck, 1978b; Livernois and Uhler, 1987; Walls, 1992). In addition to exploration effort, the amount of new resources discovered is affected by geological conditions, cumulative discoveries in the region (the depletion effect) and technology. This discovery function is a key component in nonrenewable resource exploration–extraction models, and it significantly affects future oil and gas supply.

It is important to note that while most regional-level discovery models combine discoveries at both the intensive and extensive margins, my field-level analysis focuses on the intensive margin only. The reason for this is that data are only available for fields that were actually discovered and leased, and not on tracts that were explored but not subsequently leased. My regional-level (YPE) analysis discussed below covers both intensive and extensive margins.

The field level discovery function is specified as:

$$discovery_{it} = f(technology_t, \ drill_{it}^{exp}, \ well_{it}, \ waterdepth_{it}, \ waterdepth_{it} \times year,$$

$$price_t, \ \sum_{t=1947}^{t-1} drill_{it}^{exp}, \ \sum_{t=1947}^{t-1} drill_{it}^{dev}, \ \sum_{t=1947}^{t-1} well_{it}, \ \sum_{t=1947}^{t-1} discovery_{it})$$

$$(3.1)$$

where *discovery* is the quantity of oil and gas reserves discovered in barrels of oil equivalent (BOE)[6], *technology* is the technological index for discovery, *drill*^{exp} is the average drilling distance (in feet) per exploratory well, *drill*^{dev} is the average drilling distance (in feet) per development well, *well* is the total number of exploratory and development wells, *waterdepth* is the water depth of a field in feet, *price* is the real price of oil and gas in 2000 dollars per

BOE,[7] *waterdepth* × *year* is the product of water depth and year, i is the field index and t is time (that is, *year*).

The expected sign for *technology* is positive, since technological innovations enable firms to locate new petroleum reserves. For each field, drilling effort is measured by both the number of wells drilled (*well*) and average distance drilled per well (*drill*^{exp} and *drill*^{dev}). In addition, I consider cumulative (*cdrill*^{exp}, *cdrill*^{dev} and *cwell*) drilling efforts. Although cumulative drilling may be used to capture depletion effect in an aggregate discovery model (see MacAvoy and Pindyck, 1973), I expect *cdrill*^{exp}, *cdrill*^{dev} and *cwell* to be positively associated with discovery in the field-level model. This is because the initial discovery of a field is usually a result of cumulative drillings at the site in previous years. Development drilling is included in the discovery model, since it also generates useful geological information, which leads to subsequent discoveries of new reservoirs in the same field or of adjacent fields. Positive signs are expected for these variables capturing drilling effort (that is, *drill*^{exp} and *well*; *cdrill*^{exp}, *cdrill*^{dev} and *cwell*).

As more resources are discovered in a field, subsequent discoveries in the same field become increasingly difficult, as fewer resources remain to be discovered. Thus, cumulative discovery reflects a depletion effect, and the expected sign on the associated variable (*cdiscovery*) is negative. The expected sign for *waterdepth* is positive, as exploring deeper waters will identify significant new finds. An interaction of *waterdepth* and *year* captures the changes in deep-water productivity over time. The sign of this interaction is uncertain. On the one hand, new technologies will increase productivity in deep waters over time. On the other hand, there will also be a depletion effect as deeper waters become more heavily explored over time.

No agreement exists in the literature on the effect of oil and gas price on the average productivity of resource discovery. Higher prices justify exploration in less promising areas and the development of smaller fields, so that higher prices could result in reduced average productivity. On the other hand, higher prices justify development of discoveries that are otherwise uneconomic, which would tend to increase measured productivity for exploration. Many previous studies[8] have utilized aggregate data to examine this issue. I extend these previous analyses by combining field-level data with aggregate data to explore the net effect of price on the efficiency of exploratory efforts.

Equation (3.1) is estimated as a two-way random effects model using my cross-section and time-series data. Since heteroscedasticity is present, the model uses White's heteroscedasticity adjusted standard errors. The result of the model estimates is presented in Table 3.1. The technology index (*technology*) is highly significant with a positive sign, clearly showing a strong impact of technological change on discovery at the intensive margin.

Table 3.1   Parameter estimates of field-level discovery model

Variable	Field-Level Discovery
Intercept	−25.6754
ln *technology*	6.5786***
	(15.13)
ln *drill^{exp}*	0.0623***
	(3.64)
ln *well*	0.4954***
	(5.33)
waterdepth	1.2864***
	(12.06)
waterdepth × year	0.6216***
	(12.02)
ln *price*	−3.2731***
	(−3.99)
ln *cdrill^{exp}*	0.0374**
	(1.98)
ln *cdrill^{dev}*	0.0477**
	(1.92)
ln *cwell*	0.1984*
	(1.78)
cdiscovery	−0.4743***
	(−166.74)
R^2	0.6692
Hausman statistics	204.74*

Notes:
* Significant at 10%, ** Significant at 5%, *** Significant at 1%. t statistics in parentheses.
I divided the term *waterdepth × year* by 1000 in estimation.

This is not surprising since innovations, such as horizontal drilling and 3D seismology, have drastically improved the efficiency of exploration.

The coefficients on *drill^{exp}*, *well*, *cdrill^{exp}*, *cdrill^{dev}* and *cwell* are all significant with expected positive signs. The coefficient for cumulative discovery (*cdiscovery*) is negative and highly significant, indicating the depletion effect. Both *waterdepth* and *waterdepth × ·year* are significant with positive signs, suggesting that more new oil and gas reserves can be found if firms move to deeper waters, and that productivity in deep water has been increasing over time. The sign for *price* is negative and significant, suggesting that on average there is a negative relationship between price and productivity of exploration efforts at the intensive margin.

YPE Model

To analyse the historical development of petroleum exploration and discovery in the Gulf of Mexico region, I use aggregate data from the region from 1947 to 2002 to examine the amount of reserves discovered per unit of drilling effort, a quantity called yield-per-effort (YPE) (see Hubbert 1967; Cleveland, 1992). I consider oil and gas resource discoveries in both new fields (that is, extensive margin) resulting from exploratory and development drilling and existing fields (that is, intensive margin) resulting from further exploratory drilling and development drilling. The long-run path of YPE is the net result of two opposing forces: technological change that reduces costs and depletion that increases costs (for example, Cleveland and Kaufmann, 1991). When measuring the technological change, one must isolate the effects of depletion and innovation. I use aggregated data to estimate YPE in order to test the hypothesis that technological change offsets depletion in the exploration sector in the Gulf of Mexico following Cleveland and Kaufman (1997).

Compared with onshore oil and gas operations, the offshore case is unique because water depth has played an important role in offshore exploration and discovery. In general, large fields were first discovered in shallow coastal waters and as the best prospects in shallow waters are depleted, new large fields can be found only in deeper waters. Following Cleveland and Kaufmann (1991, 1997), I specify my YPE model as:

$$YPE_t = YPE_0 \prod_i \exp(\beta_i x_{it}) \tag{3.2}$$

where *YPE* is the yield-per-effort in BOE per foot in exploratory drilling, t is time (that is, year), YPE_0 is the initial yield per effort, x_i is the i_{th} independent variable, and β_i the coefficient associated with x_i. In my analysis, I consider a number of independent variables. There are two variables capturing current drilling activities: number of exploratory wells (*well*), and average distance drilled per exploratory well (*drill*) in feet. I also use the technological index for discovery (*technology*) defined in equation (3.1) above. The expected sign of this variable is positive, since technological change leads to increases in YPE. The effect of resource depletion is measured by a depletion index (*depletion*), which captures the total resource discoveries to date. The depletion index is the cumulative proved reserves in each period (that is, cumulative production plus remaining proved reserves). As this index increases, the reserves remaining to be discovered decreases, which is associated with reductions in YPE.

Table 3.2   Parameter estimates of YPE model

Variable	YPE
Intercept	4.4043
technology	12.7823***
	(2.94)
depletion	−3.253***
	(2.94)
drill	0.6083***
	(4.65)
well	−0.3862**
	(−2.92)
waterdepth	0.3543***
	(3.68)
price	1.3975***
	(3.75)
θ_1	−1.1954***
	(−7.63)
θ_2	0.3512**
	(2.45)
R^2	0.8685
F-statistics	5.97*
Durbin-Watson	2.0321

Notes:
* Significant at 10%, ** Significant at 5%, *** Significant at 1%. t statistics are in parentheses.
Variable *year* = year − 1900

The use of separate variables measuring the combinations of technology and depletion has an advantage over the use of a single index based on cumulative exploratory drilling,[9] since it allows the decomposition of productivity change into separate effects for depletion and technological innovation. I also consider the effect of energy price (2000$/BOE) on YPE. The sign on price may be positive or negative. On the one hand, increases in price will reduce minimum economic field size, leading to a greater number of identified deposits that are economic to develop and produce. On the other hand, an increase in price will tend to encourage exploration, even at sites with lower potential, thereby reducing YPE. *Waterdepth* is the average water depth of all exploration wells at *t*. The expected signs for *waterdepth* is positive, since as water depth increases, the offshore area available for exploration expands to new frontier areas, which in turn, increases the number of undiscovered fields.

I take a double-log transformation of equation (3.2) for estimation using GLS correcting for second-degree autocorrelation of (that is, AR(2)). The result is summarized in Table 3.2. All of the coefficients are statistically significant. The signs of coefficients for *technology* and *depletion* are as expected. The positive sign on *price* is consistent with results in Cleveland and Kaufmann (1997) as well as in Forbes and Zampelli (2000). On average, there is a positive relationship between YPE and average drilling distance per well (*drill*). However, YPE is negatively related to the number of wells drilled (*well*), which likely reflects, in part, diminishing returns to increased drilling efforts holding other factors constant (for example, remaining reserves, technology).

One would expect the relative effects of technological change and resource depletion to vary over time during the study period from 1947 to 2002. Therefore, I examine the time profile of the interaction using results of two model estimates in Table 3.2. Figure 3.3 shows the impacts of technological change variable and depletion variable on the dependent variable (ln(*YPE*)). The two curves in Figure 3.3 represent the estimated effects of technological change and depletion from equation (3.2). The net effect of the two forces is depicted in Figure 3.4.

The curve in Figure 3.4 reveals a U-shaped trend. The net effect on YPE declined from 1947 to 1965, and then flattened until 1975 when it started to rise. These results indicate that during 1975 and 2002, technological change was significant enough to offset depletion, although the opposite was true during the first two decades in the study period. The technological change just offset depletion between 1995 and 1996 when the net effect equalled zero. My results are consistent with those of Fagan (1997) and Forbes and Zampelli (2000), both suggesting a more significant effect of technological change on the oil and gas industry in recent decades. The results are not consistent with those of Slade (1982) who analyses the prices of major metals and fuels. She concludes that the long-term movement of non-renewable resource price usually exhibits a U-shaped path that reflects the diminishing ability of technological change to overcome the effect of depletion. We find the opposite results in that technology was unable to outpace depletion at first, but was able to do so later.

In summary, the net effect of the technology and depletion on YPE showed a decreasing trend from 1947 to 1975. During that period, the effect of depletion dominated technological change, and YPE declined. With operations limited in shallow waters, YPE decreased since decline in resource quality (for example, field size) outweighed the effect of technological change. Since 1975, however, the pace of technological change has significantly increased. Several

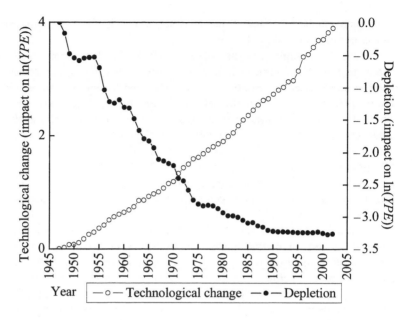

Figure 3.3   Technological change and depletion

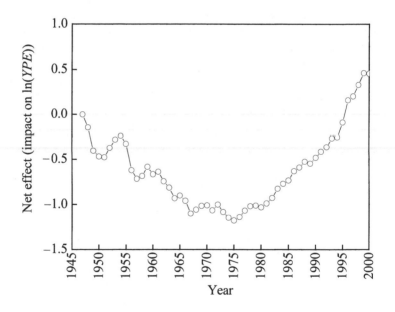

Figure 3.4   Net effect of technological change and depletion

key innovations in enabling technologies, such as platform and drilling technologies, have drastically expended the offshore areas for oil and gas exploration. In addition, digital seismic recording and analytical techniques have improved exploration efficiency. Since 1990, new technologies like horizontal drilling, 3D seismology, improved computer technologies and deep-water platforms have contributed to the rise in the net effect on YPE. As a result, the effect of technological change is able to compensate for the effect of resource depletion.

Drilling Cost Model

Drilling costs associated with exploratory and development wells account for a significant share in the total cost of offshore oil and gas operation (Lewin and Associates, 1985). Using JAS drilling cost data, Fisher (1964) analyses the cost structure in the US oil and gas industry and finds that drilling cost per well increases with drilling depth. The effect of technological change is examined by comparing regression coefficients in different years. Eddy and Kadane (1982) also examine the JAS drilling cost data, using a robust regression method. Their study is based on data from one year (that is, 1975). Norgaard and Leu (1986) use a time-trend variable and an interaction term of the time trend and drilling distance to account for technological change in their cost function. Their results show the impact of technological change on drilling cost in onshore oil operations from 1959 to 1978. They find that technological change is not drilling depth neutral. In addition, their results indicate that oil price has an inverse relationship to drilling cost, although the relationship is not statistically significant in their estimations. The Energy Information Administration (US Department of Energy, 1982) presents drilling cost models for the offshore industry. The model results suggest that offshore drilling cost is positively related to water depth.

In this study, I modify the Norgaard and Leu (1986) model as follows:

$$cost_{it} = \alpha \; technology_t^{\beta_1} \; drill_{it}^{\beta_2} \; price_t^{\beta_3} \qquad (3.3)$$

where *cost* is the drilling cost (in 2000 dollars) per well, *technology* is the technological diffusion index for drilling, *drill* is the average drilling distance in feet per well (including both exploratory and development wells), *price* is the price of oil and gas in 2000\$/BOE, *i* is the area index,[10] *t* is time (that is, year), α and β_i ($i = 1, 2, 3$) are coefficients. The expected sign for *technology* is negative, since improvements in technology are expected to reduce the costs of drilling a given well depth. Drilling footage (*drill*) should be positively associated with *cost*. The expected sign for *price* is unclear. A number of factors may affect the sign, such as drillings at the intensive margin

Table 3.3   Parameter estimates of drilling cost model

	Oil well	Gas well	Dry well
Intercept	−0.0748	7.3328	1.4905
ln *technology*	−0.3787*	−0.2729*	−0.3666
	(−3.93)	(−2.66)	(−5.12)
ln *drill*	0.1542*	0.3411*	0.8816*
	(5.31)	(11.04)	(40.81)
ln *price*	0.5450*	1.0503	1.1472*
	(3.46)	(6.27)	(9.79)
R^2	0.3577	0.5726	0.6954
White's Test	1.02	0.86	0.71
Durbin-Watson	1.803	1.873	1.716
Time period¶	1959–1996	1959–199	1955–199
# of observations	499	632	812

Notes: * Significant at 1%.
t statistics are in parentheses.
¶The data for 1957, 1958, 1994 and 1995 are missing in my data set.

(that is, existing fields) versus the extensive margin (that is, new areas). According to Norgaard and Leu (1986), drilling costs are higher in new areas.

We use seemingly unrelated regressions (SUR), since errors of three separate estimations for oil, gas and dry wells are correlated. The results are summarized in Table 3.3. The coefficients for *technology* have the correct sign and are significant for all types of wells, indicating that technological change has played a significant role in cost reduction in the offshore industry.

Fisher (1964) and Norgaard and Leu (1986) find that technological change is not drilling-depth neutral. Their results support the idea of 'depth-favoring technologies' which suggests that larger cost reductions can be achieved at greater drilling depth. To examine the issue, I examine the cross-product of the technological change variable and the drilling variable (*technology × drill*) in separate model runs. It is important to note that the results reported below reflect the distance drilled, not water depth in which drilling occurs. Using data from the same period (1959–78) as in Norgaard and Leu (1986), I am able to obtain similar results that support the idea of 'depth-favoring technologies' in the case of oil wells.[11] However, the results do not hold if I re-estimate the same model specification using extended data (1959–96), suggesting that technological change may be more depth-neutral in recent years. In all cases, the product term (*technology × drill*) is not significant for gas wells and dry holes. Thus, I conclude that technological change is generally drilling-distance neutral in the offshore case.

The coefficients for *drill* are all significant with the expected sign. The cost elasticity with respect to *drill* is 0.15, 0.34 and 0.88 for oil well, gas well and dry hole, respectively. Except for dry hole, these cost elasticities in the offshore industry are close to those (0.2 to 0.3) reported by Norgaard and Leu (1986) in their onshore study. For all well types, my results for *price* are positive and significant. Unfortunately, we are unable to examine the effect of water depth on drilling cost, since the JAS data do not report water depth. Given the importance of water depth in offshore operations, this is a significant limitation.[12]

Field-Level Production Frontier Model

The purpose of this section is to examine the role technological change in conjunction with environmental regulation has played in the offshore industry. The offshore oil and gas industry is a non-renewable resource industry and its production is affected by resource stock size (for example, oil and gas reserves) and quality (for example, field size and reservoir type). Unlike onshore production, the offshore industry must develop new offshore production technologies to accommodate increasing water depth as shallow water resources are depleted. In fact, offshore oil and gas production at any given time is conditioned on certain marine geological and technical factors. For example, without the recent deep-water technologies, production from deep-water fields would not have occurred. Finally, the industry must comply with relevant environmental regulations. Thus, for the offshore oil and gas industry, a general production function may be specified as (also see Appendix for derivation of production model):

$$\mathbf{y_t} = F(\mathbf{x_t}, D, S, R_t, E_t, t) \qquad (3.4)$$

where $\mathbf{y_t}$ is the vector of outputs (that is, oil and gas) at time t, $\mathbf{x_t}$ is the vector of factor inputs (e.g., drillings and platforms), D is the water depth, S is the field size, R_t is the depletion through time t, E is the stringency of environmental regulations,[13] and t is time. The above specification extends the classical production function (Solow, 1957) by explicitly including attribute variables D, S, R and E. The extension is essential for the study of the offshore oil and gas industry.

Generally, Equation (3.4) is valid for data at the disaggregate field level and the aggregate regional level. I will first examine the field-level production using a stochastic frontier model[14] and then estimate changes in TFP at the regional level using an aggregate model.[15]

The stochastic frontier production function was initially developed by Aigner et al. (1977) and Meeusen and van den Broeck (1977). Battese and

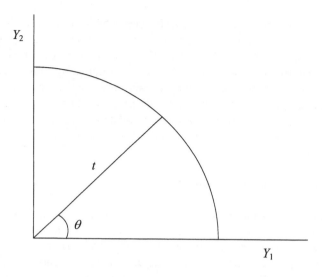

Figure 3.5   Polar representation of multiple outputs

Coelli (1992) present a stochastic frontier model for unbalanced panel data with fixed effects. The effects are assumed to be distributed as truncated normal random variables, and also permitted to vary systematically with time. Löthgren (1997) extends the stochastic frontier analysis by introducing a stochastic ray frontier model to accommodate the case of multiple outputs. In this study, there are two outputs, oil and gas. Following Löthgren, I obtain a scalar valued representation of the multiple output technology by using a polar coordinate representation of the output vector (*y*) as follows:

$$y = \iota \cdot m(\theta) \tag{3.5}$$

where ι is the Eulidean norm (length) of the output vector *y*, *m* is a function representing output mix, and θ is the polar coordinate angle.[16] Figure 3.5 illustrates the polar coordinate representation in the two-output case.

The stochastic ray frontier production function model can be specified as:

$$\iota = f(x, \theta) \exp(v - u) \tag{3.6}$$

where *v* and *u* form the composite error term in a standard stochastic frontier model, where *u* is a truncated random variable capturing inefficiency in production and *v* is a normal error term representing measurement error. My specification of (3.6) is:

$$\ln t_{it} = \alpha + \beta \ln x_{it} + \gamma \theta_{it} + v_{it} - u_{it} \qquad (3.7)$$

where i is the field index and t (=1,...,T) is time (that is, year). t_{it} is the norm of field i at time t, x_{it} is a vector of the inputs (x) and θ_{it} is an output angles. v_{it} is the random noise term, independently and identically distributed as $N(0, \sigma_v^2)$. u_{it} accounts for technological inefficiency in production, defined as $u_i \exp[-\eta(t-T)]$ with u_i being a non-negative random variable truncated at 0, and independently and identically distributed as $N(\mu, \sigma_u^2)$. α, β, γ and η are the parameters to be estimated.

In the field-level analysis, I use cumulative values for factor inputs (elements of x) and outputs (y), because for the above technology definition, it is more appropriate to express the production relationship on cumulative terms for a non-renewable industry. For example, for a field, the production at t is determined by cumulative inputs (for example, drilling) up to $t-1$.

There are two outputs: cumulative oil production in barrels and cumulative gas production in thousand cubic feet. I examine a number of input and explanatory variables (that is, elements of vector x). The effects of technological change are captured by three technical variables. *technology* is the cumulative weighted technological index for production as described before. The variable *horizontal^{exp}* represents the extent to which horizontal and directional drilling is used in exploratory wells, and is defined as the ratio of cumulative drilling distance to the corresponding vertical depth. A higher ratio reflects a greater degree of horizontal and directional drilling in the field. Similarly, *horizontal^{dev}* represents the level of horizontal drilling in development wells. The expected signs of these three technical variables are positive, since technological change leads to increases in output.

I consider five conventional factor input variables: the cumulative number of exploratory and development wells up to $t-1$ (*well*); the cumulative average drilling distance (in feet) per exploratory well (*drill^{exp}*), calculated as the cumulative drilling distance divided by the cumulative number of wells; the cumulative average drilling distance (in feet) per development well (*drill^{dev}*); the number of platforms (*platform*); and platform size, measured as average number of slots per platform for the field (*platform size*). Positive signs are expected for these variables capturing drilling and production inputs.

To account for specific field characteristics, I include several geophysical variables: the remaining reserves in the field at $t-1$ in million BOE (barrel of oil equivalent), the field size in million BOE, water depth of a field in feet, the average porosity of reservoirs in the field, measured in percentage terms, and the volume of untreated produced water in barrels.[17] The expected signs for reserves, field size and porosity are positive, since larger reserve size is generally associated with higher production, and higher porosity implies greater flow rate and lower production cost. The expected sign for *water depth* is negative, as exploration, development and production of fields tend to be more costly in deeper waters. The expected sign for *produced water* is negative, as additional inputs are needed to reduce water production for a field at a particular point in time. Finally, production is adversely affected by the stringency of environmental regulations governing offshore oil and gas operations. I measure environmental stringency as the estimated environmental compliance cost in dollars per unit of oil and gas production.

In addition to the field-level exploration–production data set, I developed a separate data set for environmental variables (E and Q). The environmental emission data set includes data on 33 different types of water pollutants in four categories from EPA[18] as well as data of oil spills from the Coast Guard. To measure the level of environmental regulatory stringency over time, I use estimates of environmental compliance costs associated with preventing water pollution and oil spills. The compliance costs are based on *ex ante* estimates, since I do not have the *ex post* cost studies.[19] The compliance cost estimates are compiled from relevant regulatory announcements published in various issues of the *Federal Register* and from relevant EPA documents (for example, US Environmental Protection Agency, 1985, 1993).

For the field-level analysis, I estimate the stochastic frontier model with three separate specifications. The first specification is for the entire data set from 1947 to 1998. Since data for stringency of environmental regulations are not available before 1968, I assess the effect of environmental regulations on offshore operations in the second specification using a separate data set including the stringency variable from 1968 to 1998, and I compare the model results with versus without the environmental variables by applying the initial specification to the data for 1968–98. All the specifications are estimated using Frontier Version 4.1 software (Coelli, 1994).

The results of the three specifications are summarized in Table 3.4. Generally, the estimated coefficients for all variables have the expected sign and reasonable magnitudes. In addition, the results are consistent across the three specifications, suggesting that the model is robust with respect to the inclusion of the environmental variable as well as variation in the length of time series.

Of the three technological variables, the technological change index (*Tech*) is highly significant in all three specifications, indicating that technological change has had a significant positive impact on the field-level production frontier. The coefficients for *horizontal^{exp}* are significant in Specifications 1 and 3, and the coefficients for *horizontal^{dev}* are significant in Specifications 2 and 3. The results suggest that horizontal drilling technology has also caused a positive shift in the production frontier.

Coefficients of all five factor input variables have the expected positive sign and are significant. The results provide a numerical description of the

Table 3.4   Parameter estimates of the stochastic frontier model

Explanatory variable	Specification 1	Specification 2	Specification 3
Technology			
ln(*Tech*)	1.634 (0.243)	1.263 (0.163)	0.567 (0.474)
ln(*horizontal^{exp}*)	1.173 (0.375)	0.154 (0.348)	0.986 (0.365)
ln(*horizontal^{dev}*)	0.363 (0.172)	2.669 (0.352)	2.616 (0.313)
Factor Inputs			
well	0.037 (0.005)	0.026 (0.006)	0.037 (0.007)
ln(*drill^{exp}*)	0.089 (0.010)	0.090 (0.010)	0.088 (0.012)
ln(*drill^{dev}*)	0.185 (0.007)	0.145 (0.008)	0.142 (0.009)
ln(*platform*)	0.076 (0.036)	0.100 (0.036)	0.072 (0.037)
platform size	0.0012(0.00004)	0.0003(0.00004)	0.0008(0.00004)
Geology			
ln(*reserve*)	0.042 (0.020)	0.054 (0.019)	0.043 (0.020)
ln(*field size*)	56.308 (2.057)	64.320 (1.098)	51.386 (2.270)
ln(*water depth*)	−104.022 (4.043)	−85.370 (1.026)	−107.347(1.028)
ln(*porosity*)	0.046 (0.035)	0.053 (0.034)	0.053 (0.033)
ln(*produced water*)	0.968 (0.006)	0.972 (0.006)	0.969 (0.006)
Environmental regulation			
ln(*env. stringency*)	—	−54.955 (1.008)	—
Time effects			
ln(*reserve*) × *t*	−0.028 (0.001)	−0.032 (0.001)	−0.027 (0.001)
ln(*water depth*) × *t*	0.053 (0.002)	0.049 (0.001)	0.055 (0.001)
ln(*env. stringency*) × *t*	—	0.029 (0.001)	—
Output Mix			
θ	5.809 (0.154)	6.815 (0.155)	6.788 (0.159)
Intercept	−17.021	−16.635	−10.986
$\sigma_s^2 = \sigma_v^2 + \sigma_u^2$	8.684 (0.097)	7.786 (0.098)	7.864 (0.089)
$\gamma = \sigma_u^2/\sigma_s^2$	0.005 (0.002)	0.004 (0.003)	0.004 (0.002)
μ	−0.422 (0.158)	0.386 (0.052)	0.385 (0.092)
η	0.069 (0.008)	0.043 (0.013)	0.029 (0.011)
log likelihood	−45245.53	−40821.35	−40852.63
Time period	1947–2002	1968–2002	1968–2002

Notes:
Dependent variable is the natural log of the norm (*t*).
Standard errors are reported in parentheses.

relationship between the production frontier and input efforts, including the number of wells (*well*), drilling depth (*drill^{exp}* and *drill^{dev}*), the number of platforms (*platform*) and *platform size.*

The field-level production frontier is affected by geological factors. As shown in the middle part of Table 3.4, most of these variables are significant and only *porosity* in Specification 2 is not. The magnitudes of these coefficients reveal that the output quantity is mostly determined by two variables: *field size* and *water depth.* While it is obvious that larger fields produce more, it is somewhat surprising to see the magnitude of the negative impact of water depth on the production frontier. The challenge posed by water depth is indeed substantial. Generally, we expect the potential for greater production to be available in deep-water areas. My results show that, on average, this is not true in these study periods. This might be because industry is focused on production from large fields in deep water and little attention is paid to small and average-sized fields. I model *produced water*, a byproduct of petroleum production, on the input side. Although the volume of produced water from a field is influenced by the geological type of its reservoirs and the age of the field, the results suggest that, on average, the quantities of produced water and petroleum output are positively related.

The offshore oil and gas industry has been subject to not only challenging marine conditions but also increasing environmental regulation. To estimate associated production frontier shift, I include a measure of the stringency of environmental regulations in Specification 2 (see Table 3.4). The significantly negative coefficient implies that environmental regulation has indeed had a measurable impact on productivity of the offshore oil and gas industry.

I include three time interaction terms with reserves (that is, remaining stock in a field), water depth and environmental stringency in our model, to examine how these factors change over time (*t*). The corresponding coefficients are all significant. The time interaction term is negative for reserves, suggesting that the positive effect of remaining resource stock on field-level production has been declining over time, which suggests that new technologies allow one to exploit small fields more efficiently. The time interaction terms are positive for water depth and environmental stringency. The former shows that the negative impacts of water depth and environmental regulations on the production frontier have been diminishing (becoming less negative) over time due to technological change, including less 'structural' components of technological change, such as learning-by-doing.

The positive sign of the parameter capturing the time-varying effect (η) indicates that efficiency at the field level has increased over time, which is likely due to learning-by-doing in the Gulf of Mexico. Finally, the estimated polar angle θ is positive and significant. The result suggests that when the frontier output mix is changed by substituting gas production for oil production, the increase in gas production is greater than the corresponding decrease in oil production, as measured in BOE.

In summary, the results of my field-level analysis indicate that the effect of technological change on the offshore oil and gas industry was substantial over the study period from 1947 to 2002. Similarly, environmental regulation also had a significant impact on offshore production.

3.4 Conclusion

Offshore oil and gas operations in the Gulf of Mexico have played an important role in energy supply in the United States. I have examined the impact of technological change on oil and gas exploration in the Gulf of Mexico from 1947 to 2002. An index variable for technological change is constructed to capture both the number and significance of technological innovations over these five decades. Using a unique micro-level data set, I have developed four sets of empirical models: a field-level discovery model; a model of yield-per-effort (YPE) at the regional level; a model of drilling cost for different well types, and a field-level production frontier model. Results of my analysis indicate that technological change has played a very significant role in the offshore industry.

The results of my field-level discovery model suggest that for a single field, the initial and subsequent resource discoveries are affected by exploration technology, exploration effort (that is, drilling), cumulative drilling, cumulative discovery (through the depletion effect), and water depth. With the field-level data, I show significant effects of technological change, resource depletion and water depth at the intensive margin (that is, within a field). Using yield-per-effort (YPE) models, I examine the net effect of technological change and resource depletion in offshore oil and gas exploration at the regional level. My results suggest that, in the exploration–discovery process alone, the effect of technological change was able to offset completely the effect of resource depletion over the five-decade period, although the depletion effect dominated technological change in the first two decades.[20] My analysis of the JAS drilling data captures a significant cost-reduction effect of technological progress on the offshore drilling industry. I lastly analyse the effect of pollution discharge (for example, produced water and oil spill) and technological change on the production frontier using a unique field-level data set. Results of my stochastic frontier model suggest that the effect of technological change on the offshore oil and gas industry at the field level was substantial. Because of technological progress, the negative effect of resource depletion on the field-level production frontier has been declining over time. Similarly, the negative impact of water depth on the production frontier has been falling. The results reveal that environmental regulation has had a significantly negative impact on offshore production, although this impact has been diminishing over time due to technological change and improved management. Finally, the stochastic frontier analysis shows that production efficiency at the field level has been decreasing, which is likely due to the depletion of reserves and resulting expansion of exploration and production in deep waters.

In this chapter, I separate the effect of technological change and the effect of resource depletion by using different variables representing the two opposing forces in my empirical models. This enables me to examine the long-term interactions between the two effects. The estimated results associated with my technological innovation index are useful for firms and management agencies to formulate research and development (R&D) policies. For example, the marginal effects of innovation on discovery, cost reduction and the production frontier provide crucial information for decisions regarding R&D investment. Similarly, my empirical results regarding the effect of resource depletion on discovery are important to firms for developing exploration–extraction strategies.

For each field in the Gulf of Mexico, the offshore operation consists of three stages: exploration, development and production. Since this chapter focuses on (1) the production stage by production frontier analysis and (2) the exploration stage, my results on the net effect of technological change and depletion do not capture the entire picture of offshore operations. In fact, the impact of technological change on the development and production stages has been substantial. New technologies in platform design and production have resulted in reductions in development and production costs, as well as an increase in producible reserves. In Chapter 2's analysis of the development and production process, I have shown that the effect of technological progress dominated that of resource depletion in the Gulf of Mexico oil and gas industry from 1947 to 1995. In modelling and forecasting of future oil and gas supply from the offshore industry, it is necessary to consider the effect of technological change in the development and production processes as well.

Appendix

Correlation in Exogenous Variables

In the petroleum discovery process of equations (3.1) and (3.2), some of the exogenous variables have been statistically established to be highly correlated and/or functionally related. In my data set, however, these are not correlated strongly compared to the studies in the literature.[21] There are two reasons for this in addition to the general view that field-level behaviour has been considered too erratic to model successfully in empirical studies (Attanasi, 1989). First, my drilling variable is drilling distance per well instead of drilling distance. Second, my data set for equation (3.1) is disaggregated field-level data instead of the data used in the literature (for example, aggregate national or broad regional data, or state-, regional- or firm-level data).

Cumulative discovery has been estimated as a function of cumulative drilling in the literature though studies in the literature use aggregated regional data (for example, Hubbert, 1967; Cleveland and Kaufman, 1991; Walls, 1992). In my field-level discovery function in equation (3.1), I use cumulative discovery, cumulative drilling per exploratory well, cumulative drilling per development well, and cumulative well as exogenous variables. This is possible since I am not able to find any statistically significant functional relationships between them.

The drilling effort and the price of oil and gas have been highly correlated in the literature (for example, Fisher, 1964; Erickson and Spann, 1971; Pindyck, 1974). Note that the elasticity estimates vary by a fairly wide margin (see Walls, 1992 for a literature review). I use both of them in exogenous variables in equations (3.1) and (3.2). They are relatively correlated in the aggregated level in equation (3.2) although they are not correlated at all in field-level data. I leave them in the exogenous variables since all of them are still statistically significant (as in Table 3.2) following the statistics literature (for example, Johnson and Wichern, 2002).

Alternative Estimation of Discovery Process

The discovery process model in equation (3.1) could be decomposed into drilling effort model and yield per unit of drilling effort (YPE). Iledare and Pulsipher (1999) estimate the number of wells and petroleum-finding rate using regional aggregated data on onshore Louisiana over 1977–94. In the drilling effort model, they use time as a proxy for technological progress and find its negative effects on the number of wells drilled. This result suggests that better drilling choices are being made as seismic technology reduces the frequency of unsuccessful drilling. Cumulative drilling has a positive impact on the number of wells (Iledare and Pulsipher, 1999). The result suggests that learning effects have a greater influence on the number of wells drilled and have a larger impact than depletion effects. In the petroleum-finding model, time as a proxy for technological progress shows positive effects suggesting hydrocarbon reserve additions per successful effort increase with technological progress. The cumulative drilling is negative, suggesting diminishing returns as drilling increases (Iledare and Pulsipher, 1999). Using field-level data, I model the drilling effort and YPE (and finding rate). I am not able to find a good statistical prediction and none of the above variables are statistically significant (complete statistical results as a technical appendix are available on request). These unsuccessful results might be caused because field-level behaviour has been considered too erratic to model successfully in empirical studies, as Attanasi (1979) noted. The following result is the only alternative successful result statistically in the discovery process using my data set.

Aggregating the field-level data, I examine the effects of regional exploration effort on the total number of discoveries per year (*discover*) at both the intensive margin and the extensive margin in the Gulf of Mexico.[22] In the simple model, I include three explanatory variables: the total footage drilled per all exploratory and development wells (*drill*) at *t* (that is, year); the total number of exploratory and development wells at *t*; and the cumulative number of discoveries from 1947 to *t*–1. The cumulative number of discoveries reflects the net effect of technological change and depletion. The model is consistent with the discovery function in Livernois and Uhler's (1987) disaggregate exploration–extraction model. The ordinary least square (OLS) results are as follows:[23]

$$\ln(discovery\ number)_t = -3.6045 + 0.8358 \ \ln(drill_t) + 0.0043 \ well_t$$
$$\qquad\qquad\qquad\qquad (4.45) \qquad\qquad\qquad (1.85)$$

$$+0.0011 \sum_{t=1947}^{t-1} discovery\ number_t$$
$$(-3.21)$$

Both the estimated coefficients on distance drilled and cumulative number of discoveries are significant at the 1 per cent level, and the number of wells drilled is significant at the 10 per cent level. The two exploratory effort variables (*drill* and *well*) have positive signs, as expected. The positive sign on the cumulative number of discoveries implies that technological change dominated the effect of depletion in the Gulf of Mexico during the entire study period.

Non-renewable Resource Model and Environmental Regulations

The empirical econometric equation of oil and gas production in this study is based on a dynamic profit-maximizing framework for the non-renewable resource industry (see Deacon, 1993; Krautkreamer, 1998; Kunce et al., 2004 for reviews of the literature). I use a simplified version of an exploration–

extraction aggregated model (for example, Livernois and Uhler, 1987). A hypothetical competitive firm makes optimal extraction and exploration decisions with respect to reserves over one or many deposits in each aggregated field. The firm faces exogenous prices, is assumed to have complete property rights, and is assumed to maximize the present value of profits from exploration and extraction operations. In particular, the following assumptions are utilized for my empirical specification. First, production cost function is assumed to have a log–log relationship to variables including factor inputs, technology, geological factors and environmental regulations applied to production. Second, the non-renewable resource is extracted from a fixed stock of homogeneous quality. Solving present value Hamiltonian and, after some tedious calculations, oil and gas production is shown to have a log–log relationship to the variables in equation (3.7).

Several studies have examined how the oil and gas industry responds to changes in environmental regulations (for example, Stollery, 1985; Jin and Grigalunas, 1993a; Denison et al., 1995; Kunce et al., 2004). Ideally, the model needs to consider the effects of the regulations on all stages of oil and gas operations: exploration, development and production (see Jin and Grigalunas, 1993a). Empirically, however, it is difficult to obtain the data of the regulations. For example, a recent study by Kunce et al. (2004) looks at the environmental regulations pertaining to drilling. Drilling fluids, drill cuttings, deck drainage, well treatment fluids, proposal sand and sanitary and domestic wastes are also important factors in the regulations in addition to the environmental regulations applied to production. I only consider the compliance cost of the regulations applied to production, since these data are not available at the field level. This may not be a bad assumption since there is more regulation on the production side than on drilling (see US Environmental Protection Agency, 1976, 1985, 1993, 1999 for a detailed history of the regulations).

NOTES

1. See Erickson and Spann (1971), Khazzoom (1971), MacAvoy and Pindyck (1973), Uhler (1976) and Pindyck (1978a).
2. See Rose et al. (1986), Deacon (1993), Walls (1994), Iledare and Pulsipher (1995, 1999).
3. The data were from the Financial Reporting System at the Department of Energy and are not available to the general public.
4. They also used data from the Financial Reporting System.
5. There is a possibility of double counting of the observation since costs of individual wells were not obtainable and average costs are given by depth and area.
6. In the field-level data, most of my data set (71 per cent of MMS observations) includes both oil and gas reserves. From these observations, it is impossible to distinguish the oil and gas drilling efforts associated with each oil production and gas production, respectively.

Therefore, I do not distinguish oil and gas in equation (3.1) and equation (3.2) as shown below.

7. This is the total oil and gas revenue divided by the sum of oil and gas production in BOE.
8. See Fisher (1964), Erickson and Spann (1971), Pindyck (1974), Iledare and Pulsipher (1999) and Forbes and Zampelli (2000).
9. Cleveland and Kaufmann (1991, 1997) use cumulative drilling to examine the net impact of technological change on depletion in their YPE models.
10. JAS group offshore drilling data by the following areas: offshore Texas, offshore Louisiana, offshore federal Gulf of Mexico and Gulf of Mexico north.
11. The OLS results are:

    $\ln(cost_{it}) = -7.8354 + 1.3684 \ln(tech_t) - 0.0875 \ln(tech_t) \times \ln(drill_{it}) + 1.4645 \ln(drill_{it})$
    $\qquad\qquad\qquad\quad (3.22) \qquad\qquad\quad (-2.47) \qquad\qquad\qquad (-7.32)$
    $\qquad + 0.6645 \ln(price_t)$
    $\qquad\quad (3.32)$

    t statistics are in parentheses; adjusted $R^2 = 0.93$; number of observations = 237.
12. There are several other problems. For example, the data do not differentiate exploration from development drilling, while exploration wells tend to take longer to drill. Also, royalty regime and availability of drilling rigs are other potentially important variables in the analysis.
13. See Stijn et al. (2002) for the literature review of stochastic frontier analysis in pollution control.
14. Although stochastic frontier models have been used for measuring technological change, the results are usually sensitive to parameterization (see Hjalmarsson et al., 1996). In the study, I will not estimate technological change using the stochastic frontier model.
15. Some cost data are available only in aggregated form and therefore I utilize the cost elasticity information to estimate TFP.
16. For a detailed description of the method and calculation of θ, see Löthgren (1997).
17. I follow the usual convention in environmental economics of treating pollution emissions as an input to production (for example, Baumol and Oates, 1988; Cropper and Oates, 1992). Thus, a reduction (increase) in untreated produced water, with all other inputs and outputs held fixed, represents an increase (decrease) in productivity.
18. The four categories are conventional pollutants, non-conventional organic pollutants, non-conventional metal pollutants and radionuclides. Conventional pollutants include oil and grease, and total suspended solids (TSS). Non-conventional organic pollutants include benzene, benzo(a)pyrene, chlorobenzene, di-n-butylphthalate, ethylbenzene, n-alkanes, naphthalene, P-chloro-M-cresol, phenol, steranes, toluene, triterpanes, total xylenes, 2-butanone, and 2,4-dimethylphenol. Non-conventional metal pollutants include aluminium, arsenic, barium, boron, cadmium, copper, iron, lead, manganese, mercury, nickel, silver, titanium and zinc. Radionuclides include radium 226 and radium 228.
19. Harrington et al. (2000) examined *ex ante* versus *ex post* cost estimates of environmental regulations, and concluded that for EPA and OSHA rules, *ex ante* estimates of unit pollution reduction cost were often accurate.
20. Future research includes the co-integration approach which is a useful technique describing the long-run impact of technology and depletion on the petroleum discovery process (Cuddington and Moss, 2001).
21. The detailed technical appendix of correlation matrix and alternative models discussed in this section is available on request. However, note that none of the alternative models shows a good prediction.
22. I also examined several other models including a regional-level discovery quantity model and a binary choice model of discovery. All these models had poor results.
23. $R^2 = 0.79$; F-statistic = 57.81; DW = 1.78. t statistics are in parenthesis. F-statistics are significant at the 1 per cent level.

4. Environmental regulations and technological change: testing the Porter hypothesis

4.1 Introduction

Substantial efforts have been made to regulate pollution in most industrialized countries, and the stringency of pollution regulations have continued to increase worldwide. Technological progress can play a key role in maintaining a high standard of living in the face of these increasingly stringent environmental regulations. However, the extent of its contribution depends on how well environmental policies are designed and implemented. Successful environmental policies can contribute to technological innovation and diffusion (for example, Kneese and Schultze, 1978; Jaffe et al., 2003), while poor policy designs can inhibit innovation.

Traditionally, economists have subscribed to the idea that painful consequences of environmental regulations cannot easily be avoided, and environmental regulation necessarily involves additional cost to industry (Jaffe et al., 1995; Palmer et al., 1995). Within this context, the key issue is how to design environmental regulations to attain environmental goals while minimizing productivity loss, and thereby controlling the adverse impact on industry to the extent feasible.

Recently, however, researchers have challenged this conventional view with an alternative hypothesis that tougher environmental regulations can stimulate innovation and motivate increases in x-efficiency, potentially increasing productivity and profitability.[1] This is the well-known Porter hypothesis (Porter, 1991; Porter and van der Linde, 1995).

The Porter hypothesis is counter to the intuition of many economists, as it could be interpreted as evidence that firms are not making rational production choices prior to regulation. Thus, many believe that such a finding would require a re-examination of the theory of the firm. Yet, recent economic literature concludes that the Porter hypothesis is not necessarily incompatible with economic rationality. First, I note that there are market failures in technological innovation (for example, Romer, 1990) that are: (1)

technological knowledge is a public good, which is a non-rival and non-excludable good; (2) many beneficiaries (free-riders) do not contribute to the cost of technological knowledge; and (3) uncertainty – unable to make estimations of technical and commercial returns to innovations. At the same time, there are situations where environmental regulations can lead to long-term benefits to industry (Ulph, 1996; Simpson and Bradford, 1996; Bovenberg and Smulders, 1996; Xepapadeas and De Zeeuw, 1999; Mohr, 2002). For example, the standard literature on technological change shows that firms have the incentive to underinvest in the development of new technologies since they cannot capture the full benefits, particularly with respect to advances in basic knowledge (for example, Romer, 1990). Under these circumstances, environmental regulations that encourage new technological development could improve efficiency. Recent literature has also identified other conditions under which environmental regulations may lead to long-term benefits to industry (Bovenberg and Smulders, 1996; Simpson and Bradford, 1996; Ulph, 1996; Xepapadeas and de Zeeuw, 1999; Mohr, 2002).[2] Thus, the Porter hypothesis does not necessarily violate the basic tenets of profit maximization by rational producers.

The notion of the Porter hypothesis is somewhat ambiguous. This study provides two different interpretations of the hypothesis (see Jaffe et al., 1995 for more interpretations). One form of the hypothesis is that, in the long run, environmental regulations are nothing to worry about, because they really will not be all that expensive. This is so since the regulations encourage innovations and these innovations might, in general, more than fully offset the compliance cost and lead to a net benefit for the regulated firm (Porter and van der Linde, 1995). Many economists disagree with this hypothesis since addition of constraints on a firm's set of choices cannot be expected to result in an increased level of profits (for example, Palmer et al., 1995). The other interpretation of the Porter hypothesis is that tougher environmental regulations make firms more internationally competitive than weaker environmental regulations. This interpretation was first advanced as a response to the claim that US firms had become less competitive due to strict environmental regulations. Porter (1991) argues that the critics were wrong, and that the right form of more stringent regulation could spur competitiveness. I define competitiveness in terms of productivity following Hall and Winsten (1959) and Banker et al. (1996). This is because technological change lies at the heart of long-term economic growth and social benefit (for example, Romer, 1990).

The Porter hypothesis may take on alternative formulations, depending on how the index is measured (for example, Jaffe et al., 1995). In this study, I examine two versions of the Porter hypothesis. In the standard version, productivity is measured in terms of market outputs only (for example, oil and gas production). I also examine a version of the Porter hypothesis which considers so-called 'green' productivity, based on a joint production model including both market outputs and non-market outputs (that is, pollutant emissions). For example, when faced with new environmental regulations, firms might develop innovative methods for complying, thereby shifting out the multi-product production frontier.[3] Under this second form of the Porter hypothesis, a reduction in pollution holding market output constant is also credited as a gain in productivity.

The extent to which the multi-product production frontier shifts in response to new environmental regulations is clearly an important issue for management agencies. For example, the US Environmental Protection Agency (EPA) is required to determine the cost imposed on industry for certain types of new regulations, such as EPA's designation of best conventional technology (BCT). However, analyses of the costs of potential new regulations are necessarily carried out using *ex ante* data on production methods. To the extent that tougher environmental regulations lead to induced innovation, these cost estimates tend to overstate the actual *ex post* costs. However, industry representatives often counter this argument, stating that unanticipated problems invariably arise when implementing new environmental controls, so that actual *ex post* costs are generally higher then *ex ante* cost estimates. Hence, the degree to which induced innovation reduces the burden of the associated regulations is an important policy issue.

This chapter explores the interactions among environmental regulations, technological innovation and productivity growth in the offshore oil and gas industry. Applying data envelopment analysis (DEA) to a unique micro-level data set from the Gulf of Mexico, I first measure various components of total factor productivity within a joint production model, which considers both market and environmental outputs. I compute the change in productivity indexes over time and decompose productivity change to provide a better understanding of the relative importance of various components over the study period. I then explore the Porter hypothesis. To do so, I employ standard statistical tests of causality to identify relationships between the stringency of environmental regulations and various productivity-related indexes computed with DEA. In the short term, more stringent environmental regulations clearly reduce total factor productivity (TFP) in the production of market outputs. With technological change, however, the short-run costs of regulation could conceivably be offset, in part or in full, if the regulations stimulate innovation and increase productivity in the longer term. I identify both the immediate and longer-term impacts of regulations on productivity by testing the Porter hypothesis within a dynamic context through the period when impacts dissipate.

An important challenge faced in empirical tests of the Porter hypothesis is to identify the direction of causality between technological innovation and environmental regulations. New, tougher environmental regulations might spur research and development efforts leading to innovation, as implied by the Porter hypothesis. However, innovation might also precede and drive tougher new regulations in at least two ways. First, technical innovations, especially those in pollution control technologies, may lead federal agencies to develop tougher environmental regulations that capitalize on these new technologies (for example, Meyer, 1993). For example, the US EPA's technology-based standards are based on concepts like best conventional technology (BCT) or best available technology (BAT), which implies that the current state of technology will tend to drive the stringency of environmental regulations. Development of new technologies may thus lead to subsequent increases in the stringency of environmental regulations due to 'supply-side' effects, such as improvements in the technical and/or economic feasibility of pollution control. Additionally, economic development might lead to an increased demand for environmental quality, as embodied in the environmental Kuznets curve.[4]

Thus, causality between environmental regulations and innovation might go in either (or both) directions, and it is critical to identify the direction of causality between environmental regulations and advances in environmental technology when testing the Porter hypothesis. These questions seek empirical answers, and my study attempts to contribute to the literature, empirically and methodologically. I apply two methods to identify the direction of causality between stringency of environmental regulations and innovation, and I identify the extent to which there is empirical support for demand-side (environmental Kuznets curve) and/or 'supply-side' increases in stringency of environmental regulations in response to increases in productivity.

4.2 Literature Review

There have been several empirical investigations using indirect data of the relationship between the stringency of environmental regulation and the development of new technologies in the 1990s. Limited evidence suggests that patent counts and research and development (R&D) expenditures increase with the stringency of environmental regulation. Lanjouw and Mody (1996) conducted a study of Germany, Japan and the US, which found a positive relationship between environmental compliance cost (a proxy for environmental regulation stringency) and patenting of new environmental technologies. Lanjouw and Mody (1996) provide support for the 'weak' version of the hypothesis. Jaffe and Palmer (1997) defined the weak version of the Porter hypothesis as that environmental regulation stimulates only innovations contributing to the production of environmental commodities. In addition, Jaffe and Palmer (1997) used US data to investigate the relationship between environmental compliance expenditure and R&D expenditure. Their results show no significant relationship between environmental compliance cost and patents. However, they found a significant relationship between compliance costs and R&D expenditure (Jaffe and Palmer, 1997).

Jaffe et al. (1995) reviewed empirical studies that estimate the influence of environmental regulations on productivity. For example, Jorgenson and Wilcoxen (1990) have estimated that the long-run cost of environmental regulation is a reduction of 1.91 per cent in the level of the US gross national product. In contrast, the recent study of US oil refiners by Berman and Bui (2001) suggests that environmental regulation is productivity enhancing.

Alpay et al. (2002) use the profit function approach to assess the effects of environmental regulations on profitability and productivity in food manufacturing in Mexico and the United States. They conclude that environmental regulations have had no significant effect on profitability or productivity in the United States, but regulations have significantly enhanced productivity in Mexico, supporting the Porter hypothesis. These studies, however, have been criticized for not considering the full range of impacts of environmental regulations, including possible positive external impacts on other producers (for example, Barbera and McConnell, 1990; Repetto, 1996). Furthermore, studies using patent counts and R&D expenditures are based on indirect measures of productivity change.

4.3   Modelling Approach

I use data envelopment analysis (DEA) to calculate productivity change (see, for example, Charnes et al., 1978; Färe et al., 1994b). DEA is a set of non-parametric mathematical programming techniques that estimate the relative efficiency of production units and identify best practice frontiers.[5] A principal advantage of DEA is that it can be used to decompose productivity measures and to measure changes over time in the components. In addition, DEA is not conditioned on the assumption of optimizing behaviour on the part of every individual observation, nor does DEA impose any particular functional form on production technology. Avoiding these maintained hypotheses may be an advantage, particularly for analyses with micro data that extend over a long time series, where production units face significant uncertainty, irreversibility and fixed (and/or sunk) costs. In such cases, assumptions of static efficiency of every production unit in all time periods would likely be suspect.

Decomposition of Productivity Indexes

Malmquist indexes (for example, Caves et al., 1982a) are used to quantify productivity change, and are decomposed into various constituents, as described below. Malmquist total factor productivity (TFP) is an output-based index of the relative productivity of two observations, measured as the ratio of the two associated distance functions (for example, Caves et al., 1982b). When applied to observations in different periods, the TFP index is interpreted as a measure of productivity change over time. Under variable returns to scale (VRS), the Malmquist index can be decomposed into measures associated with technological change, efficiency change and scale change:

$$TFP_{VRS} = TC_{VRS} \cdot EC_{VRS} \cdot SC_{VRS} \qquad (4.1)$$

where TC_{VRS} is technological change under VRS, EC_{VRS} is efficiency change, and SC_{VRS} is scale change. Technological change measures shifts in the production frontier. Efficiency change measures changes the position of a production unit relative to the frontier, so-called 'catching up' (Färe et al., 1994b). Scale change measures shifts in productivity due to changes in the scale of operations relative to the optimal scale.

Under the assumption of constant returns to scale (CRS), technological change may be decomposed into input-biased technological change (IBTC), output-biased technological change (OBTC), and magnitude change (MC):

$$TC_{CRS} = IBTC_{CRS} \cdot OBTC_{CRS} \cdot MC_{CRS} \qquad (4.2)$$

Here the magnitude component (MC_{CRS}) is a measure of Hicks-neutral technological change.[6] If both IBTC and OBTC are equal to 1, then the technological change is Hicks-neutral.

In the endogenous growth theory framework, technological change is decomposed into two categories: innovation and learning-by-doing (for example, Young, 1993). This relates to the two models of technological change: innovation (for example, Romer, 1990), that focuses on the creation of distinct new technologies; and learning-by-doing (for example, Arrow, 1962), that looks at incremental improvements in productivity with existing technologies.

I use different models to measure and to decompose productivity change in terms of market outputs, environmental (pollution) outputs, and joint production (so-called 'green' productivity) (see Table 4.1). A detailed discussion of the decomposition methods is contained in Chapter 2. Here I briefly describe the general logic of the approach.

Table 4.1   Model specifications

Index calculated	Model 1 Base model: Joint TFP	Model 2 Production TFP	Model 3 Innovation LBD & Diffusion (joint)	Model 4 Innovation LBD & Diffusion (oil & gas)
Output variables				
Oil production (bbl)	X	X	X	X
Gas production (Mcf)	X	X	X	X
Water pollution	X		X	
Oil spill	X		X	
Input variables				
Number of platforms	X	X	X	X
Av. platform size (#slot/#platform)	X	X	X	X
Number of exploration wells	X	X	X	X
Number of development wells	X	X	X	X
Average drilling distance for exploratory wells	X	X	X	X
Average drilling distance for development wells	X	X	X	X
Produced water	X	X	X	X
Weighted innovation index			X	X
Horizontal & directional drilling (exploratory)			X	X
Horizontal & directional drilling (development)			X	X
Environmental compliance cost	X		X	
Attribute variables				
Water depth	X	X	X	X
Depletion effects (oil)	X	X	X	X
Depletion effects (gas)	X	X	X	X
Oil reserves in the field	X	X	X	X
Gas reserves in the field	X	X	X	X
Porosity (field type)	X	X	X	X

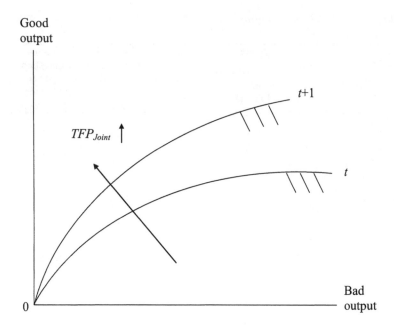

Figure 4.1   Non-market technology with market technology

I decompose TFP change into changes in productivity for market and environmental outputs:

$$TFP_{Joint} = TFP_{Market} \cdot TFP_{Env} \qquad (4.3)$$

where TFP_{Joint} is the joint measure of TFP change, including both changes in productivity of market outputs (TFP_{Market}) and changes in productivity of environmental outputs (TFP_{Env}). A base model (Model 1 in Table 4.1) is used to calculate an overall measure of TFP change of joint outputs. A second model (Model 2) is created which excludes variables associated with non-market outputs. When applied to Model 2, DEA calculates TFP change of market outputs only. Figure 4.1 illustrates the sum of the productivity of nonmarket output (that is, the reduction in environmental risks) plus market output, denoted by TFP_{Joint}. Figure 4.1 shows one good output case and one bad (that is, non-market) output case. The TFP change associated with environmental outputs is then calculated as:

$$TFP_{Env} = TFP_{Joint} / TFP_{Market} \qquad (4.4)$$

Thus, dividing the joint measure of productivity change from Model 1 by the productivity change measure of market outputs from Model 2 provides the residual measure of productivity change in the environmental sector.

I use a similar methodology for decomposing joint TFP change into that associated with innovation (TFP_{Innov}) and learning-by-doing (TFP_{LBD}). In this case, the components of TFP are defined as:

$$TFP_{Joint} = TFP_{Innov} \cdot TFP_{LBD} \qquad (4.5)$$

I developed Model 3 in Table 4.1 to carry out this decomposition. Model 3 includes an input variable that measures specifically identifiable new technological discoveries, discussed in detail in later section below. Applying DEA to Model 3 provides a measure of residual TFP change beyond that which can be explained by changes in the input of specifically identifiable new technologies. The DEA result with Model 3 is interpreted as TFP associated with non-structural effects, including learning-by-doing. TFP associated with specifically identifiable new technologies is then calculated as:

$$TFP_{Innov} = TFP_{Joint} / TFP_{LBD} \qquad (4.6)$$

Similarly, I decompose both technological change (TC) and efficiency change (EC) into indexes representing identifiable new technologies and a residual that is not explained by identifiable technologies.

Productivity Indexes and Directional Distance Functions

Chung et al. (1997) define an output-oriented Malmquist–Luenberger productivity index that is comparable to the Malmquist productivity index, but that includes productivity changes with respect to both desirable and undesirable outputs. Note that Malmquist-Luenberger productivity index is named as a combination of Malmquist productivity index and Luenberger productivity indicator. In contrast to the Shephard output distance function that measures efficiency by expanding all outputs simultaneously, the directional distance function measures efficiency due to increasing desirable outputs (market goods) while decreasing undesirable outputs (for example, pollution emissions). Using the directional distance function specification, our problem can be formulated as follows. Let $\mathbf{x} = (x_1,...,x_M) \in \mathbf{R}_+^M$, $\mathbf{b} = (b_1,...,b_L) \in \mathbf{R}_+^K$, $\mathbf{y} = (y_1,...,y_N) \in \mathbf{R}_+^N$ be row vectors of inputs, pollution outputs (undesirable outputs) and market outputs, respectively. Define the technology set ($\mathbf{Q}$) by:

$$\mathbf{Q}^t = \{(\mathbf{x}^t, \mathbf{b}^t, \mathbf{y}^t): \mathbf{x}^t \text{ can produce } (\mathbf{y}^t, \mathbf{b}^t)\}. \qquad (4.7)$$

Thus, $\mathbf{Q}^t$ represents the set of all output vectors, $\mathbf{y}^t$ and $\mathbf{b}^t$, that can be produced using the input vector, $\mathbf{x}^t$. The directional distance function at time t is defined as:

$$\vec{d}_o^t(\mathbf{y}^t, \mathbf{x}^t, \mathbf{b}^t; \mathbf{g}^t) = \sup\{\phi : (\mathbf{y}^t, \mathbf{x}^t, \mathbf{b}^t) + \phi\, \mathbf{g}^t \in \mathbf{Q}^t\}, \qquad (4.8)$$

where $\mathbf{g}^t$ is defined as the vector $(\mathbf{y}^t, \mathbf{0}, -\mathbf{b}^t)$, that is, desirable outputs are proportionately increased, inputs are held fixed and pollution outputs are proportionately decreased:

$$[\vec{d}_o^t(\mathbf{y}_{k'j'}^i, \mathbf{x}_{k'j'}^i, \mathbf{b}_{k'j'}^i; \mathbf{g}_{k'j'}^i \mid VRS)] = \max_{\lambda_{kj}\phi^{k'j'}} \phi^{k',j'} \qquad (4.9)$$

Since I use a vintage model, the DEA formulation differs from that in Chung et al., (1997). My DEA formulation is as follows. Let k be the index of an oil and gas field, t be time (that is, year), i_k be the discovery year for field k and j_k be the number of years since discovery of field k (that is, field year). Thus, for each field, $j_k = t - i_k$. In the vintage model, I consider all fields discovered in the same year to be a vintage group, and I calculate separate distance functions for each field in each vintage group. I then calculate the Malmquist productivity index by comparing distance functions in two different vintages (i and $i+1$).

For discovery year i, the distance function for field k' in field year j' is calculated as:

$$subject\ to \quad (1+\phi^{k',j'})y_{k'j'n}^i - \sum_{k \in K(i)} \sum_{j=0}^{J(k)} \lambda_{kj} y_{kjn}^i \geq 0, \quad n=1,\ldots,N,$$

$$(1-\phi^{k',j'})b_{k'j'l}^i - \sum_{k \in K(i)} \sum_{j=0}^{J(k)} \lambda_{kj} b_{kjl}^i = 0, \quad l=1,\ldots,L,$$

$$x_{k'j'm}^j - \sum_{k \in K(i)} \sum_{j=0}^{J(k)} \lambda_{kj} x_{kjm}^j \geq 0, \quad m=1,\ldots,M,$$

$$d_{k'j'g}^i - \sum_{k \in K(i)} \sum_{j=0}^{J(k)} \lambda_{kj} d_{kjg}^i \geq 0, \quad g=1,\ldots,G,$$

$$\sum_{k \in K(i)} \sum_{j=0}^{J(k)} \lambda_{kj} = 1, \quad k \in K(i),\ j=1,\ldots,J(k),$$

$$\lambda_{kj} \geq 0, \quad k \in K(i), \quad j=1,\ldots,J(k).$$

where $K(i)$ includes all fields discovered in i and $J(k)$ is the last field year for field k. Note that the above linear programming problem (4.8) is used to estimate the distance function for a single field in a particular period (that is, year i). To estimate the productivity change over time and its components (for example, equation (4.1)), it is necessary to calculate several different distance functions including both the single-period and mixed-period distance functions for each field and time period. For the mixed-period distance function, there are two vintage years i and $i+1$. For example, the output constraint in (4.9) becomes:

$$(1+\phi^{k',j'})y^i_{k'j'n} - \sum_{k\in K(i+1)} \sum_{j=0}^{J(k)} \lambda_{kj} y^{i+1}_{kjn} \leq 0, \quad n=1,...,N, \qquad (4.10)$$

This constraint identifies the maximum feasible radial expansion (ϕ) of outputs from field k' of vintage i that does not exceed a linear combination of efficient output vectors from fields of vintage $i+1$. The larger the maximum feasible value of ϕ, the greater the productivity change in fields of vintage $i+1$ relative to vintage i.

In this study, time (t) and vintage year (i) extend from 1968 to 2002; the vectors of outputs ($\mathbf{y}$ and $\mathbf{b}$), inputs ($\mathbf{x}$) and attributes ($\mathbf{a}$) for each model are listed in Table 4.1. A weighted innovation index, detailed below, is assigned to each vintage, and held constant across time for fields of that vintage. Other than the two depletion variables, all attribute variables (for example, water depth) vary across fields, but are constant over time for a given field.

Assessment of the Porter Hypothesis

Contemporaneous analysis of a regulation is needed to find the immediate cost of implementing the regulation. But the ultimate impact of environmental regulations will be felt several years later when the induced innovation process has been completed. I test the Porter hypothesis by examining whether levels of the stringency of environmental regulations are associated with subsequent increases in productivity. The DEA methods discussed above are used to measure productivity change and the various constituents of productivity change over time. I then use two approaches, the Almon distributed lag model (Almon, 1965) and Granger causality tests (Granger, 1969), to identify causal relationships between the stringency of environmental regulations and the various productivity measures.

The Almon lag model relates the productivity indexes (TFP change and TC) to lags in the stringency of environmental regulations using the functional specification:

$$P_t = \alpha + \sum_{i}^{N} \beta_i E_{t-i} + \varepsilon_t \qquad (4.11)$$

where P_t denotes the productivity index at time t, α is a constant term, E_{t-i} denotes lagged values of the regulation stringency index, β_i is the coefficient of the i_{th} lag and ε_t is a stochastic term. In general, the Almon polynomial distributed lag model allows coefficients to follow a variety of patterns as the length of the lags increases. Typically, an inverted U-shaped pattern is expected, and a second-degree polynomial is often considered adequate to characterize the lag structure. Following common practice (for example, Harvey 1990), I choose the lag length that minimizes the Akaike Information Criteria (AIC).[7]

I also apply the Granger causality test (Granger, 1969; Johansen and Juselius, 1990) to examine the direction of causality between environmental regulations and productivity indexes. The Granger test provides a simple means to identify cause-and-effect relationships when the structure of the relationship is not clear.[8] A time series, y^1, is said to 'Granger cause' y^2 if the prediction of y^2 can be improved upon by the inclusion of lagged values of y^1 in the information set, in addition to lags on y^2. In this case, the Porter hypothesis is consistent with my finding that lags on the stringency of environmental regulations have positive and statistically significant coefficients, when I add this result to a distributed lag model for productivity change.

The Granger test proceeds as follows. First, data vectors for productivity change (PC) and environmental stringency (ES) are partitioned into current values and a series of time lags $[\mathbf{PC}_t, \mathbf{ES}_t]$ and $[\mathbf{PC}^-, \mathbf{ES}^-]$, where the superscripts indicate $\mathbf{PC}^-$ and $\mathbf{ES}^-$ are vectors of lags on productivity change and environmental stringency. Then the Granger causality test is employed in the multivariate setting using a vector autoregression (VAR) (Johansen 1988; Johansen and Juselius, 1990), as follows:

$$\begin{bmatrix} \mathbf{PC} \\ \mathbf{ES} \end{bmatrix} = \begin{bmatrix} \Delta_{11} & \Delta_{12} \\ \Delta_{21} & \Delta_{22} \end{bmatrix} \begin{bmatrix} \mathbf{PC}^- \\ \mathbf{ES}^- \end{bmatrix} + \begin{bmatrix} \varepsilon_1 \\ \varepsilon_2 \end{bmatrix}$$

I test the null hypotheses that stringency of environmental regulations does not 'Granger cause' productivity change ($\Delta_{12} = 0$) and the hypothesis that productivity change does not 'Granger cause' environmental stringency ($\Delta_{21} = 0$). The Porter hypothesis is consistent with the sum of the lagged coefficients (the elements of Δ_{12}) being positive. In contrast, the traditional view that environmental regulation can only decrease productivity is consistent with the result of all elements of Δ_{12} being non-positive.

My second hypothesis is that past levels of technological change induce future increases in the stringency of environmental regulations ($\Delta_{21} \geq 0$). This could be the case, for example, because environmental regulations are technology based, and therefore technological advances could result in a subsequent increase in the stringency of environmental regulations. Additionally, increased productivity results in higher income levels, potentially increasing the demand for environmental quality through an environmental Kuznets curve. Thus, increased productivity could result in more stringent environmental regulations through at least two different mechanisms.

Application

I apply the above methods to oil and gas production in the Gulf of Mexico, one of the first areas in the world to begin large-scale offshore oil and gas production. Offshore operations in the Gulf of Mexico have played an important role in domestic energy production and supply stabilization.

Reducing the environmental impact of offshore operations is among the most pressing challenges facing the oil and gas industry in the US today. In recent decades, compliance with environmental regulations has become increasingly costly and complex. For example, in 1996, the petroleum industry, including refining, spent an estimated $8.2 billion on environmental protection; approximately the same amount that it spent exploring for new domestic supplies (American Petroleum Institute, 2001).

Because the early data did not include environmental reporting, I use the data for the period from 1968 to 2002. Thus, the project database is comprised of well-level data for oil output, gas output and produced water output, and field-level data for the number of exploration wells, total drilling distance of exploration wells, total vertical distance of exploration wells, number of development wells, total drilling distance of development wells, total vertical distance of development wells, number of platforms, total number of slots, total number of slots drilled, water depth, oil reserves, gas reserves, original proved oil and gas combined reserves (in BOE), discovery year and porosity.

Although I have well-level production data, the well is not a good unit for measuring technological efficiency due to spillover effects across wells within a given field. Rather, the field level is a more appropriate unit for measuring technological efficiency. For this reason the relevant variables were extracted from the MMS data files and merged by year and field, so that the final data set was comprised of 32 years of annual data at the field level. On average there are 410 fields operating in any particular year, and a total of 12 465 observations.

I use the cost of complying with environmental regulations as the measure of environmental stringency. Environmental compliance cost is based on *ex ante* estimates from US Environmental Protection Agency sources, since I do not have the *ex post* cost studies.[9] I compiled a data file for water pollution and oil spill prevention costs from Federal Register (FR) documents, five EPA documents, engineering documents and Coast Guard documents which contain the *ex ante* capital cost, operation and maintenance cost estimates for each set of regulations. These environmental regulations require phased implementation over a period of years and regulations are occasionally revised, which implies a variation in stringency over time. Each of the capital, operation and maintenance costs are estimated based on the project type, whether the field is an oil and gas joint project, an oil-only project, or a gas-only project.

The output variables in my model are oil production, gas production, water pollution and oil spills (see Table 4.1). The input variables include the following: the number of platforms, platform size, number of development wells, number of exploration wells, average distance drilled for exploratory wells, average distance drilled for development wells and environmental compliance cost. Field attributes are the water depth, initial oil reserves, initial gas reserves, field porosity and an aggregate measure of resource depletion. My water pollutants data set is composed of 33 different types of pollutants in the four EPA categories. The four categories are conventional pollutants, non-conventional organic pollutants, non-conventional metal pollutants and radionuclides. Conventional pollutants include oil, grease and total suspended solids (TSS). Non-conventional organic pollutants include benzene, benzo(a)pyrene, chlorobenzene, di-n-butylphthalate, ethylbenzene, n-alkanes, naphthalene, P-chloro-M-cresol, phenol, steranes, toluene, triterpanes, total xylenes, 2-butanone and 2,4-dimethylphenol. Non-conventional metal pollutants include aluminium, arsenic, barium, boron, cadmium, copper, iron, lead, manganese, mercury, nickel, silver, titanium and zinc. Radionuclides include radium 226 and radium 228.

One important innovation of recent decades is the extent of horizontal drilling, which refers to the ability to guide a drillstring at any angle. This allows the wellbore to intersect the reservoir from the side rather from above, allowing a much more efficient extraction of resources from thin or partly depleted formations. Horizontal drilling is also advantagous for formations with certain types of natural fractures, low permiability, a gap cap, bottom water, and for some layered formations. A measure of horizontal drilling and our weighted innovation variable are used as input variables in Model 3 (see Table 4.1). When applied to Model 3, DEA calculates the residual fraction of TFP change which cannot be explained by the input of specifically identifiable new technologies, and is therefore attributed to less structural effects. The fraction of TFP change associated with identifiable technological innovations is calculated by dividing joint TFP change from Model 1 by the residual measure of TFP change from Model 3. I also apply the same approach to decompose both technological change and efficiency change into the portions associated with specifically identifiable new technologies and the residual portions that are attributed to less structural effects.

4.4   Empirical Results

Data Envelopment Analysis

The DEA framework is used to measure productivity change and to carry out the various decompositions described above, contributing to a better understanding of nature of technological change for our application. Figure 4.2 presents the results for joint TFP change, and TFP change decomposed into the market and environmental sectors. Overall, joint TFP increases by about 65 per cent from 1968 through 2002, which implies a geometric mean of about 1.9 per cent per year. Over the first 16 years (1968–84) joint TFP increases by about 17 per cent, or a rate of about 1.0 per cent per year. In the next 20 years (1985–2002) joint TFP increases by about 47 per cent, or a rate of about 2.3 per cent per year. This is consistent with the increasing rate of technological progress that has been observed in the industry (for example, Bohi, 1998). TFP change in the market sector accounts for about 75 per cent of the joint, while TFP change in the environmental sector accounts for about 25 per cent.

The decomposition of technological change (TC) into the joint, market and environmental sectors are presented in Figure 4.3. Joint TC accounts for an increase in productivity of about 59 per cent over the study period. Again, the largest share of TC occurs in the market sector, which accounts for about 90 per cent of the joint TC. In contrast, the environmental sector accounts for about 10 per cent of TC.

Thus, there has been a considerable increase in productivity in market outputs despite increasingly rigorous environmental regulations. In contrast, the rate of productivity change in the environmental sector has lagged behind that in the market sector. These results confirm the conceptual literature, which finds that because command-and-control based environmental policies provide little latitude for innovation, they are likely to inhibit productivity growth. Nevertheless, despite these institutional barriers, industry has been able to increase productivity of environmental technologies to some extent, hence moderating compliance costs.

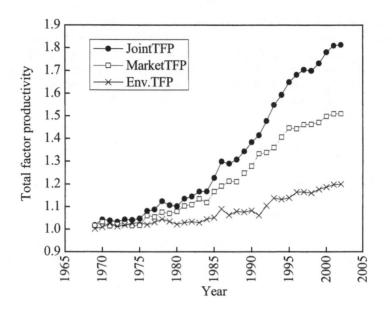

Figure 4.2   Decomposition of TFP change by sector

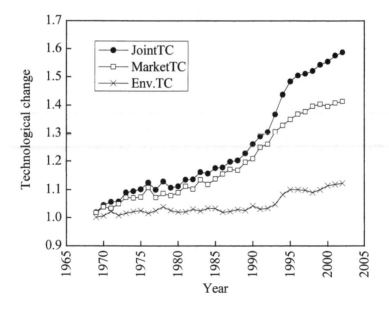

Figure 4.3   Decomposition of technological change by sector

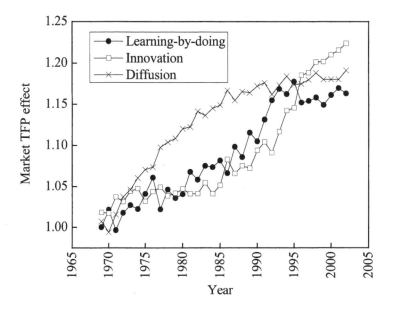

Figure 4.4   Decomposition of TFP change for market outputs

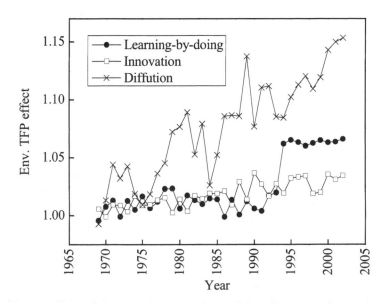

Figure 4.5   Decomposition of TFP change for environmental outputs

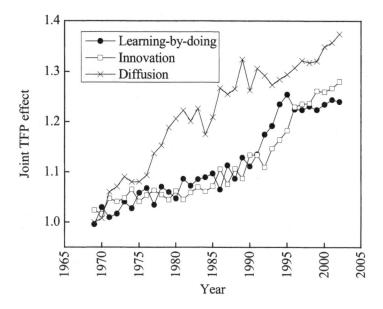

Figure 4.6   Decomposition of TFP change for joint outputs

Figures 4.4 to 4.6 depict trends of TFP change, decomposed into learning-by-doing (LBD), innovation (INNOV) and diffusion (DIFF). Overall effects of joint production are presented in Figure 4.6. TFP increases by approximately 34 per cent for innovation, 29 per cent for LBD and 45 per cent for diffusion over the study period. Note that diffusion plays the most important role until the end of the time horizon, when there is a clear trend towards LBD and innovation. The increased productivity due to innovation mainly comes from the market sector (oil and gas production), rather than the environmental sector, while the increased productivity due to LBD comes more equally from the market and environmental sectors. Again, this is consistent with prior expectations. Technology-based regulations are likely to restrict firms' incentives for developing and implementing new environmental technologies. However, firms may retain some latitude for cost savings through less structural innovations (for example, learning-by-doing), such as more careful management of the technologies upon which the regulations are based.

Additional insights into the nature of technological change can be obtained by identifying the extent to which it conforms to Hicks-neutrality. Hicks-neutrality of technological change for joint production implies parallel shifts in isoquants on the input side and parallel shifts in the production frontiers on the output side. In contrast, biases in technological change imply relative changes in productivity across inputs and/or outputs, which imply non-parallel shifts of isoquants and/or production frontiers. DEA is capable of decomposing technological change into output-biased technological change (OBTC), input-biased technological change (IBTC) and magnitude change (MC) (see equation (4.2)). The DEA measure of OBTC identifies the extent to which technological change increases the productivity of each output relative to all other outputs. Similarly, IBTC identifies whether technological change increases the productivity of each input relative to all other inputs. When the DEA measures of OBTC and IBTC simultaneously equal 1, productivity change is Hicks-neutral. However, DEA only provides overall measures of bias, which are aggregated over all inputs (IBTC) or outputs (OBTC) (Färe and Grosskopf 1996). In contrast, the parametric measurements of technological change (for example, Antle and Capalbo, 1988) can provide measures of bias for each individual input and output.

Considering market outputs only (Model 2 in Table 4.1) gives an IBTC measure of 1.71 and OBTC measure of 2.42. Therefore, the overall technological change bias index, which is the product of IBTC and OBTC, is 4.14. Unfortunately, DEA is not a statistical technique, and therefore does not allow one to test for statistical significance. However, the overall bias index is sufficiently far from 1 to suggest that Hicks-neutral technological change may not hold in Model 2. In comparison, with the joint production model (Model 1), which includes market and environmental outputs, one finds a larger overall technological change bias index (IBTC = 2.91, OBTC = 2.05, and the overall bias index = 5.97).

Testing the Porter Hypothesis

As discussed above, I conduct two tests of the Porter hypothesis. First, I use Almon distributed lag models to test whether increases in the stringency of environmental regulations are associated with future changes in productivity indexes (TFP change and TC). The results for the Almon lag model are reported in Table 4.2. The results show statistically significant relationships between the stringency of environmental regulations and joint productivity for both TC and TFP change. Most individual lag coefficients are statistically significant at the 5 per cent or 1 per cent level for both productivity measures, and the aggregate effects are significant at better than the 1 per cent level. The initial lags are negative in sign, indicating that the immediate effect of environmental regulation is to reduce both productivity indexes. But the longer-term lags and the sum of all lags are positive for TC and TFP change. The result indicates that joint productivity increases in the longer term, and that longer-term increases more than offset the short-term decreases. Thus, I find empirical support for the hypothesis that more stringent environmental

Table 4.2   Almon distributed lags for impact of environmental regulations on alternative productivity measures

Time		Joint production of environmental & market outputs		Market outputs only	
		Technological change	Total factor productivity	Technological change	Total factor productivity
Time	0	−0.187*	−0.373***	0.009	−0.003
lag		(−2.12)	(−3.59)	(0.08)	(−0.05)
	1	0.023***	−0.111*	−0.029	−0.012
		(3.84)	(−1.83)	(−0.35)	(−0.16)
	2	0.125**	0.103***	−0.031	0.080
		(2.55)	(4.99)	(−0.22)	(0.07)
	3	0.119**	0.258***	0.007	0.058
		(2.52)	(18.45)	(0.17)	(0.47)
	4		0.356***		
			(10.26)		
	5		0.398***		
			(8.74)		
	6		0.380***		
			(7.77)		
	7		0.29***		
			(6.55)		
	8		0.15***		
			(7.34)		
Sum of		0.080***	1.498***	0.038	0.049
lags		(3.85)	(28.48)	(0.41)	(0.81)
Adj. R²		0.384	0.976	0.153	0.124
AIC		88.9	94.5	194.8	182.3

Notes:
* Significant at 10%, ** Significant at 5%, *** Significant at 1%.
t-statistics are reported in parentheses.

regulations induce both TFP change and TC of the joint production model (Model 1).

However, I find no support for induced productivity change or technological change when considering market outputs only (Model 2). As indicated in Table 4.2, the individual lags and the sum of all lags are not statistically significant at standard levels. Hence, the Almon lag results do not support the standard version of the Porter hypothesis, which states that increases in the stringency of environmental regulations can induce increases in the productivity of market outputs, potentially leading to increased profits in the long term.

Next I use Granger causality tests to explore causal directions between the stringency of environmental regulations and changes in the relevant productivity measure (TFP change or TC). When TC is the dependent variable, the model provides a test of shifts in the production frontier. When TFP change is the dependent variable, the model provides a test for changes in overall productivity (technological change, efficiency change and scale change).

First I test one direction of causality, where the relevant productivity measure is the dependent variable and environmental stringency is the independent variable. In this case I regress the current level of productivity on lags of productivity and lags of environmental stringency, and test for statistical significance of lags on environmental stringency. Next I test for causality in the reverse direction with a model where environmental stringency is the dependent variable and productivity change is the independent variable. I also carry out separate analyses for market outputs (oil and gas), and for joint production of market and environmental outputs. In all cases, the null hypotheses of the Granger tests are for non-causality. Thus, rejecting a null hypothesis is consistent with a finding of causality.

The optimal number of lags is also a critical issue in the Granger causality test. I tested several information criteria: the Akaike Information criteria (AIC), the Schwarz Bayesian criteria (SC) and the Akaike final prediction error criterion (FPE). I found identical results for the appropriate number of lags with each of the three criteria and, therefore, I report results for the AIC only.

As indicated in Table 4.3, the Granger tests indicate that environmental stringency causes TC in the joint production model, which is consistent with the restated version of the Porter hypothesis. The finding is consistent with the notion that increases in environmental stringency shift the joint production frontier of market and environmental outputs. In contrast, I find no significant causality between stringency of environmental regulations and productivity of market goods, thus rejecting the standard form of Porter hypothesis. Of course, it should be emphasized that the result is for this application only, and that special circumstances might lead to this result. For example, environmental regulations in the offshore industry are command-and-control oriented, so that there is not much flexibility to develop new technologies that comply with environmental regulations. The results could differ in a context where regulations were more flexible, such as when financial incentives are employed.

Table 4.3 Granger causality test for productivity and environmental stringency

Productivity measure		Null hypothesis 1		Null hypothesis 2	
		Environmental stringency $\nrightarrow$ Productivity		Productivity $\nrightarrow$ Environmental stringency	
		χ^2	Prob. $> \chi^2$	χ^2	Prob. $> \chi^2$
Joint production of environmental and market outputs	TC	11.75	0.0345	4.23	0.5135
	TFP	2.64	0.2833	2.12	0.3634
Market outputs only	TC	0.98	0.6138	10.74	0.0303
	TFP	0.22	0.8915	1.05	0.5832

Finally, I test whether higher productivity leads to more stringent environmental regulations. As indicated in Table 4.3, I find a causal link from technological change of market outputs to environmental stringency, but not of joint production. This finding supports the case for causality on the demand side, whereby increases in real income stimulate demand for environmental goods. However, the finding does not support causality on the supply side, where lower costs of environmental control drive adoption of tougher environmental standards.

4.5   Discussion and Conclusion

Technological progress plays an important role in addressing environmental problems while simultaneously improving standards of living. From the 1960s, economists have greatly improved our understanding of the process of technological innovation. We have progressed from 'confessions of ignorance', where time is the only 'explanatory' variable in technological progress, towards a better understanding of the mechanisms that drive productivity change, and improved measurements of various components of productivity change.

This chapter contributes to the literature on productivity change in several ways. First, I applied data envelopment analysis to a unique micro-level data set to measure various components of total factor productivity within a joint production model, which considers both market and environmental outputs. This contributes to our understanding of the impact environment controls have had on various components of total factor productivity in this industry, and thereby the potential for technological change to maintain productivity in the face of increasingly stringent environmental regulations.

The results show an upward trend in productivity in the Gulf of Mexico offshore oil and gas industry, despite resource depletion and increasingly stringent environmental regulations. My findings indicate improved productivity of environmental technologies, but environmental productivity change has lagged behind that for market outputs. Over the 28-year study period, technological change can be partitioned into approximately 80 per cent in the market sector (oil and gas production), and about 20 per cent in the environmental sector. This result may be due in part to the command-and-control nature of most environmental regulations, which allow much less flexibility for innovation in the environmental sector, as compared to the level of flexibility for innovation in production of market outputs.

I also analysed the contribution of technological change and efficiency change for both market and environmental outputs. I developed an index for decomposing technological change into technological innovation, which is associated with discovery of identifiable new technologies, and learning-by-doing, which embodies the less structural components of productivity change. The results indicate that diffusion has had a significantly larger impact on TFP than technological innovation and learning-by-doing. This is important for providing an improved understanding of the process of technological change, and could contribute to the design of effective policy. For example, the significance of technological diffusion as a determinant of productivity change suggests that it is very important for policies to encourage the sharing of new technologies in this industry.

Next I applied two models in order to understand the dynamics of the causal relationships between the stringency of environmental regulations and productivity, and thereby test the Porter hypothesis. The Porter hypothesis states that environmental regulations could spur innovation, leading to long-run increases in productivity and potentially to increased profits for the regulated industry. I recast the Porter hypothesis to explore the relationship between environmental regulations and productivity more fully. Specifically, I tested whether environmental regulations enhance joint productivity of environmental and market outputs, in addition to the standard Porter hypothesis, which applies to productivity of market outputs only.

My results support the recast version of Porter hypothesis, which examines productivity of joint production of market and environmental outputs. But I found no evidence supporting the standard formulation of the Porter hypothesis regarding increased productivity of market outputs. This finding could be due in part to the command-and-control design of environmental regulations in offshore oil and gas, which historically has not provided much latitude for innovation in achieving environmental goals.

My result suggests we must be careful to maintain a realistic view of the potential for environmental regulations. An overly naive conviction that there exists a near universal potential for win–win solutions in environmental problems could be used to justify poorly conceived environmental policies.

NOTES

1. Note that productivity improvement in a comparative static sense is not sufficient to guarantee increased profits. For example, the presence of short-run fixed capital can imply that adoption of new, productivity-enhancing technologies could reduce the present discounted value of profits (see Alpay et al., 2002). In this case, it may be economically rational for incumbent market leaders to resist new technologies, potentially yielding a comparative advantage to new entrants. Additionally, productivity improvements may shift output supply and/or input demand functions, which might affect prices in some markets, possibly resulting in lower profits.
2. Simpson and Bradford (1996) and Ulph (1996) rely on a two-country, game-theoretic framework where each country hosts one producer. Gains come from exploiting market

power, so the models apply only to a subset of environmental industries. Bovenberg and Smulders (1996) explore the role of environmental policy in an endogenous growth model and characterize conditions under which more stringent policies are likely to lead to higher growth. Mohr (2002) derives the results using a less restrictive model, starting with the observation that new productive capital is often less polluting than prior generations of capital as in Xepapadeas and de Zeeuw (1999). Using a general equilibrium model with a large number of agents, the model shows that environmental policy can simultaneously increase productivity and welfare. These gains come even without accounting for the value of a cleaner environment.

3. Note that in many cases one might expect new regulations to hurt established firms in favour of innovators that develop new approaches for addressing environmental constraints (Jaffe et al., 1995).

4. The environmental Kuznets curve hypothesizes an inverted U-shape relation between pollution intensity and per capita income. At low income levels, economic development leads to increasing levels of pollution emissions. However, as economic growth and income continue to increase beyond a threshold, demand for environmental quality increases and pollution emissions decline (see Tisdell, 2001).

5. Other techniques to measure TFP include Solow's growth accounting using input and output indexes (for example, Denison, 1979) and econometric estimation of the shifts in production, cost or profit function (for example, Ray and Segerson, 1990). Both methods require substantial cost and/or price data that are unavailable in the offshore oil and gas industry.

6. Hicks-neutral technological change implies parallel shifts in isoquants on the input side and parallel shifts in the production frontiers on the output side. In contrast, input-biased technological change implies non-parallel shifts of isoquants, and output-biased technological change implies non-parallel shifts in production frontiers.

7. Note that for this case, this same lag also maximizes adjusted R^2, which is an alternative recommended criterion.

8. The Granger causality test is a more rigorous test than the Almon lag test in two ways. First, the Granger test identifies whether the lagged independent variable (stringency of environmental regulations) adds explanatory power, relative to a model based on the lagged dependent variable (productivity change). This allows the Granger test to distinguish between an instance of two variables independently following time trends, versus a causal relationship between the two variables. In contrast, the Almon lag test considers the whether the lagged independent variable has any explanatory power, not considering lags on the dependent variable. Secondly, the Granger test examines causality in both directions, so that it can potentially distinguish between models where causality goes in either or both directions

9. Harrington et al. (2000) looked at *ex ante* cost estimates of environmental regulations compared to the *ex post* cost estimates and compared the accuracy of estimates of the direct costs of more than two dozen regulations. They concluded, at least for EPA and OSHA rules, that unit pollution reduction costs estimates are often accurate.

5. Sector-specific contribution of innovations: exploration, development and production technologies

5.1 Introduction

Oil and gas industry practice has changed a great deal from the 1980s. The industry faces significant challenges to productivity improvements in finding, producing and processing new reserves of oil and gas while complying with regulations at an acceptable cost. The exploration, development and production sectors of the industry have relied heavily on technology to improve the process of exploration for new resources and to exploit existing resources.

A firm first needs drill rigs to begin exploratory drilling when acquiring a previously unexplored tract of land. This is called the exploration process. After exploration has taken place, a firm subsequently invests in the production platforms needed to develop and extract the reserve. This stage is called development. The firm then starts petroleum production. Modern sector processes include the use of three-dimensional (3D) and four-dimensional (4D) seismic processing, reservoir monitoring and modelling, and sophisticated plant and platform design and modelling capabilities.

Major contributions to future domestic supplies must come from new frontiers in such geologically challenging and operationally complex settings as deep-water offshore drilling. Today's producers are applying a host of new technologies and strategies to minimize the environmental impact of oil and natural gas operations in these frontier regions.

However, the extent to which new exploration, development and production technologies contribute to the increase in production and environmental efficiency (or productivity) is not known. This chapter estimates and compares the effects of innovations in each sector. Many recently developed technologies and methods are used in the offshore industry. In particular, offshore technology in the Gulf of Mexico is expected to achieve significant accelerated growth in production in order to stabilize the supply of required energy. This chapter applies detailed field-level data from the Gulf of Mexico to explore the effects of new innovations by comparing their effects on the exploration, development and production sectors.

In exploration, the speed of technological improvements has been slow, but their contribution, once developed, is large. On the other hand, in the development sector, the speed of technological improvements is relatively fast, though their effectiveness is probably not as great. The speed of technological improvements in production technologies is probably fastest, but yet again their contribution may not be so great. I aim to measure the relevance of innovation to Total Factor Productivity (TFP) in the US offshore oil and gas industry.

Additionally, I am interested in the question as to which sector – exploration, development or production – employs more pro-environmental technological advances. One may consider that the effects are relatively similar because the industry considers environmental preservation an important issue; therefore, the degree of environmental advances might be similar.

The oil and natural gas industry takes many steps to assure that exploration, development, and production operations can take place with little environmental impact. Careful planning and consideration of the conditions at the site allow operations to be conducted in a responsible manner. One example of a successful production operation with environmental management is directional drilling technology, which allows access to oil and gas resources that underlie a sensitive area from a nearby area where a drilling rig can be safely located. This is a representative example of where oil and gas production and environmental protection are not mutually exclusive.

The US oil and gas industry has integrated environmental applications into its business operations. The industry has come to recognize that high environmental standards and responsible development are good business, and demonstrates its commitment to protecting the environment in research and technology investments, policies and practices, and participation in a host of voluntary environmental protection programs. The industry's use of smarter, more efficient technology complements these trends (US Department of Energy, 1993, 1996).

5.2 Background of Technologies

Technology advances make the exploration, development and production of oil and gas less expensive, ensure more efficient production, and provide protection of the environment. Exploration, development and production of oil and gas in the Gulf of Mexico are carried out through international

Table 5.1   Project flow of oil and gas project flow

Process	Technology	Cost

Exploration	Regional geological survey
	Remote sensing
	Determinants of test well location
	Test well drilling
	Analysis of source rock and
	   reservoir rock data
	Analysis of logging and well data
	Overall assessment, examination
	   of profitability, renunciation of
	   mining rights
		Exploration
		   investment
		Test drilling
		   investment

Development	Development plan
	Drilling of development well
	Placement of production
	   equipment
		Development
		   investment

Production	Production	Operating cost
		Reinvestment to
		   expand
		   production
		   competence

collaboration, and various types of firms participate, including civil engineering, construction and service firms. Various technologies at each step of exploration, development and production advance over time, though their speed of advance and workflow are different in each stage. Table 5.1 shows an outline of oil and gas operation workflows. The exploration stage of the project usually takes three to five years, with the regional geological survey and remote sensing taking two years, and test well drilling taking another two to three years. The development and production processes then require another one to five years for completion.

The use of modern technology has permitted greater efficiency in the search for oil and gas. Nowadays, more resources are found using fewer wells. At the same time, wells are drilled deeper and faster than before and fewer dry holes are encountered. Oil and gas exploration technologies consist of several steps, including regional geological surveys, remote sensing and drilling. Table 5.2 summarizes some important exploration technologies. Remote sensing, in particular, encompasses the steps of: (1) a prolific survey of the subject area; (2) application for mining rights, negotiation and bidding for the acquisition of mining rights; (3) an aerial geological survey; (4)

Table 5.2   Key technologies in exploration

Technology	Explanation
Preliminary survey	Assessment of geology through literature review and purchased materials Economic and political survey
Resource exploration	Detection of sedimentary land from surface condition through remote sensing using exploration satellites
Geographical exploration	Estimation of underground geological structures through measurement of gravity and magnetism over wide areas. This estimation is required to obtain an overview of land with sedimentary layers differing from surroundings in gravity and magnetism
Seismic exploration	Artificial earthquakes are generated and the seismic waves reflected back from strata surfaces are captured by seismographs to examine the depth and shapes of the boundaries between underground formations. Earthquakes are generated using vibrations from compressed air in oceans and from gunpowder or steel plates on land. The observed reflected waves are digitized and processed using computer.

geophysical exploration; (5) geochemical exploration; (6) seismic exploration; and (7) the comprehensive analysis of all expectations.

A few of the technologies currently employed have made exploration less costly with a higher success rate, and at the same time have reduced their environmental impact. These include advances in high-resolution 3D seismic and 4D time-lapse imaging. The main technologies in this sector are: (1) advanced 3D seismic imaging technology; (2) advanced 4D time-lapse imaging technology; (3) remote sensory technology used in conjunction with seismic imaging; (4) sub-salt imaging technology used to interpret hidden formations; (5) the environmental pollution control technology; and (6) seismic explorations using artificial earthquakes, a technology used in the final stage to determine drilling sites which is particularly important in this stage. Economic benefits are realized from these latest oil and gas exploration technologies.

In the drilling, rotary-type drills are used for test and production well drilling. Bits – located at the tip of the drill – play an important role in drilling and have a complex structure. As such, material development technology and precision machining are both necessary. Drilling circulates mud along a drill pipe. The mud is slurry water, and serves to bring the drill cuttings to the surface, thereby helping to transmit underground data. This facilitates geophysical exploration. Therefore, the development of mud has played an important role in making deep drilling possible.

A drilling rig represents structural equipment used to drill for oil and gas from underground reservoirs or to obtain mineral core samples. The term can refer to a land-based rig, a marine-based structure commonly called an offshore rig, or a structure that drills oil wells called an oil rig. Drilling rigs can be: (1) small and portable, such as those used in mineral exploration drilling; or (2) large, capable of drilling through thousands of metres of the earth's crust. Large mud pumps are used to circulate drilling mud through the drill bit and the casing for cooling and to remove the cuttings while the well is drilled. A floating vessel upon which a drilling rig sits can be a floating rig or a semi-submersible rig because the whole purpose of the structure is for drilling. Sometimes a drilling rig is also used to complete an oil well, preparing it for production. However, the rig is not involved with the extraction of the oil; its primary function is to make a hole in the ground so that oil can be extracted.

Test drilling allows various types of loggings within wells, enabling the detection and prediction of oil and gas reservoirs. Logging technologies are summarized as follows:

1. Mud drilling: detection of oil and gas reservoirs.
2. Core cuttings: (a) detection of oil reservoirs; (b) lithofacies survey (sandstone, mudstone and volcanic rock); (c) fossil survey (determination of geological age and deposit environment); (d) survey of reservoir rock competence (porosity, oil saturation and permeability); and (e) survey of source rock competence (quantity, quality and maturity of kerosene).
3. Wireline logging: (a) survey of strata depths and lithofacies; (b) survey of geological structure (strata slope); and (c) survey of reservoir rock competence (porosity, oil saturation and permeability).
4. Testing oil and gas from reservoir: (a) type of fluid (oil, gas and water); (b) production capacity survey (fluid pressure, permeability and obstacles to completion); and (c) component analysis of extracted fluid.

Oil and natural gas extracted together from underground are separated into oil and gas, then further refined through the removal of water and salt. Crude oil or gas is allowed to flow into production wells drilled into the reservoir and flows through steel oil well pipes to the surface, where control equipment at the well mouth sends it to separating equipment and storage tanks. Controls at the well mouth use valves and flow controllers comprising thermometers and pressure gauge chokes. Flowing wells, pumping wells and gas lift wells are different types of production wells. Flowing wells are where gas and water pressure in the reservoir cause the oil to flow naturally. This pressure declines during production. As a result, methods such as drawing out the crude oil with a pump, or injecting gas to lighten the oil's specific gravity to assist flow, are then used to extract the oil.

Currently, approximately 25 per cent of US oil and natural gas production comes from offshore areas. Technology has enabled the industry to explore deeper waters in the Gulf of Mexico and to make many new discoveries, while minimizing the impact on the environment. The industry's offshore activities, including the technology used and the operational steps, are expected to help protect health and the environment. In the field, the operator needs to prepare to develop site-specific waste management, and manages exploration, development and production wastes. Although technology and management methods are developed in each stage of exploration, development and production, the contribution of each step is not yet known.

5.3   Methodology

I use several different versions of the model to measure and decompose productivity changes. Table 5.3 shows the model specification. First, a base model as in Chapter 2 is used to calculate the gross productivity change, which measures the gross effect of increases in productivity due to improvements in all exploration, development and production technology. A gross productivity change index greater than zero implies there is a productivity progress, while a gross productivity change index less than zero implies there is a productivity regress. We decompose the measure of productivity change into indexes that represent specific technological innovations and a residual. Thus, the index of productivity change is decomposed as:

$$TFP_{Gross} = TFP_{Sector(i)} \cdot TFP_{Res(i)}$$

where TFP_{Gross} is the gross index of productivity change, $TFP_{Sector(i)}$ is the productivity change associated with identifiable new technologies (the weighted innovation index and the measures of horizontal drilling) of sector i (i is exploration, development or production) and $TFP_{Res(i)}$ is the net index of productivity change that cannot be explained by the specifically identifiable new technologies. This chapter only analyses the size of $TFP_{Sector(i)}$ without any concern for $TFP_{Res(i)}$.

TFP change from Model 1, which incorporates all forms of technological change, is divided by TFP as calculated in Model 2 (Model 3 or Model 4), which includes the weighted technological innovation index and the measure of horizontal drilling discussed above treated as 'inputs'. Thus, applying data

Table 5.3   Model specifications without environmental variables

Index calculated	Model 1 Base model: Gross TFP	Model 2 Exploratory innovation	Model 3 Development innovation	Model 4 Production innovation
Output variables				
Oil production (bbl)	X	X	X	X
Gas production (Mcf)	X	X	X	X
Input variables				
Number of platforms	X	X	X	X
Av. platform size (#slot/#platform)	X	X	X	X
Number of exploration wells	X	X	X	X
Number of development wells	X	X	X	X
Average drilling distance for exploratory wells	X	X	X	X
Average drilling distance for development wells	X	X	X	X
Produced water	X	X	X	X
Water depth	X	X	X	X
Depletion effects (Oil)	X	X	X	X
Depletion effects (Gas)	X	X	X	X
Oil reserves in the field	X	X	X	X
Gas reserves in the field	X	X	X	X
Porosity (field type)	X	X	X	X
Innovation index (exploratory)		X		
Innovation index (development)			X	
Innovation index (production)				X
Horizontal & directional drilling (exploratory)		X		
Horizontal & directional drilling (development)			X	

envelopment analysis (DEA) to Model 2 (Model 3 or Model 4) calculates an index of productivity change after accounting for the effects of specific measurable technological innovations. Therefore, Model 2 (Model 3 or Model 4) measures shifts in the frontier that cannot be accounted for by specific new innovations. This method allows an explanation of a portion of productivity change associated with specific innovations, and to narrow the 'confession of ignorance' to a residual effect. Thus, the fraction of TFP associated with specific innovations is:

$$TFP_{Sector(i)} = TFP_{Gross}/TFP_{Res(i)}.$$

Because TFP_{Sector} is measured for each of the exploratory, development and production stages, it is possible to find and compare directly the technological change associated with specific innovations. For example, Model 2 includes variables that measure innovations in the exploration sector. Thus, the effect of innovation in the exploratory sector over time is calculated by dividing the results of Model 1 by the results of Model 2. Similarly, Model 3 includes a variable that measures technological innovations in the development sector. So, the effect on productivity of changes in the development sector over time is calculated by dividing the results of Model 1 by the results of Model 3. The contribution of the production sector is calculated by dividing the results of Model 1 by the results of Model 4.

The speed of technological improvements has been slow, but their contribution, once developed, is large in the exploration sector. In the development and production sectors, on the other hand, the speed is relatively fast, though their effectiveness is probably not so large. I measure and compare the relevance of each sector's contribution, $TFP_{Sector(i)}$, to changes in the gross TFP. I am especially interested in how large the contribution of the exploration sector is compared with the other two sectors.

Next, I discuss the measurements of environmental productivity associated with specific innovations. Table 5.4 shows the model specification with environmental variables. The TFP change associated with environmental inputs and outputs is then calculated as:

$$TFP_{Env, Sector(i)} = TFP_{Joint, Sector(i)}/TFP_{Market, Sector(i)}.$$

Thus, in the case of the exploratory sector, dividing the joint measure of productivity change from Model 5 by the productivity change measure of market outputs from Model 2 provides the residual measure of productivity change in the environmental sector. In each model, an appropriate innovations index is included in the model. For example, only market and environmental technological innovations in the exploratory sector are included in Model 5, while only market technological innovations in the exploratory sector are included in Model 2. In the same manner, the measurement of environmental productivity associated with specific innovations in the development (production) sector is calculated by the TFP in Model 6 (Model 7) divided by

Table 5.4　Model specifications with environmental variables

Index calculated:	Model 5 Exploratory innovation	Model 6 Development innovation	Model 7 Production innovation
Output variables			
Oil production (bbl)	X	X	X
Gas production (Mcf)	X	X	X
Water pollution	X	X	X
Oil spill			X
Input variables			
Number of platforms	X	X	X
Av. platform size (#slot/#platform)	X	X	X
Number of exploration wells	X	X	X
Number of development wells	X	X	X
Average drilling distance for exploratory wells	X	X	X
Average drilling distance for development wells	X	X	X
Produced water	X	X	X
Water depth	X	X	X
Depletion effects (oil)	X	X	X
Depletion effects (gas)	X	X	X
Oil reserves in the field	X	X	X
Gas reserves in the field	X	X	X
Porosity (field type)	X	X	X
Innovation index (exploratory)	X		
Innovation index (development)		X	
Innovation index (production)			X
Horizontal & directional drilling (exploratory)	X		
Horizontal & directional drilling (development)		X	
Environmental compliance cost	X	X	X

the TFP in Model 3 (Model 4). By comparing the three contributions of environmental technological innovations, $TFP_{Env,Sector(i)}$, it is possible to answer the question as to whether the exploration, development or production sector has more pro-environmental technological advancements.

5.4　Results

This study decomposes TFP change in the Gulf of Mexico OCS exploration, development and production sectors using the weighted innovation index and horizontal drilling variables discussed earlier. I use these innovation variables as attributes to account for the effects of specifically identifiable new technologies.

Figure 5.1 presents the trends for the effects of innovations in each sector of exploration, development and production processes over the period from 1947 to 2002. The highest score in the latest year is set as 100. This shows that the contribution from the exploration sector is approximately twice as large as the contribution from the production sector on average. The developing sector's contribution to the TFP increase is around 20 per cent greater on average than that of the production sector. Among these three sectors, the exploratory sector contributes most to the TFP increase. This implies that although technological innovation for the development and production sectors is crucial for increasing production and improving TFP, there are significantly more productivity gains from the exploratory sector's innovations. Thus, though speed of technological improvements has been relatively slow in the exploration sector and the number of innovations is relatively small, their contribution is larger once developed. Over the study period, the effects of exploratory innovations continuously contribute to increases in TFP, indicating large diffusion effects as suggested in Chapter 2.

The largest effects are attributed to several important innovations described below. Many disciplines in science play important roles in oil and gas exploration technological development. Geophysics has been used to survey subsurface structures since about 1930, although oil and gas exploration technology started in the early twentieth century. One of the most recent important innovations in oil and gas exploration technological development is the use of computers. Employing advances in computer performance, the accumulation of vast amounts of data and the use of analysis systems and quantitative modelling simulations enable the precise description of geological conditions and oil and gas reservoirs, enabling the projection of future oil and gas production. Seismic exploration closely links the locations of epicentres and receivers. It measures multiple reflected waves with different phases and allows 3D imaging of geological formations. Precision measurement enables the estimation of oil and gas reservoirs with large differences in density sandwiched between other geological formations.

When advancing technological levels, protection of the environment is also an important issue. Complete technical development for exploration, development and production technologies suited to the natural environment together with appropriate materials and systems are needed.

Figure 5.2 shows the results for environmental technologies. The results indicate that the highest score appears in the production sector, while the exploratory and development sectors represent the second- and third-highest

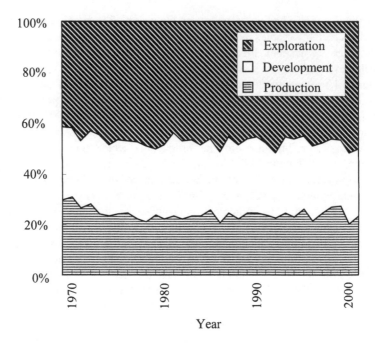

*Figure 5.1   Market technology innovation: exploration, development and
production*

scores, respectively. Each share is about 40 per cent, 35 per cent and 25 per
cent on average for production, exploration and development, respectively. In
contrast to the results for market technologies, the production sector plays an
important role in increasing environmental productivity. One may consider
that the effects are relatively similar because the industry considers
environmental preservation an important issue; therefore, the degree of
environmental advances might be similar. However, the production sector
involves the environment most directly, and therefore the significance of its
contribution is the greatest. The contributions measured by these indices
include innovations from both the market side (pollution prevention
technologies) and the non-market side (exploration, development and
production technologies that require changes in their uses of technologies and
therefore affect pollution management).

With the increase in environmental stringency, an increasing number of
pollution prevention technologies have been developed for the offshore oil
and gas industry. Market-side technologies affecting environmental
management include drilling, the use of computers and deep-water
technologies, amongst others. For example, advanced drilling technology is

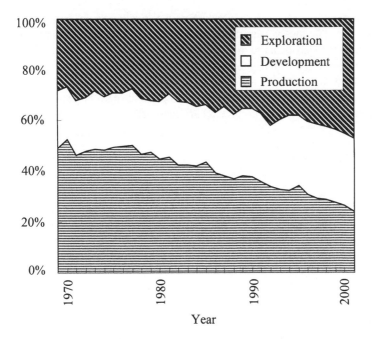

*Figure 5.2   Environmental technology innovation: exploration,
            development and production*

the key to extracting more oil and gas from deep water. Inclined wells and long horizontal wells are being used to avoid surface obstacles and to extract oil from the reservoirs spreading horizontally from vertical wells. Multilateral well systems are already used: these combine one vertical well with multiple horizontal wells. These systems increase the economic viability of oil and gas extraction. Drillers use steerable down-hole motors to create well bores that bend and turn at all angles. They also create sensory systems next to the drill bit to determine its location, angle and the composition of the rock layers as they are encountered. Drilling requires accurate control to determine the underground position precisely. Therefore, measurement while drilling (MWD) is used to obtain bottom-hole data at the point of drilling, which is fed back to surface control systems. Automatic control of databases that need to be compared, control programs, positioning using satellite data, quick collection of drill-head data and other developments are constantly improving over time.

Furthermore, systems have been developed to obtain data using sensors of geological conditions and to send them to the surface in addition to data obtained on bit load, torque and other drilling parameters at the drilling point.

This enables the use of an application called logging while drilling (LWD), which simultaneously performs drilling and logging. Improving the transmission speed of large amounts of data is another area of development. The development of mud pulses, mud sirens and pipe transmission methods and systems that use mud as a medium have also been made. Environmentally, these technologies save pollution emissions per unit of oil and gas production, and therefore improve environmental productivity.

5.5   Conclusion

Advances in technologies are expected to play an important role in meeting the challenges of effectively and productively finding, producing and processing new reserves of oil and gas while complying with environmental regulations at an acceptable cost. It is necessary to develop technologies furthermore using the integrated science of geophysics, geochemistry surface and applied engineering fields.

One key innovation is advances in oil and gas reservoir evaluation technologies. The acquisition, analysis and interpretation of data on liquid pressure and movement from rock, oil, gas and stratum water obtained from wells can be combined with information from geological exploration, well building, logging and oil reservoirs to create quantitative models of oil field and gas field shapes and conditions. Predictive simulations have also been created, and these are being developed as a method for assessing oil and gas reservoirs at the drilling fields. The flow of liquid within oil reservoirs can also be modelled, and outside forces (for example, changes in flow when water or carbon dioxide is injected from the surface) can also be simulated. This is expected to improve recovery rates.

Samples obtained from oil reservoirs are being used for measuring physical properties deep underground to estimate the physical properties of deep oil reservoirs. When these analyses are collected from multiple wells on a site, they can be used to create a detailed image of geological and oil reservoirs in an area. In the process of production work, repeated 3D seismic exploration and oil reservoir evaluations that track changes over time allow for 4D monitoring and simulation. Extending this over time may yield remarkable improvements in the accuracy of predicting oil reservoir productivity and reserves.

Second, enhanced oil recovery (EOR) technology is expected to contribute to increasing productivity management. The amount of oil that can be recovered through natural pressure or pumping as the primary recovery volume is usually 20–30 per cent of the resources in an oil reservoir. In order to continue recovery beyond this point, water or steam and gas may be injected, raising pressure in the oil reservoirs. This secondary recovery raises the rate of recovery to about 30–40 per cent. In addition, insertion of steam and surfactants to lower oil viscosity, the injection of carbon dioxide to separate oil from rock, and its dilution with chemicals or solvents can raise the recovery rate to 40–60 per cent. Improvements in such recovery methods are a major reason that recoverable reserves are now increasing. Over time, production is accompanied by changes in oil components. Production can also be reduced or halted by obstacles in geological formations. Technologies using water pressure or explosives to remove geological obstacles are also being developed. In complex geological formations containing faults, oil reservoirs are broken up. For this reason, such technologies are an important means of improving recovery rates.

However, it is not possible to tell a priori which particular innovations in exploration, development and production processes over the period from 1947 to 2002 most contribute to the increase in TFP. I find that although the speed of technological improvements has been slow in exploration, or the number of innovations is small, their contribution is large once developed. Over the study period, the effects of exploratory innovations continuously contribute to the increase in TFP, indicating large effects of diffusion as suggested earlier. In contrast to the results for market technologies, I find that the production sector plays an important role in increasing environmental productivity. Though one may consider that the effects are relatively similar because the industry regards environmental preservation as an important issue, and therefore the degree of environmental advances might be similar, the production sector engages with the environment most directly and therefore the significance of its contribution would be the greatest. The contributions measured by these indices include innovations from both the market side (pollution prevention technologies) and the non-market side (exploration, development and production technologies that require changes in their uses of technologies and therefore affect pollution management).

6. Returns to pollution abatement and the environmental Kuznets curve

6.1 Introduction

Recently, there has been a focus on the relation between environmental quality and economic development. The environmental Kuznets curve (EKC) postulates an inverse U-shaped relationship between environmental quality and per capita income levels. That is, the income elasticity of environmental quality turns from positive at lower levels of per capita income to negative at higher levels. Many empirical studies have examined this relationship for various pollutants, starting with the seminal work of Grossman and Krueger (1993, 1995). Researchers have found an inverted U-shaped relationship, monotonically decreasing or increasing between environmental quality and a rising per capita income level. Stern (2004) has provided a summary of the empirical literature. These studies have shown there is no single relationship between environmental quality and per capita income that fits all types of pollutants.

One of the more important criticisms of these empirical studies is that they yield little insight into the mechanisms of the inverted U-shaped relationship. In the EKC literature, theory has played a limited role in its development (Copeland and Taylor, 2004). This has created difficulties in interpreting the empirical inverted U-shaped curve. A simple explanation for the EKC is provided by Andreoni and Levinson (2001). In their study, pollution abatement efficiency is expected to increase as the pollution abatement effort increases. These efficiency increases make abatement less expensive and, therefore, pollution can decrease, even if environmental policies stagnate. If this is feasible, increasing returns to abating pollution may exist, and this relationship can explain the EKC. In this framework, the inverted U-shaped EKC does not require any complicated political-economy models of collective decision making, externalities and economic growth. One implication of Andreoni and Levinson's study is that EKCs can exist whether policies are socially efficient or inefficient because of increasing returns to scale.

Recent work by Zaim and Taskin (2000) undertakes an efficiency approach in the EKC literature. They measure the environmental efficiency of

Organisation for Economic Co-operation and Development (OECD) countries over 1980–90 using data envelopment analysis (DEA) with a proxy for ·environmental quality as the EKC dependent variable. Finding the determinants of the factors underlying the changes in the environmental efficiency are their main concern. They find a Kuznets curve in the efficiency.

This study tests the hypothesis that there are increasing returns to the abatement of pollution using the environmental efficiency approach. This chapter analyses the environmental efficiency resulting from US offshore production using data from 1975 to 2002. I estimate regressions at the oil and gas field level for first-differences models.

The chapter is structured as follows. Section 6.2 provides a review of the literature. Section 6.3 discusses the research methods. Section 6.4 presents the econometric results and section 6.5 presents a summary and some concluding remarks.

6.2   Background: The Environmental Kuznets Curve

There exist theoretical explanations supporting the empirical evidence that an EKC exists. Four main theoretical explanations, which could each interact with the others (for example, Copeland and Taylor, 2004), are as follows.

Firstly, phase of development, where increasing output requires more inputs, which implies more emissions as a by-product. Thus, economic growth exhibits a scale effect that has a negative impact on the environment in the early stages of development. However, economic growth also has positive impacts on the environment through a composition effect. As income grows in the later stages of development, the structure of the economy changes and there is an increase in cleaner activities that produce less pollution. In the case of general industrial pollutants, environmental degradation tends to increase during the structural transformation of an economy from the agricultural to the industrial phase, and subsequently starts to fall with another structural change from an energy-intensive industry to a technology-intensive industry based on services and knowledge. In the case of pesticide risk from agriculture, the focus of this study, environmental degradation tends to increase with the use of toxic and organic chemical loadings as the economy grows, and starts to fall as the share of agriculture in the economy decreases.

Secondly, income effects, where the shape of the EKC reflects changes in the demand for environmental quality, or pesticide risk in this study, as income rises. This explanation suggests that the relationship between pollution and income should vary across pollutants according to their perceived damage.

Thirdly, threshold effects, where an environmental policy is implemented after some threshold has been reached. Threshold effects can arise in either the abatement opportunities, as in Stokey (1998), or in the political process, as in Jones and Manuelli (2001). Israel and Levinson (2004) referred to the first type of threshold effect as the *technology constraint explanation*. It assumes an abatement production function where the marginal product of abatement is bounded. In Stokey (1998), dirtier technologies are used if income is below a critical threshold, whereas progressively cleaner methods are utilized as income rises above that level and the marginal cost of abating pollution makes abatement worthwhile. The second type of threshold effect is called an 'institutional constraint explanation' by Israel and Levinson (2004). It assumes that some obstacle prevents poor countries from establishing the social institutions necessary to regulate pollution. In Jones and Manuelli (2001), political and economic barriers are considered to be fixed costs, so that the appointment costs of institutions stick up for the environment. Once income has risen sufficiently, these fixed costs become worth incurring, environmental protection agencies are established, and pollution begins to decrease with economic growth. Jones and Manuelli (2001) argued that the EKC relationship is determined by a society's ability to make collective decisions, whereas Stokey (1998) described an economy that needs to pass certain threshold levels of development before obtaining access to cleaner production technologies.

Fourthly, increasing returns to abating pollution, where the abatement efficiency increases with increases in the scale of abatement. This indicates that doubling the clean-up efforts more than doubles the amount of pollution abated. Andreoni and Levinson (2001) modelled the abatement technology directly and demonstrated that whether policies are socially efficient or inefficient, EKCs can exist because of increasing returns to scale. The authors argued that most theoretical explanations of the EKC hypothesis are based on some sort of scale economy. For example, the fixed costs in Stokey (1998) gave rise to scale economies in pollution abatement. Similarly, the fixed costs in Jones and Manuelli (2001) generated scale economies from a societal perspective. The third and fourth explanations of the EKC, that is, threshold effects and increasing returns to abating pollution, share a common theme, which is the importance of technology. The model by Andreoni and Levinson (2001) generated many of the implications of existing models without requiring dynamics, predetermined patterns of economic growth, multiple equilibria, released constraints, political institutions, bundled commodities, irreversible pollution or even externalities. Thus, increasing returns to scale in abatement broadly encompass many of the existing models that derive inverse U-shaped pollution–income paths. An important implication of Andreoni and Levinson's research is that explanations of abatement and production technologies are central to understanding the EKC phenomenon. In the case of offshore pollution from oil and gas production, the inefficiency caused by the lack of cross-field externalities, such as technology spillovers, might be reduced by scaling up abatement and implementing more effective waste water controls.

Empirical evidence of increasing returns to pollution abatement is limited. Andreoni and Levinson (2001) regressed data on pollution abatement operating costs (PAOC) by US states and two-digit SIC codes on a quadratic industry-level gross state product (GSP). The negative sign of the quadratic term on the GSP indicated that larger industries spend proportionally less on pollution abatement. However, I am not aware of any study that has attempted to test whether efforts to abate environmental degradations involve increasing returns. Furthermore, in any such study, it would be important to control the level of abatement technology because, in practice, the technology employed changes over time.

6.3   Econometric Methods

In the existing literature, time trend variables have been taken into account to test for efficiency or technology level (see, for example, Hilton and Levinson, 1998). However, the time trend may capture any effects changing over time, such as changes in relative energy prices (Agras and Chapman, 1999). Explicit consideration of a technology is necessary to capture the efficiency factors. In a review of the EKC literature, Stern (1998) noted the importance of understanding technological progress. This study employed DEA and illustrated the important role played by the environmental efficiency level in calculating environmental quality directly instead of using pollution per area as a dependent variable and time trend as an explanatory variable. This measurement is especially useful when there is multiple environmental pollution. This is so because DEA estimates the efficiency using multiple environmental pollution.

This study estimates a quadratic EKC using field-level data. The usual approach when facing heteroscedasticity of unknown form is to use the generalized method of moments (GMM) as introduced by Hansen (1982). The GMM makes use of orthogonality conditions to allow for efficient estimation in the presence of heteroscedasticity of unknown form (see Mátyás, 1999). My specification of the model is given by:

$$Y_{it} = \alpha_0 + \alpha_1 I_t + \alpha_2 I_t^2 + \alpha_3 \, Abate_{it} + \varepsilon_{it} \qquad (6.1)$$

where Y is the environmental efficiency for field i and year t, I is the real gross domestic product (GDP), and *Abate* is the pollution abatement effort.

Technology and skills have been important elements in the theoretical and empirical literature on the determinants of pollution. In this study, my specification allows for technological differences over fields and years. As I would like to look at the abatement level and the efficiency level of the environmental management, this specification includes the efficiency level of environmental technologies as the dependent variable and the abatement level as the explanatory variable.

The Y variable is estimated from two non-parametric efficiency estimates: (1) efficiency of market output (that is, oil and gas production), denoted by EFF_{Market}; and (2) the sum of the efficiency of non-market output (that is, the reduction in water pollution) plus market output, denoted by EFF_{Joint}. EFF_{Market} includes the usual production inputs and outputs, and EFF_{Joint} includes environmental degradation and abatements effort, as well as production inputs and outputs. Given the input level, an increase in output raises the usual productivity, EFF_{Market}. Holding inputs and environmental output constant, an increase in good output raises EFF_{Joint}. Furthermore, holding inputs and good output constant, a decrease in the environmental output raises EFF_{Joint}. Thus, the residual effects of two factors explain the productivity resulting from changes in technology for the nonmarket goods (environmental degradation). This is given by:

$$Y = EFF_{Joint} - EFF_{Market} \qquad (6.2)$$

where an increase in Y implies an improvement in abatement efficiency, which might consist of either a greater reduction of environmental degradation given the same level of abatement effort, or a reduction of abatement efforts given the same level of environmental degradation level, or both.

I expect a negative sign for the abatement effort variable, *Abate*, because an increase in the pollution abatement effort reduces the environmental degradation in an efficient way, holding all else constant. The next specification includes the quadratic term of the abatement effort to test the increasing returns, as follows:

$$Y_{it} = \beta_0 + \beta_1 I_t + \beta_2 I_t^2 + \beta_3 Abate_{it} + \beta_4 Abate_{it}^2 + \varepsilon_{it}. \qquad (6.3)$$

A statistically significant negative sign on the quadratic term of abatement implies the existence of increasing returns to pollution abatements. In contrast, a significant positive sign on the quadratic term of abatement implies the existence of decreasing returns to abatement. An insignificant sign implies that no significant evidence of returns to scale has been found. If the quadratic term of I is significant with a negative sign in (6.1) and insignificant in (6.3), and if the quadratic term of *Abate* is significant with a negative sign, this implies that the inverted U-shaped relationship of the EKC is explained by increasing or decreasing returns to abating pollution.

I estimate the model with the fixed and random effects. In the presence of field-specific stochastic trends, neither random effects nor fixed effects estimators will be consistent. Differencing the data will eliminate potential stochastic trends in the series. Therefore, I take a first-differences model as follows:

$$\Delta Y_{it} = \alpha_0' + \alpha_1' \Delta I_t + \alpha_2' \Delta I_t^2 + \alpha_3' \Delta Abate_{it} + \varepsilon_{it},$$ (6.4)

$$\Delta Y_{it} = \beta_0' + \beta_1' \Delta I_t + \beta_2' \Delta I_t^2 + \beta_3' \Delta Abate_{it} + \beta_4' \Delta Abate_{it}^2 + \varepsilon_{it},$$ (6.5)

which I estimate with a fixed effects transformation by only considering time effects. The time effects are expected to capture common time-related effects.

6.4   Results

The usual approach when facing heteroscedasticity of unknown form is to use the GMM introduced by Hansen (1982). The environmental efficiency models are estimated using the GMM estimation method. Using J-statistics, it is not possible to reject the hypothesis that all instruments satisfy the orthogonality conditions. The Sargan test of the overidentifying restrictions yields p-values of 0.26, which imply that the instruments used in the GMM estimation are valid. The null of a unit root is rejected at all standard significance levels. Table 6.1 reports the results of estimating equation (6.1) and equation (6.3). The unique feature of this study is to use the environmental efficiency of production technologies instead of environmental quality. In all of the specifications in Table 6.1, it is possible to obtain statistically significant results and find that the quadratic term of income per capita had negative effects on the environmental efficiency. All results show that the EKC has an inverted U-shape.

Next, I add the quadratic term of abatement effort as in equation (6.2) and equation (6.4). Table 6.2 shows the estimated results. The J-statistics show that it is not possible to reject the hypothesis that all instruments satisfy orthogonality conditions. The estimates of the quadratic term of per capita GDP are not significant.

All of the estimates of the quadratic term of the abatement effort show negative signs and all are significant at the 10 per cent level. Note, however,

Table 6.1   GMM parameter estimates (equations (6.1) and (6.3)): base model

Dependent variable	Fixed effects	Random effects	Fixed effects (*First differences*)
Per capita GDP	1.375	1.337 **	0.762 *
	(1.65)	(2.76)	(1.96)
(Per capita GDP)^2	−0.942 **	−0.362 ***	−0.283 *
	(−2.11)	(−3.12)	(−2.09)
Abatement effort	−0.771 ***	−0.388 **	−0.329 **
	(−3.45)	(2.32)	(−2.43)
J-statistic (*p-value*)	0.2538	0.2147	0.2134
Unit root test	Reject	Reject	Reject
Hausman test		Reject	

Notes:
*** Significant at 1%, ** Significant at 5%, * Significant at 10%.
t statistics are in parentheses.
Coefficients of dummy variables are estimated but not reported in this table.

Table 6.2   GMM parameter estimates (equations (6.2) and (6.4)): test of increasing returns to abating

Dependent variable	Fixed effects	Random effects	Fixed effects (*First differences*)
Per capita GDP	1.621	1.563 **	1.312 *
	(1.37)	(2.55)	(1.87)
(Per capita GDP)^2	−0.992	−0.967	−0.629
	(−0.98)	(1.09)	(−1.25)
Abatement effort	0.219	0.121 **	0.541
	(1.01)	(2.45)	(1.23)
(Abatement effort)^2	−0.177 **	−0.104 **	−0.099 **
	(−2.36)	(2.56)	(−2.55)
J-statistic (*p-value*)	0.2538	0.2147	0.2134
Unit root test	Reject	Reject	Reject
Hausman test		Reject	

Notes:
*** Significant at 1%, ** Significant at 5%, * Significant at 10%.
t statistics are in parentheses.
Coefficients of dummy variables are estimated but not reported in this table.

that the linear abatement term is positive and statistically significant. In these cases, it is possible that an increased abatement cost is associated with a decreasing rather than an increasing environmental efficiency. Overall, my hypothesis of increasing returns to pollution abatements is supported.

In particular, the quadratic terms of per capita GDP are no longer significant and those of abatement are significant. This implies that increasing returns to abating pollution explain the inverted U-shaped relation of the EKC with greater statistical significance than does the income level. Thus, the driving force for increasing environmental efficiency in the US oil and gas industry is the increase in pollution abatement rather than the increase in income.

In this study, I show that increasing returns to pollution abatement play an important role in determining the pollution level over the period of the study. Thus, in support of Andreoni and Levinson (2001), an important implication of this research is that explanations regarding abatement technology are central to understanding the phenomenon of the EKC.

6.5   Conclusion and Discussion

Theory has played a limited role in the development of the EKC literature (Copeland and Taylor, 2004), which has created difficulties in interpreting the empirical inverted U-shaped curve. Andreoni and Levinson (2001) provided a simple explanation for the EKC: pollution abatement efficiency might increase as the abatement effort rises. The efficiency increases make abatement less expensive and, thus, environmental quality can increase even if environmental policies are stagnant. Thus, increasing returns to abating pollution might exist and this relationship can explain the EKC. In this framework, the inverted U-shaped EKC does not require any complicated political-economy models of collective decision making, externalities and economic growth. One implication of Andreoni and Levinson's study is that EKCs can exist whether policies are socially efficient or inefficient, because of increasing returns to scale.

This study tests for increasing returns to pollution abatement in an EKC framework by analysing the environmental risk in the US oil and gas industry with field-level data for the period 1975–2004. Although Andreoni and Levinson (2001) assumed no change in pollution policy, several environmental regulations have been implemented in the US offshore industry. Thus, rather than determining whether environmental policy is required, this test aimed to understand the impact of abatement on the pollution level. Contamination by water pollution can potentially damage the offshore environment. Considering the importance of the environmental issue, detecting the relationship between abatement and environmental damage is important. I utilized a data set involving environmental efficiency. My estimates for the US offshore industry for the period 1975–2002 support the hypothesis of increasing returns to abatement.

The numerical results have to be interpreted with care because inverted U-shaped relationships may become N-shaped curves in the longer run. That is, they may initially exhibit the same pattern as the inverted U-shaped curve, but beyond a certain income level, return to exhibiting a positive relationship between environmental pressure and income (Pezzey, 1989; Opschoor, 1990; de Bruyn et al., 1998). Thus, delinking might be considered a temporary phenomenon. Opschoor (1990), for example, argued that once technological advances in resource use or abatement opportunities have been exhausted, or have become too expensive, further income growth will result in an increase of environmental degradation. In the same way, the evidence of increasing returns to abatement might be short-run results. In the long run, if the environmental technology level remains constant, scale economy effects might be exhausted and change to decreasing returns to abatement. Therefore, further evidence of technology analysis in this literature is required to answer this question.

The relationship between offshore oil and gas production and the environment is also complex, depending on such location-specific factors as the assimilative capacity of the natural environment, which often have not been fully explored scientifically. Hence, any estimate of prospective environmental impacts from oil and gas production is subject to considerable risk. Nevertheless, deriving quantitative estimates of the likely environmental impacts of offshore water pollution abatement might help to focus and advance the policy debate.

7. Direction of environmental technological change: pollution saving or cost saving?

7.1 Introduction

Debates on environmental economics in the past decades have been largely focused on the effects of environmental policy on technological progress (Jung et al., 1996). An understanding of the process of technological progress is imperative because the environmental impact of economic activity is strongly affected by the direction of technological change. Newly available technologies might alleviate existing polluting activities or cause more pollution. The cumulative effects of technological changes are expected to be large because the effects of environmental problems and policy are assessed over a long time.

There are two possible sources of pollution reduction, and therefore there are technological options to reduce pollution. Emissions can be reduced by decreasing output and/or by means of 'end-of-pipe' treatments. The first term implies pollution-saving technological progress in the production process itself, which shifts down the emission coefficient. The innovations developed or discovered to reduce the amount of pollution generated per unit of output without changing production cost are included in this term. The second term implies cost-saving technological progress in end-of-pipe treatments, which shift down the cost function.

Theoretically, the conventional approach in the literature to technological change and environmental policy assumes a fixed output level and concentrates on minimizing pure abatement cost caused by end-of-pipe measures (plus transfers in the case of a pollution emission tax). Conventional studies, mainly analysing the second source which minimizes pure abatement costs, usually claim that market-based instruments such as emission taxes induce a stronger incentive for technological change to reduce pollution than command-and-control type emission standards (for example, Zerbe, 1970; Wenders, 1975; Downing and White, 1986; Milliman and Prince, 1989). This claim is justified by the fact that under a tax policy there is a positive price for every unit of pollutant, whereas emission standards imply a price of zero in the case of compliance. Therefore, economists prefer market-based instruments, such as emission taxes, rather than direct controls through emission standards.

A recent study by Dietz and Michaelis (2004), however, claims that this crucially depends on some rather unrealistic assumptions. The policy may induce different output levels such that the impact of innovation on profits also depends on environmental regulations. As a consequence, the appropriate measure of the incentive to innovate is not only measured by the reductions in pure abatement cost, as assumed in the conventional model, but also by increases in profits. They assume both possibilities and show this is not true. Instead, they show that the impact on innovation in pollution control caused by taxes and standards strongly depends on the scale of technological progress, as well as on the cost structure of the firm under consideration, such that there is no unique ranking of the two policies. Dietz and Michaelis (2004) show that which instrument provides a higher incentive to innovate depends on the specific circumstances of the case considered.[1] If the pollution-saving technological progress is expected to come as a big bang or non-marginal change, then the conventional view holds and emission taxes induce a higher incentive to innovate compared with emission standards. However, the reverse is true if pollution-saving technological progress is expected to come as a marginal change or as a sequence of comparatively small steps independent of each other. As a consequence, no general political advice can be given in favour of taxes or standards, and there a dilemma may emerge concerning the choice of the appropriate instrument.

In this chapter, instead of directly measuring the marginal cost of production and the marginal cost caused by the abatement of additional units of the pollutant under consideration, I measure and compare the effectiveness for pollution reduction by estimating the pollution-saving technological progress in the production process and the cost-saving technological progress in end-of-pipe treatments. I then analyse two different types of technological progress in pollution control for the offshore oil and gas industry. The information provided should ensure a better process of environmental policy making between governmental authorities and the firms involved.

Policy makers may be interested in deciding the use of market mechanisms such as taxation or emission trading if they are more efficient than conventional command-and-control type regulation. If the pollution-saving technological progress is expected to come as a non-marginal change, then emission taxes induce a higher incentive to innovate and therefore the taxes should be recommended in practice. If the technological progress is expected to come as a marginal change, however, the emission standards induce a higher incentive to innovate and need to be recommended in practice. In general, the emission standards have been applied in practice for a long time and altering the policies would be significant cost to the government and industries. Therefore, the emission standards might not be recommended if the additional benefits from changing the policy were relatively small. However, the empirical procedure used in this chapter might be helpful to identify the benefits of two different technological changes. Additionally, for the industry, the information on the origin of the growth of environmental technological progress might be important for the research and development (R&D) strategy.

7.2 Model

The conventional model of innovation in pollution control under different policy regimes is based on two doubtful assumptions about the optimization behaviour of the innovating firm as well as about the nature of the emission standard. The approach in the literature assumes a fixed output level given by the environmental regulations.

The second deficiency relates to the description of the emission standard. As is common in the pollution control literature, the studies employ fixed levels of absolute quantities (for example, tonnes per year) as emission standards. In practice, however, emission standards are regularly fixed in terms of the concentration of pollutants in waste water or waste gas. This difference is significant because pollution concentration standards can equally be applied to a wide range of different sources, while standards in terms of absolute quantities have to be differenced according to the size of each single emission source.

As in Dietz and Michaelis (2004), the firm under consideration is endowed with two possible measures for reducing emissions in my model. Emissions can be reduced by decreasing output and/or by using end-of-pipe treatments. Consider a firm within a competitive industry that consists of a large number of firms emitting a homogenous pollutant into the environment. Denote the output of the firm under consideration by y and the market price by p.

Assume that production costs are given by a continuous cost function $c_1(y)$. The amount of pollutants abated is denoted by v and the amount of pollutants finally emitted to the environment is denoted by $e = \varepsilon y - v$, where ε is the emission coefficient. Finally, assume that the cost of abatement through end-of-pipe measures is given by a continuous cost function $c_2(v)$. The pollution control authority levies an emission tax of t per unit of emitted pollutant or imposes an emission standard. Assuming a linear relationship between output y and the amount of waste water or waste gas, this translates into an emission standard that allows a maximum of $\kappa < \varepsilon$ units of pollutants per unit of output. The amount of pollutants to be abated is given by $v = y(\varepsilon - \kappa)$.

The firm seeks to maximize the profit function $\pi = py - c_1(y) - c_2(v)$ subject to the constraint $v = y(\varepsilon - \kappa)$ in the case of the emission standard. This leads to the following optimality condition indicating the optimal output under the emission standard:

$$p = c_1'(y^*) + (\varepsilon - \kappa)c_2'\left[y^*(\varepsilon - \kappa)\right] \tag{7.1}$$

This condition requires the equalization of price and marginal cost. The latter is composed of two parts: the marginal cost of production plus the marginal cost caused by the abatement of $(\varepsilon - \kappa)$ additional units of the pollutant under consideration. Substituting $y^*(\varepsilon - \kappa)$ by $(\varepsilon y^* - e)$ yields:

$$p = c_1'(y^*) + (\varepsilon - \kappa)c_2'(\varepsilon y^* - e) \tag{7.2}$$

In principle, the above model allows the analysis of two different types of technological progress in pollution control: pollution-saving progress in the production process itself, which shifts down the emission coefficient ε, and cost-saving progress in end-of-pipe treatments, which shifts down the cost function $c_2(v)$. The earlier term implies innovations are developed or discovered that reduce the amount of pollution generated per unit of output without changing the production cost. Theoretically, it cannot be known which factor is larger. Although it is certainly not clear, there is evidence in manufacturing industries to assume that end-of-pipe technologies are almost fully developed, whereas changes in the production process itself still offer a wide range of opportunities to reduce emissions (for example, German Council of Environmental Advisors, 1994). However, there are no previous empirical tests comparing two factors using econometric methods, and no predictions for the oil and gas industries are currently available.

In this chapter, instead of directly measuring marginal cost of production and the direct abatement of pollution, I measure and compare the effectiveness for pollution reduction by estimating the pollution-saving technological progress in the production process and the cost-saving technological progress in end-of-pipe treatments. I employ a parametric pollution production function approach in which pollution is a by-product of oil and gas production. Pollution levels are determined by pollution abatement associated with environmental regulations, technology and production. I express the terms by using pollution abatement cost expenditure for the pollution abatement level, the innovation index of both cost-saving technological progress and pollution-saving technological progress for the technology level, and oil and gas production levels for the production. In summary, I specify the environmental pollution function as:

$$\ln \sum_{t=1947}^{t} (pollution_{it}) = \alpha_i + \lambda_t + \beta_1 \ln \sum_{t=1947}^{t} (production_{it}) + \beta_2 \ln(abatement_{it})$$
$$+ \beta_3 \ln(innov\_prod_{it}) + \beta_4 \ln(innov\_abate_{it})$$
$$+ \beta_5 \ln \sum_{t=1947}^{t} (production_{it}) \ln(innov\_prod_{it})$$
$$+ \beta_6 \ln(abatement_{it}) \ln(innov\_abate_{it}) + \varepsilon_{it}$$

$$(7.3)$$

where *pollution* is a proxy for environmental pollution, α are field-specific intercepts, the λs are time-specific intercepts, *production* is the quantity of oil and gas produced, as measured by million barrels of oil equivalent, *abatement* is the estimated cost of complying with environmental regulations, *innov_prod* is the innovation index of pollution-saving technological progress, and *innov_abate* is the innovation index of cost-saving technological progress. I use produced water as a proxy for environmental pollution. The dependent variable needs to explain the discharged pollution level after the treatment; therefore, untreated produced water before treatment needs to be adjusted by the treatment level.

The expected sign for *innov* is negative because improvements in the level of innovation are expected to reduce pollution. The expected sign for *abatement* is negative because more stringent regulations are expected to reduce pollution. The expected sign for *production* is positive because pollution is a by-product of production. The product of the innovation variable and the production level variable are expected to have minus signs because higher innovation levels (or pollution-saving technological progress in the production process) given the same level of production are expected to be associated with a lower pollution level. In the same manner, the product of the innovation variable and the abatement level variable are expected to have minus signs because a higher level of innovation (or cost-saving technological progress in end-of-pipe treatments) given the same level of abatement level is expected to be associated with a lower level of pollution.

The cumulative value of *pollution* may be an integrated variable. The estimates may be spurious if the pollution function regressions do not co-integrate. Additionally, permanent unobserved heterogeneity is addressed by differencing the data to remove possible correlations between explanatory variables and field-specific effects. Therefore, differencing the data will eliminate potential stochastic trends in the series. A first-differences model could be inappropriate if there is in fact co-integration in each field. However, it is unlikely that there is a single global co-integrating vector imposed by the regression model. Therefore, I estimate this model using the generalized method of moments (GMM):

$$\Delta \ln \sum_{t=1947}^{t} (pollution_{it}) = \lambda + \beta_1 \Delta \ln \sum_{t=1947}^{t} (production_{it}) + \beta_2 \Delta \ln(abatement_{it})$$
$$+ \beta_3 \Delta \ln(innov\_prod_{it}) + \beta_4 \Delta \ln(innov\_abate_{it})$$
$$+ \beta_5 \Delta \left[\ln \sum_{t=1947}^{t} (production_{it}) \times \ln(innov\_prod_{it}) \right]$$
$$+ \beta_6 \Delta \left[\ln(abatement_{it}) \times \ln(innov\_abate_{it}) \right] + \varepsilon_{it}$$

$$(7.4)$$

Several econometric concerns need to be addressed in order to obtain consistent parameter estimates from the pollution function. Most of these arise from the nature of the equation error ε_{it}. If the equation error is independently and identically distributed, and hence uncorrelated with input choices, the ordinary least squares (OLS) estimates will be consistent but inefficient. Parameter estimates will be inconsistent and oversized if input choices are correlated with unobservable factors (factors normally observable to firm managers, but unobservable to the analyst) or omitted variables for that matter. Unobservable factors can arise from difficulties in observing and quantifying differences in the quality of innovations and effects of demand shocks across fields. This information is rarely captured by the data set and is included in the random term, causing the input variables to be correlated with the error term. In this case, the innovation variables may be endogenous. Moreover, oil and gas production data is surely endogenous, and simple OLS could lead to biased estimates.

These estimation problems are dealt with as follows. Input endogeneity is addressed by adopting an instrumental variable estimation procedure. Lagged levels are used as instruments in the pollution function in its procedure. If the random factor, ε_{it}, is non-persistent, a standard GMM will be both consistent and efficient (Arellano and Bond, 1991). When the dynamic error processes are highly persistent, however, lagged levels have been shown to be poor instruments for contemporaneous differences and lead to finite sample biases (Blundell and Bond, 1998; Blundell et al., 2000). Both lagged differences and lagged levels are used as instruments in estimating parameters of the pollution function, and the resulting system GMM estimator is both consistent and efficient (Blundell and Bond, 1998). Standard errors are robust and corrected for finite sample biases based on Windmeijer (2005). This system GMM estimator encompasses the standard GMM estimator. Lastly, as explained above, permanent unobserved heterogeneity is addressed by differencing the data to remove possible correlation between explanatory variables and field-specific effects.

I apply the above methods to oil and gas production in the Gulf of Mexico, one of the first areas in the world to begin large-scale offshore oil and gas production. Reducing the environmental impact of offshore operations is among the most pressing challenges facing the oil and gas industry in the US today. In recent decades, compliance with environmental regulations has become increasingly costly and innovations associated with the environmental compliance have increased. I use the data for the period from 1968 to 2002 at the field level.

7.3   Results

In testing the effects of the technological progress hypotheses, namely, cost-saving technological progress in end-of-pipe treatments and pollution-saving technological progress in the production process, the results from system GMM estimation techniques are presented and discussed. Table 7.1 summarizes the results for the total sample. All GMM estimates are based on a two-step system GMM estimator with robust standard errors adjusted for finite sample biases.

The first specification examines the presence of oil and gas production in terms of BOE and the abatement effort to reduce pollution. The coefficients on these two variables are statistically significant and their signs are positive and negative, respectively, implying that pollution is a by-product of oil and gas production and that abatement actually contributes to the reduction of pollution. Their signs and statistically significant results are consistent over all specifications.

The second specification shows that both the cost-saving technological progress and the pollution-saving technological progress are statistically significant and negative. This implies that increases in the innovation level of end-of-pipe treatments and the production process contribute to a significant decrease in pollution. Higher elasticities of the cost-saving technological progress in the end-of-pipe treatments compared with the pollution-saving technological progress in the production process implies that a marginal increase in the end-of-pipe treatment technology level reduces more pollution. Examples of end-of-pipe treatment technologies include water dumps of radio-wave interfaces, new waxes in inhibitors and the use of progressing cavity pumps in the water produced. Other examples include solid control technology where additional cost savings are often realized by increasing the

Table 7.1   GMM parameter estimates: cost-saving technological progress and pollution-saving technological progress

Dependent variable	Specification 1	Pollution level Specification 2	Specification 3
Production	0.943 ** (2.75)	0.923 ** (2.71)	0.901 ** (2.65)
Abatement	−0.912 ** (−2.46)	−0.812 * (−2.19)	−0.616 * (−1.66)
Innov_prod		−0.216 ** (−2.23)	−0.189 * (−1.95)
Innov_abate		−0.375 ** (−2.54)	−0.289 ** (−1.95)
Innov_prod · Production			−0.021 * (−1.79)
Innov_abate · Abatement			−0.084 * (−1.85)
J-statistic (*p-value*)	0.2236	0.2373	0.2561
Unit root test	Reject	Reject	Reject

Notes:
*** Significant at 1%, ** Significant at 5%, * Significant at 10%.
t statistics are in parentheses.

drilling rate and reduced hole problems. On the other hand, a well-known example of pollution-saving technological progress in the production process is horizontal drilling, which directly reduces pollution emissions because the number of drilling wells is reduced.

The third specification tests the question regarding the sizes of cost-saving and pollution-saving technological progress. Multiplication of the innovation variable and the production level variable (*Innov_prod · Production*) is negative and statistically significant. This implies that a higher level of innovation in the pollution-saving technological progress in the production process is associated with a lower pollution level. In the same manner, multiplication of the innovation and abatement level variables (*Innov_abate · Abatement*) yields a statistically significant negative sign. This is because a higher level of innovation in cost-saving technological progress in end-of-pipe treatments given the same abatement level is associated with a lower level of pollution.

Using the estimated parameters and data on oil and gas production, as well as the pollution and innovation variables, it is possible to predict the magnitude of these effects. Figure 7.1 shows the overall pollution reduction from both the cost-saving technological progress in end-of-pipe treatments

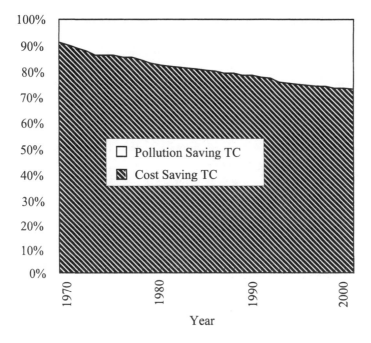

Figure 7.1   Magnitude of cost-saving technological progress and pollution-saving technological progress

and the pollution-saving technological progress. I calculate the contribution from the innovation variables by estimating the single and multiplied values of the innovations. The cost-saving technological progress in end-of-pipe treatments clearly contributes more to the reduction of pollution, which is consistent with the third specification of Table 7.1.

The share of cost-saving technological progress is always more than 70 per cent over time. In 1969, the share of pollution-saving technological progress was only 9 per cent. However, the share kept increasing over time, reaching 27.7 per cent in 2002. A decreasing trend in cost-saving technological progress may imply that end-of-pipe technologies are almost fully developed, but the production process itself still offers a wide range of opportunities to reduce emissions. In addition, the results show there is no significant change in its magnitude over time, that is, technological progress is expected to arrive as a marginal change or as a sequence of comparatively small independent steps. Following Dietz and Michaelis (2004), the conventional view that emission taxes induce a greater incentive to innovate compared with emission standards may not hold. This implies that we need to be more careful about future recommendation of environmental policies.

7.4 Conclusion

This chapter examines the nature of technological progress for pollution reduction using field-level data on the offshore oil and gas industry in the Gulf of Mexico. A pollution function augmented to include measures of both cost-saving technological progress in end-of-pipe treatments and pollution-saving technological progress in the production process is estimated using GMM estimation. This estimator enables the control of the input endogeneity, possible measurement errors, unobservable effects and persistent errors often encountered in empirical estimation.

I analyse two different types of technological progress in pollution control in the offshore oil and gas industry. With respect to the effects of technological change, this chapter finds evidence in support of the existence of cost-saving technological progress in end-of-pipe treatments and pollution-saving technological progress in the production process. The findings also indicate that cost-saving technological progress is more significant than pollution-saving technological progress.

Furthermore, my findings also show that the conventional view that emission taxes ensure greater incentives to innovate compared with emission standards may not hold. This implies that we need to be careful about future choices of environmental policy. Information about these estimates may encourage the better process of environmental policy making between governmental authorities and the firms involved.

NOTE

1. Dietz and Michaelis (2004) focus on the analysis of marginal and non-marginal pollution-saving technological progress. There is abundant evidence to assume that end-of-pipe technologies are almost fully developed, whereas changes in the production process itself still offer a wide range of opportunities to reduce emissions (see, for example, German Council of Environmental Advisors, 1994). An important exception is recent attempts to develop end-of-pipe measures for removing carbon dioxide emissions from power plants and similar facilities (see, for example, Grimston et al., 2001).

8. Alternative technology indexes

8.1 Introduction

Productivity and technology improvements play a critical role in determining long-term economic progress. They are therefore an important policy concern, including for research and development (R&D) strategy.[1] However, because technology is difficult to measure and model, empirical estimates are rarely used in productivity analysis.[2] Several alternative technology indexes have been utilized in the literature. Early research on productivity change (for example, Solow, 1957) focused on time as the sole 'explanatory' variable for technological change. This has since been recognized as a 'confession of ignorance' (for example, Arrow, 1962). Later, patent counts were used as a closer approximation of innovation and the level of technology (for example, Griliches, 1984). Because simple patent counts do not distinguish the importance of individual patents, refinements have employed the number of times the patent has been cited as a weight to measure the importance of the patent (see Hall et al., 2000, 2001).[3]

A finding in the literature is that citations appear to be correlated with the value of innovations. For example, Trajtenberg (1990) and Popp (2002) found greater usefulness in the patent count weighted by citations than patent counting alone for computed tomography scanners and energy-saving technologies as a proxy for the value of innovation. The claim specifies in detail the components of the patent innovation, and therefore their number may be an indication of the breadth and extent of the innovation (see, for example, Lanjouw and Schankerman, 1999).

However, patent statistics can be misleading, because many patents never see commercial application. Many innovations are also not patented, and some are subdivided into multiple patents, each covering one or more aspects of the innovation. Also, changes in patent policies over time may again make patent counts a misleading measure of innovation, particularly over longer time periods.[4] For these reasons, more recent studies have included innovation count refinements (for example, Moss, 1993; Cuddington and Moss, 2001). This is where reports of technology adoption in trade journals and other sources are used to construct an index of technological innovation. Again, a simple count of new technologies does not capture the relative importance of individual technologies. Therefore, innovation indexes based on a simple count of technology adoption have been refined by weighting innovations by their relative importance.

The question of which technology index best explains productivity change can only be answered empirically. Studies of computed tomography scanners (Trajtenberg, 1990) and energy-saving technologies (Popp, 2002) have shown that patent counts weighted by citations perform better as a proxy of productivity measurement than simple patent counts. However, no available work compares the competing indexes of technological measurement.

This chapter examines the usefulness of ten alternative technology indexes as a proxy of productivity change within the context of an industry case-study. I chose the Gulf of Mexico offshore oil and gas industry because it has played a significant role in the energy supply in the US.

8.2   Models and Data

In order to compare the performance of alternative proxy measures of technology, a more refined measure of productivity change is required to serve as a criterion. I use data envelopment analysis (DEA) to estimate the productivity change using a unique and extensive micro-level data set.

DEA is a non-parametric mathematical programing technique for estimating the relative efficiency of production units and identifying best practice frontiers (for example, Charnes et al., 1978; Färe et al., 1985). DEA is not conditioned on the assumption of optimizing behaviour on the part of each individual observation, nor does DEA impose any particular functional form on the production technology. Avoiding these restrictions may be an advantage, particularly for micro-level analyses that extend over a long time series, where assumptions of technological efficiency of every production unit across all time periods may be suspect. Moreover, in a non-renewable resource industry with sunk and irreversible costs, input use may appear contemporaneously suboptimal, even when it is optimal from a dynamic viewpoint.

The data used in this analysis were obtained from the US Department of the Interior, Minerals Management Service (MMS), Gulf of Mexico OCS Regional Office. The data are used to measure productivity change for offshore oil and gas over 1971–99. I then compare each of the ten alternative technology indexes discussed to understand their relative performance. I test both a long- and a short-term case. The long-term and short-term cases show the cumulative and incremental innovation, respectively.

The model is expressed as:

$$Y_{it} = x_{it-j}\beta + V_{it}, \quad i = 1,\ldots,N, \, t = 1,\ldots,T, \, j = 0,\ldots,t-1 \tag{8.1}$$

where Y_{it} is the Total Factor Productivity (TFP) estimated using DEA at time t, and x_{it-j} represents each alternative technology index at time $t-j$. The time-lag effect of each alternative variable is considered because it takes time for some innovation to exert effects on the market. This is especially true for patents. The time-lag, j, is chosen based on the best fit in terms of R^2 in each estimation in (8.1). β is an unknown parameter and the V_{it} are random error terms assumed to be independent and identically distributed $N(0, \sigma_V^2)$.

My analysis utilizes ten alternative technology indexes (that is, independent variables in 8.1): technology diffusion counts, importance-weighted diffusion counts, innovation counts, importance-weighted innovation counts, three patent counts, two importance-weighted patent counts and a simple measure of time.

Following the estimation of equation (8.1), I test differences in the correlation coefficients of each independent variable by taking pairwise differences in correlation coefficients, applying Fisher's z transformation, and dividing by the associated standard error: this can then be interpreted like a standard t-statistic (for example, Pearson and Bennett, 1942; Zar, 1999). If the estimations show statistically significant results, it suggests that one independent variable explains productivity significantly better than an alternative index.

My use of technology diffusion and innovation counts is explained by the following. First, Moss (1993) and Cuddington and Moss (2001) constructed a technology diffusion index that counts technology diffusion reported in industry trade journals. I modify the Moss index to reflect innovation by counting only the first time a particular technology is reported. Accordingly, my index measures technological innovation rather than diffusion. The cumulative weighted technology diffusion and innovation index at time t is calculated as:

$$Weighted\ Diffusion_t = \sum_{t=t_0}^{t}\sum_{i=1}^{I} w_{i,t} \times Diffusion\,Counting_{i,t} \tag{8.2}$$

$$Weighted\ Innovation_t = \sum_{t=t_0}^{t}\sum_{i=1}^{I} w_{i,t} \times Innovation\,Counting_{i,t} \tag{8.3}$$

where *Weighted Diffusion_t* and *Weighted Innovation_t* are the cumulative weighted technology diffusion and innovation index at time t, respectively;

$w_{i,t}$ is the weight for technology in category i at time t; and *Diffusion Counting*$_{i,t}$ and *Innovation Counting*$_{i,t}$ are the non-weighted technology diffusion and innovation counts in category i at time t, respectively.

I employ patent counts data for the crude oil and natural gas industry granted in the US for SIC 0711 from Johnson (1999). This includes both patents that are created in the chosen sector (IOM = industry of manufacture) and patents used in the chosen sector (SOU = sector of use).[5] Theoretically, I expect SOU to be a more appropriate type of data than IOM because my interest lies in the development of technology for use in the industry rather than in the technology developed by the industry. For example, a new form of drill developed by the machinery sector for use in oil excavation would be included in the SOU, but not in the IOM. The SOU and IOU data are referred to as 'patent count by use' and 'patent by manufacture', respectively.

I independently count the patents for the offshore oil and gas industry with the data provided by the US Patent Office.[6] The actual timing of the patented innovation is closer to the application date than to the subsequent grant date because innovators have an incentive to apply for a patent as soon as possible.[7] Thus, I use application year and truncate the citations from the five-year lag grant date. I need to limit the date because in order to maintain consistency between older and newer patents, that is, recent patents do not have as many citations as older patents. Another reason is that longer time lags do not show the importance of the patent in a particular year, that is, it may yield an important reference for new innovations, but it does not show the importance of the cited patent itself in a particular year.

The number of citations and claims are used to construct weights that represent the importance of patents. The weights for each patent i are given by the actual number of citations and claims subsequently received, denoted by c_i following Trajtenberg (1990) and Lanjouw and Schankerman (1999), respectively.[8] The weighted patent at time t is calculated as:

$$Weighted\ Patent_t = \sum_{i=1}^{n_t} (1 + c_i) \tag{8.4}$$

where *Weighted Patent*$_t$ is either the citation or claim-weighted patent count and n_t is the number of patents issued during year t.

8.3 Results

I estimate two measures of TFP. The first is a measure of TFP incorporating all related variables: that is, including environmental (that is, non-market) and market variables. The second is a measure of TFP using only market

Table 8.1   Estimation of alternative technology indexes: long term (value in the table shows the R^2)

R^2	Total factor productivity	
	Total	Oil & gas
Diffusion count	0.895	0.954
Weighted diffusion	0.944	0.990
Innovation count	0.845	0.924
Weighted innovation	0.867	0.941
Patent count		
Manufacture	0.883	–
Use	0.895	–
Patent	0.871	0.951
Weighted patent		
Claim	0.858	0.943
Citation	0.871	0.940
Time	0.857	0.831

Table 8.2   Estimation of alternative technology index: short term (value in the table shows the R^2)

R^2	Total factor productivity	
	Total	Oil & gas
Diffusion count	0.318	0.065
Weighted diffusion	0.450	0.317
Innovation count	0.113	0.173
Weighted innovation	0.101	0.044
Patent count		
Manufacture	0.428	–
Use	0.342	–
Patent	0.082	0.192
Weighted patent		
Claim	0.042	0.092
Citation	0.136	0.216

variables. When I estimate TFP with environmental variables, I employ a technology index including all technology developments, including environmental technologies. Thus, the more efficient reduction of pollution and/or the more efficient increase in market output given inputs is considered as an increase in TFP.

In this chapter, I highlight only the major findings. The estimated results for the long-term case are shown in Table 8.1. All of the models in Table 8.1 fit quite well, with most R^2s exceeding 0.80. The weighted diffusion count and weighted innovation count consistently have a higher R^2 than the unweighted diffusion and innovation counts, implying the importance weighting appears to have on explanatory power. The weighted diffusion count has the highest score for both cases. The variable *time* has the lowest and second-lowest scores for the two cases. As expected, the SOU patent count has a higher R^2 than the sector of manufacture. The estimated results for the short-term case are shown in Table 8.2. As in Table 8.1, the weighted diffusion count has the highest score for both cases.

Next, my interest is whether weighted diffusion count is statistically significantly better than the alternative measures. I test differences in correlation coefficients following Pearson and Bennett (1942) and Zar (1999). The results of these tests in the long-run oil and gas productivity case are presented in Table 8.3. The superiority of the weighted diffusion count is clear for the total case (that is, with environmental variables) because the difference in R^2 between the weighted diffusion count and the second-best score is larger in the total case than in the oil and gas production case. As shown, the weighted diffusion count as an index of technology is clearly superior to all other indexes considered. Employing *time* as an index of technology is clearly inferior to the other indexes, with the exception of the simple innovation count. The main result is that the weighted diffusion count as an index of technology is superior to all other indexes, notwithstanding the cases in the provided tables. The remaining indexes do not have clear superior or inferior statistical relationships.

8.4   Conclusions and Discussion

Developing and assessing R&D plays an important role in developing technologies. Technologies and productivity play a critical role in determining long-term economic progress and are therefore an important policy concern. The objective of this study is to analyse how useful the technology index proxies found in the literature are as an approximation of technology. Non-parametric mathematical programming techniques such as DEA are developed to account for the characteristics of non-renewable

Table 8.3   t-statistics for tests of alternative technology indexes – dependent variable: oil and gas industry total factor productivity

		Diffusion		Innovation		Patent			Year
		Diffusion count	Importance weighted	Innovation count	Innovation Importance weighted	Patent count	Weighted by claim	Weighted by citation	
Diffusion	Count		2.56*	0.86	0.42	0.11	0.36	0.45*	2.27*
	Importance weighted			3.42**	2.98**	2.67*	2.93**	3.01***	4.83***
Innovation	Count				0.43	0.75	0.49	0.41	1.41
	Importance weighted					0.32	0.06	0.03	1.84*
Patent	Count						0.26	0.35	2.16*
	Weighted by claims							0.09	1.90*
	Weighted by citations								1.81*

Notes:
Value in lower-left is symmetric to upper-right.
Significance levels: * 10%, ** 1%, *** 0.1%

resource industries in Chapter 2. DEA measures the efficiency and productivity of the industry using input-output data. Because of difficulties in obtaining data and the limits of computational time, finding an alternative technology index may be helpful for future R&D policy making.

Alternative technology indexes are tested to provide an understanding of the performance of alternative proxies for technology in the offshore oil and gas industry. My analysis compares ten technology indexes: technology diffusion counts, importance-weighted diffusion counts, innovation counts, importance-weighted innovation counts, three patent counts, two importance-weighted patent counts, and a simple measure of time. I find that all proxies fit adequately as an approximation, but the weighted diffusion count as an index of technology is clearly superior to all other indexes considered. From a theoretical perspective, the weighted diffusion count may be the better index because it takes into account the actual field application of new technologies and the importance of each technology. I employ expert opinion regarding the importance of innovations, as recognized by the industry experts surveyed by the National Petroleum Council (NPC). The NPC analyse the expected level of impact of a specific technology, in both the short and long term. This weighting scheme proves to be useful to approximate the level of productivity.

In practical econometric analysis, time is often used as a proxy for technological change. This is because forecasting the future value of time, that is, a simple time trend, is trivial compared with the difficulty of forecasting a diffusion index with, for example, expert surveys (for example, Iledare and Pulsipher, 1999). Practical considerations are important when choosing a model to forecast technological and productivity change. Theoretically, however, it is difficult to envision policies to affect time. Thus, as a policy scenario analysis, time is inappropriate. My results show that utilizing time as an index of technology is clearly inferior to most other indexes, and using more refined measures of technology, such as diffusion counts, improve the results in our application. One could image developing structural models of technology diffusion or patents, and therefore R&D policy helps the structural modelling for productivity analysis (for example, the endogenous technological change literature). One important application of a technology index lies in forecasting energy supply (for example, US Department of Energy, 2006). Oil price-induced innovation, where different hypothesized oil prices affect different patterns of induced technology in the future, may be the best application of the weighted diffusion count.

The currently accelerating rate of technological change in the offshore oil and gas industry is discussed in Chapter 2; therefore, time as a proxy is not appropriate in any stricter sense. It remains to be seen, however, whether we can maintain this pace of increasing productivity in the future, or whether recent productivity gains will soon be lost as reserves lying in deeper waters are depleted. Forecasting future trends is always dangerous, but it may not be realistic to expect to maintain indefinitely the current accelerating rate of technological change in offshore production technology. Because my results empirically show that other indexes are superior to *year* statistically, I do not recommend the use of time as an alternative for a technology index during the period of this analysis.

NOTES

1. See Jaffe et al. (2003) for detailed innovation policy.
2. Time is often used as a proxy for technological change (for example, Iledare and Pulsipher, 1999). As an alternative proxy, Lach (1995) uses patent data to estimate the contribution of knowledge to productivity change at the industry level.
3. References cited in US patent documents, referred to as citations, serve an important legal function since they delimit the scope of the property rights awarded by the patent. Simple patent counts measure innovative activity, and citation-weighted patent counting measures the success in innovative activity (Hall et al., 2000).
4. For a detailed analysis of patent policy, see Jaffe and Trajtenberg (2002) and Gallini (2002).
5. These exclude establishments primarily engaged in the production of crude oil from surface shales or tar sands or from reservoirs where the hydrocarbons are basically semi-solids and conventional primary crude production is not possible.
6. Detailed data files can be found at http://www.uspto.gov.
7. See, for example, Griliches (1984). The average time lag between application and grant date is 1.88 years for the offshore oil and gas industry.
8. See Hall et al. (2001) for a detailed analysis of patent weighting.

9. Forecasting energy supply and pollution

9.1 Introduction

Sound energy and environmental policies require reliable forecasts of production and pollution, as well as supply response to policy actions. Predicting when oil will be depleted is relatively straightforward once one has good estimates of future rates of production and the amount of oil that remains to be produced. Proven reserves, however, do not represent total oil resources, but are an estimate of the minimum amount that would be produced if no further discoveries were made, no advances in technology occurred, and if there were no changes in prices or other economic conditions. In fact, these parameters are in a constant state of flux. Therefore, economic and political factors play an important role in forecasting future production, and an enormous amount of data is required to capture various complexities in the analysis (Lynch, 2002).

Evidence in Chapter 2 suggests that increases in productivity have offset depletion effects in the Gulf of Mexico offshore oil and gas industry over a 49-year period from 1947 to 2002. Initially, depletion effects outweighed productivity-enhancing effects of new technology, but in the later periods, technological advance offset depletion. This result is consistent with common reports of Gulf of Mexico production. The Gulf of Mexico was referred to as the 'Dead Sea' in the early 1980s, but with recent reports of new technologies, a rapid pace of productivity enhancement led the Gulf of Mexico to be one of the most promising petroleum production areas in the world (Bohi, 1998). This should not, however, be taken as an indication that productivity will necessarily continue to follow this U-shaped curve of increasing productivity. It remains to be seen whether this pace of increasing productivity can be maintained in the future, or whether recent productivity gains will soon be lost to depletion as reserves in deep waters are depleted.

Reducing the environmental impact of offshore operations is one of the most pressing challenges facing the oil and gas industry in the US today. In recent decades, environmental concerns led to the imposition of numerous new regulations on oil and gas operations. Indeed, some have argued that environmental concerns may be more important than physical scarcity of oil

(Adelman, 1975). Although these regulations have provided the basis for many environmental improvements by industry, compliance has become costly and increasingly complex. In 1996, the petroleum industry, including refining, spent as much on environmental protection as it spent on searching for new domestic supplies: $8.2 billion (American Petroleum Institute, 2001). Jin and Grigalunas (1993a, 1993b) examined the impact of environmental regulation on firms in the oil and gas industry using the optimal control model assuming constant technology. Their results indicate that rising environmental compliance costs lead to reductions in investment and production, implying that fewer resources will be developed and associated economic benefits will decline.

The objective of this chapter is to forecast oil and gas production based on different economic and policy scenarios. Historical data are used to simulate the evolution of the industry to date. Following the Energy Information Administration (EIA) (US Department of Energy, 2006), I use disaggregated data to forecast regional production. I estimate oil and gas production and the resultant pollution formation at the field level using sub-model results and then aggregate over the fields to the regional level. My estimated model is used to construct a simulation model of the industry over time. I then simulate the future of the offshore oil and gas industry under alternative assumptions regarding future oil and gas prices, technological change and alternative environmental policies. I address various policy questions, such as identifying potential cost savings that could result from innovative pollution control measures and the associated benefits that can be derived from flexible regulatory approaches, such as market-based approaches for pollution control. I also provide an aggregate model extending a rational expectations econometric model by Walls (1994) and compare the results.

9.2 Literature Review

In the forecasting literature, most projections take a top-down (or aggregated) approach (Hubbert, 1967; Cleveland and Kaufmann, 1991; Pesaran and Samiei, 1995; Moroney and Berg, 1999).[1] They use overall estimates of resource potential and estimate future production. Other aggregated models include rational expectations econometric models (e.g., Epple, 1985; Walls, 1994). For example, Walls (1994) used a hybrid approach to model oil and gas supply from the Gulf of Mexico outer continental shelf. Her model contains components of both econometric and geologic-engineering models. Although they have an advantage of incorporating uncertainty and capturing the dynamics of the exploration processes, the models must be highly simplified in order to obtain analytical solutions to the optimization problems.

There are clear advantages to using micro-level data, since aggregation of data across distinctive geologic provinces may obscure the effects of economic and policy variables on the pattern of exploratory activities (Pindyck, 1978a). Typically, field-level forecasts of discovery and production account for depletion (Smith and Paddock 1984; Eckbo et al., 1978; Drew et al., 1982; Nehring, 2001). However, none of these models include an explicit treatment of technological change. As a result, forecasts of future oil and gas supply from a region usually show a declining trend, which reflects only the effect of resource depletion (Porter, 1990; Energy Modeling Forum, 1991; Walls, 1994). Impacts of technological change have been analysed using a disaggregated model (US Department of Energy, 2006) and an aggregated finding-cost model (Cuddington and Moss, 2001). However, neither of these models accounts for increasing stringency of environmental regulations, nor do they consider pollution levels. Thus, the trade-off between production and pollution from environmental regulation has not been investigated in the offshore oil and gas industry.

9.3   Methodology and Estimation Results

I model the oil and gas production and pollution systems considering the technological change using field-level data in the Gulf of Mexico. The model uses regression techniques in both the aggregated industry level and disaggregated field level. The general logic of the model is illustrated in Figure 9.1. This section discusses the methodology and estimation results for each of the following steps: determine technological change (Step 1), determine the number and size distribution of fields (Step 2), determine inputs (Step 3), determine outputs of oil, gas and pollution levels (Step 4). The detailed flow of my methodology is illustrated in Figure 9.2. First, I specify the policy scenario. This includes information such as R&D expenditure (to induce technological change), oil and gas prices (to encourage new field discoveries), stringency of environmental regulation, and the associated regulatory regime (command-and-control versus flexible regulations). These policy options are indicated in bold in Figure 9.2. First, I provide the field-level disaggregated models with some combination of aggregate model and their results. Then, I also provide an aggregate model modifying the rational expectations econometric model and the results.

Step 1: Technological Change

In this section, I provide the determinants of the level of production technology from information on research and development (R&D)

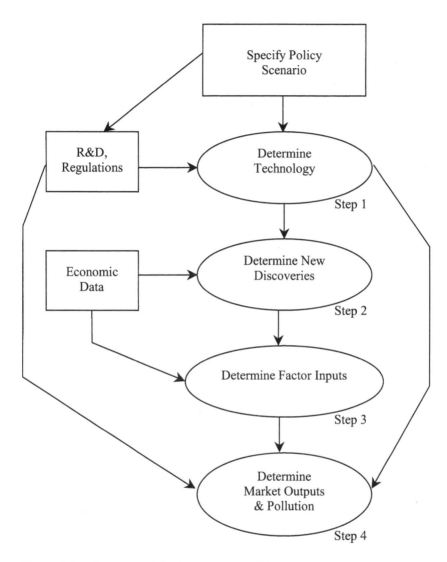

Figure 9.1   Overview of the forecasting model

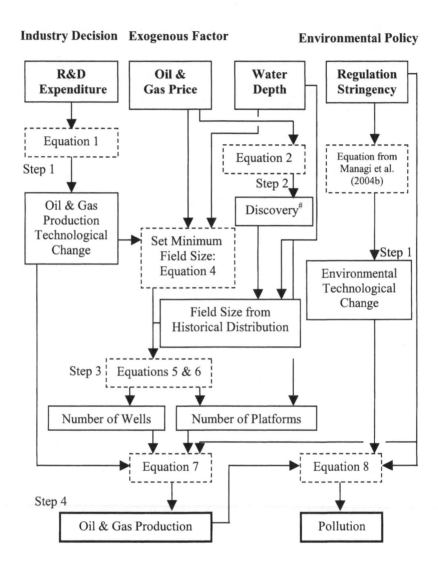

Figure 9.2   Flow chart of the methodology

expenditures and the level of environmental technology from environmental regulations. Recently, energy models have been expanded to represent endogenous technological change through R&D or learning-by-doing. For example, Goulder and Schneider (1999) investigated the impact of including induced technological change in the form of R&D efforts (see Jaffe et al.,

2003 for a theoretical review). R&D in a particular year will affect technological change several years down the road when the induced innovation process has been completed (Griliches, 1984).[2] The process of technological change, however, is quite complex and still poorly understood. Contemporaneous impact analysis of R&D is needed to determine the immediate cost of R&D. But time lags are needed to consider the longer-term gains associated with innovation and consequent improvements in productivity. I expect the R&D to have a positive, long-term impact on technological change.

R&D expenditure for oil and gas recovery is obtained from the Energy Information Administration's Financial Reporting System (FRS) database over 1977 to 2004.[3] This R&D includes funding from the federal government and private companies. FRS database does not distinguish onshore and offshore R&D. The impact of new technologies is most obvious offshore, but they have made possible many new onshore developments as well. Therefore, I use a summation of onshore and offshore R&D. There are also international spillover effects that have not been considered in this study. The R&D expenditure of the oil companies shows a declining trend on average since 1990. Creusen and Minne (2000) show that oil companies are reluctant to commit themselves to risky projects to improve their market position and to introduce radically new products. On the other hand, industry at least in the United States was rapidly reorganizing the way it did research from the 1980s to exploit ever greater economies from joint efforts, partnerships, consortia and a general migration of the R&D function from the producers to the service industry and universities.

The functional specification relating improvements in technologies and R&D is given by the following equation:

$$Y_t = \alpha + \sum_i^N \beta_i X_{t-i} + \varepsilon_t, \tag{9.1}$$

where Y_t denotes technological change indexes (that is, change in *tech*) at time t, which is explained below, and X_t denotes R&D expenditure at time t. The technological change variable is the index of the Luenberger productivity indicator plus 1, that is, Technological change = (1+Luenberger productivity indicator), since the Luenberger productivity indicator is a difference-based model. The term β_i is the coefficient of X_{t-i}, which indicates how technological change is affected by R&D expenditure i years lagged. The term α is a constant term and ε_t is a stochastic term, which together comprise the 'unexplained' components of technological change. The expected dynamic lagged effects of independent variables can be examined by imposing theoretical restrictions on the coefficients of the lagged values of these variables.

I used the Luenberger productivity indicator of data envelopment analysis (DEA) to estimate the technological change indexes using a unique and extensive micro-level data set. Technological change measures shifts in the production frontier. DEA is a set of non-parametric mathematical programing techniques for estimating the relative efficiency of production units and for identifying best practice frontiers (for example, Färe et al., 1994a). DEA does not impose any particular functional form on production technology, and it is not conditioned on the assumption of optimizing behaviour on the part of each individual observation. Avoiding these maintained hypotheses may be an advantage, particularly for micro-level analyses that extend over a long time series, where assumptions of technological efficiency of every production unit in all time periods might be suspect. Further, in a non-renewable resource industry, input use might appear contemporaneously suboptimal due to sunk and irreversible costs even when it is optimal from a dynamic point of view. The data for DEA estimation include field-level annual data for the following variables: oil output, gas output, the number of exploration and development wells drilled, the total drilling distance of exploration and development wells, the number of platforms, water depth, oil reserve, gas reserve, untreated water produced and discovery year.

I employ the Almon polynomial distributed lag model, which is an estimation procedure for distributed lags that allows the coefficients of the lagged independent variables to follow a variety of patterns as the length of the lags increases (Almon, 1965). The use of Almon polynomials remedies the problem of collinearity. The use of Almon lags requires the determination of the maximum lag length, where I choose the lag length in order to minimize the Akaike information criteria (AIC) (Harvey, 1990). The results of replicating the Almon lag model are reported below:[4]

$$\Delta tech_t = 100.645 + 2.064 \ \ln(R\&D_{t-2}) \ + 1.715 \ \ln(R\&D_{t-3})$$
$$\qquad\qquad\qquad (2.73) \qquad\qquad\qquad\qquad (2.73)$$
$$\qquad + 1.379 \ \ln(R\&D_{t-4}) \ + 1.026 \ \ln(R\&D_{t-5})$$
$$\qquad\qquad (2.73) \qquad\qquad\qquad\quad (2.73)$$
$$\qquad + 0.691 \ \ln(R\&D_{t-6}) \ + 0.354 \ \ln(R\&D_{t-7})$$
$$\qquad\qquad (2.79) \qquad\qquad\qquad\quad (2.78)$$
$$\qquad - 0.444 \ \ln(\Delta tech_{t-1})$$
$$\qquad\qquad (-2.23)$$
$$\text{Adj. } R^2 = 0.533 \qquad\qquad \text{AIC} = 37.243 \qquad \text{Durbin h} = 0.243.$$

The results show statistically significant results.[5] The creation of dynamic effects of R&D investments on production technological change has a two- to seven-year lag relationship.

Similar to the estimation of production technological change, environmental technological change is estimated using DEA estimation. The evidence in Chapter 4 uses environmental output data composed of 33 different types of water pollutants in the four EPA categories, oil spill volume data from the Coast Guard, and environmental input data from compliance cost of environmental regulation. The four categories of EPA are conventional pollutants, non-conventional organic pollutants, non-conventional metal pollutants and radionuclides. Conventional pollutants include oil and grease and total suspended solids (TSS). Environmental technological change measures the shifts in the environmental abatement frontier. Since higher stringency of environmental regulations adds significantly to industry costs, industry might increase R&D to develop better environmental technologies to reduce the compliance cost. Therefore, environmental regulation will stimulate the innovation and diffusion of technologies that facilitate compliance (see Jaffe et al., 2003 for a literature review of theoretical and empirical analysis). I used lagged measures of the stringency of environmental regulations to identify the dynamic impacts on environmental technological change. Then, I found the long-term positive impact of environmental regulation on environmental technological change. This model is used to forecast environmental technological change in this chapter.

Step 2: New Field Discovery

I generate new discoveries of oil and gas fields, including size and water depth of each new field discovery, where oil and gas price is the factor explaining the number of new field discoveries. A random field size based on historical field size distribution at each water depth is used, and the distribution can change over time to consider depletion.[6] Then, I determine which prospects are economic by setting the minimum profitable field based on the real price of oil and gas in 2000 dollars per barrels of oil equivalent (BOE), technology level and water depth using stochastic frontier analysis. Thus, if field size is smaller than minimum profitable field size, I eliminate it from the simulation process.

The number of newly discovered fields is specified as a function of oil and gas prices.[7] I expect a positive sign on the price of oil and gas, since higher prices offer an incentive for firms to place greater effort on exploration (see Erickson and Spann, 1971 for a detailed discussion of price and discovery). I specify the discovery number function as:

$$disc.number_t = f(price_t).$$ (9.2)

A linear model is used for parameter estimation, where n is the number of observations:[8]

$$disc.number_t = 7.8566 + 0.5953\ price_t$$

$$(2.32)$$

$$R^2 = 0.4654 \qquad n = 56 \quad DW = 2.1865 \qquad \rho = -0.05385,$$

where ρ is the estimate of the first-order serial correlation. The coefficient on price is of the correct sign and is statistically significant at the 10 per cent level.

Eckbo et al. (1978) modelled the minimum economic field size based on the information of oil and factor prices. The minimum field size that is profitable for a firm in my model is determined by the state of technology, the oil and gas prices and water depth, since the level of technology and water depth determine the factor prices.[9] Other things being equal, minimum field size will decrease if technology and/or price increase and if water depth is shallower.

I used the stochastic frontier production model to determine the minimum field size (Aigner et al., 1977; Meeusen and van den Broeck, 1977). In this study, the stochastic frontier function for minimal field size is specified as:

$$y = f(x)\exp(v+u),$$ (9.3)

where v and u form the composite error term in a standard stochastic frontier model, with u being a truncated random variable capturing the divergence of field size from the minimum profitable field (that is, the observed field size is greater than the frontier minimal), and v is a normal variable that comprises measurement error. A logarithmic transformation is applied to linearize equation (9.3):

$$\ln y_i = \ln x_i \beta + v_i + u_i,$$ (9.4)

where i is the field index, and x_i is a vector of the explanatory variables (*price*, *technology* and *water depth*); v_i is the random error term, independently and identically distributed as $N(0, \sigma_v^2)$; and u_i is a non-negative random variable truncated at zero and independently and identically distributed as $N(\mu, \sigma_u^2)$.

The minimum economic field size is the output variable. I examined a number of explanatory variables (that is, elements of vector x). The results of the parameter estimates are summarized below.[10] All of the coefficients have the correct sign and are statistically significant at a high level ($p < 0.0001$):

$$\ln y_i = 11.654 - 10.543 \ln tech_t + 0.476 \ln water\ depth_i$$
$$\quad\quad\quad (-9.855) \quad\quad\quad (8.754)$$

$$- 0.349 \ln price_t$$
$$(-2.588)$$

$$\sigma^2 = \sigma_v^2 + \sigma_u^2 = 1.987 \quad\quad \gamma = \sigma_u^2/\sigma_v^2 = 0.765 \quad\quad \mu = -0.198$$
$$(14.234) \quad\quad\quad\quad (0.066) \quad\quad\quad\quad (-0.323)$$

$$\text{log likelihood} = -1453.286 \quad\quad\quad\quad n = 933,$$

where γ is an indication of the relative contribution of v to error term, and μ is the mode of the normal distribution.[11] A higher value of γ shows that a one-sided error component (that is, u) dominates the symmetric error components (that is, v) (Kumbhakar and Lovell, 2000).[12]

Step 3: Factor Inputs

For fields that are economically producible, factor inputs, such as the number of platforms and the number of wells in the field, are generated using information on field size and water depth. When newer, larger fields are discovered and developed, there is a derived demand for new offshore structures that serve as inputs to production.[13] I use the cumulative number of platforms and wells for the same reason as in the production function described below. I specify the platform and well number functions as:

$$\sum_{t=1947}^{t} platform_{it} = f(field\ size_{it}, \ water\ depth_{it}) \quad\quad\quad (9.5)$$

$$\sum_{t=1947}^{t} well_{it} = f(field\ size_{it}) \quad\quad\quad\quad\quad\quad (9.6)$$

I expect the field size (note: this is the actual size and not the minimum economic size) to have a positive effect on the number of wells and platforms and water depth to have a negative effect on the number of platforms, since a smaller number of larger platforms are typically installed in deeper waters. In each field, field size increases over time because of reserve addition and revision and decreases because of resource extraction. In contrast, water depth remains constant over the year for each field. Thus, both the number of platforms and wells increases when field size increases and decreases when field size decreases. Considering the predictability of past platforms and wells, I use a two-way random effects model to estimate this relationship.[14] The following shows the results of linear model parameter estimation.[15] The estimated coefficients are significant and have the expected sign:

$$\sum_{t=1947}^{t} platform_{it} = 2.643 + 0.0368 \; field \, size_{it} - 0.001143 \; water \, depth_{it}$$
$$(57.06) \qquad\qquad\qquad (-4.52)$$
$$R^2 = 0.9505 \qquad DW = 1.7753 \qquad \rho = 0.09743$$

$$\sum_{t=1947}^{t} well_{it} = 12.4854 + 0.3842 \; field \, size_{it}$$
$$(62.59)$$
$$R^2 = 0.9343 \qquad DW = 1.8553 \qquad \rho = 0.09542.$$

Step 4: Production and Pollution

Finally, I generate production and pollution paths over time. Production of oil and gas is determined by technology, the stringency of environmental regulations, the number of platforms and the number of wells. Pollution levels are determined from environmental regulations, technology and production. I then aggregate these field-level estimates to the regional level. In the field-level analysis, I use cumulative values for factor inputs (for example, wells and platforms) and outputs (*oil, gas* and *pollution*), since it is more appropriate to express the production relationship in cumulative terms for a non-renewable industry. For example, for any field, the production at t is determined by cumulative inputs (for example, the number of wells drilled) and extraction up to $t-1$. In addition, the industry must comply with relevant environmental regulations, so I use environmental stringency as an explanatory variable. I specify field-level production function as:

$$\sum_{t=1947}^{t} production_{it} = f(tech_t, \; env.stringency_t, \; \sum_{t=1947}^{t-1} platform_{it}, \; \sum_{t=1947}^{t-1} well_{it})$$
$$(9.7)$$

where *production* is the quantity of oil and gas produced in million barrels of oil equivalent (10^6 BOE); *tech* is the technological change index; and *env. stringency* is the stringency of environmental regulations governing offshore oil and gas operations, measured as environmental compliance cost in dollars per unit of oil and gas production in the region.[16] The variable *platform* represents the total number of platforms, *well* is the total number of exploratory and development wells, i is the field index, and t is time (that is, year). Note that my simplistic model does not take into account the many important institutional changes (for example, fiscal regime, acreage auctions, leasing conditions) that affect production in the US Gulf of Mexico (see Boué, 2002 for detail).

I use a two-way random effects model to estimate this relationship. The expected sign for *tech* is positive, since improvements in technology are expected to increase production (Lynch, 2002). The expected sign of *env. stringency* is negative, since more stringent regulations are expected to reduce production, with technology held fixed (Jin and Grigalunas, 1993a, 1993b). The expected signs for the cumulative number of platforms and wells are positive. As explained in Step 3, both the platform and well values decrease once the field size starts to decrease. Therefore, these two variables eventually put an end to annual production. The estimation results of the production model are:[17]

$$\sum_{t=1947}^{t} production_{it} = -21.6342 + 35.4234 \ tech_t \ -2.4525 \ env.stringency_t$$
$$(5.32) \qquad\qquad (-4.53)$$

$$+1.9734 \sum_{t=1947}^{t-1} platform_{it} + 0.5982 \sum_{t=1947}^{t-1} well_{it}$$
$$(50.05) \qquad\qquad\qquad (5.32)$$

$$R^2 = 0.9766 \qquad DW = 1.7532 \qquad \rho = 0.09532.$$

All the coefficients have the correct sign and are significant at a high level ($p < 0.0001$). The coefficient on *tech* is highly significant with a positive sign; therefore, if technological change increases with other variables held fixed, production increases. My results indicate that technological change plays a significant role in production in the offshore oil and gas industry in the Gulf of Mexico. This is not surprising since technological progress, such as 3D seismology and horizontal drilling, have drastically improved the efficiency of production. In forecasting production, I assume production ends if estimated cumulative production starts to decrease compared to last year's cumulative production. This assumption is required since I am not able to establish the decision-making process of shut-in of wells and/or removal of platforms.

Pollution is the by-product of oil and gas production and hence is also expressed in cumulative terms.[18] My environmental output data set is composed of 33 different types of water pollutants in the four EPA categories and oil spill volume data from the Coast Guard. However, since there are no techniques that integrate 34 different pollution outputs, I use produced water as a proxy for environmental pollution. The dependent variable, however, needs to explain the discharged pollution level after the treatment; therefore, untreated produced water needs to be adjusted by the treatment level. I use environmental total factor productivity (TFP), as calculated in Chapter 4, as a measurement of treatment level. In general, a productivity index is defined as the ratio of an index of output growth divided by an index of input growth over two periods. TFP is the comprehensive productivity index that attempts to include all outputs and all inputs used in the production process. Changes in the TFP index can tell us how the amount of total output produced from a unit of total input has changed over time. In addition to this standard measure of TFP, I estimated TFP, including environmental compliance cost (as a proxy for the regulation compliance efforts), on the input side and environmental pollution on the output side. Thus, this TFP with environmental data implies more market output and less environmental pollution can be produced given standard market and environmental input. Taking the ratio of TFP with and without environmental factors, defined as environmental TFP [(TFP with environment) / (TFP without environment)], it is possible to measure the productivity (or efficiency) of pollution abatements. Therefore, an increase in the environmental TFP implies that less environmental pollution can be released for the given environmental input. Dividing the untreated produced water before treatment by environmental TFP, I create a proxy for discharged pollution level after the treatment. The initial value of environmental TFP is 1, and the improvement in environmental abatement technology is shown as a value of environmental TFP to be more than 1. In summary, I specify the environmental pollution function using the two-way random model as:

$$\sum_{t=1947}^{t} pollution_{it} = f(env.tech_t, \ env.stringency_t, \ \sum_{t=1947}^{t} production_{it}) \quad (9.8)$$

where *pollution* is a proxy for environmental pollution, *env.tech* is the environmental technological change index as detailed in Chapter 4, environmental stringency is measured by the estimated cost of complying with environmental regulations, and production is the quantity of oil and gas produced, as measured by million BOE.

Standard TFP can be decomposed into measures associated with technological change and efficiency change using DEA (for example, Färe et al., 1994a). I applied this decomposition to the environmental TFP, and the environmental technological change index is estimated using DEA. Since technological change measures shifts in the production frontier, the interpretation of environmental technological change is that it measures shifts in the pollution abatement frontier (that is, the measurement of the best environmental technology level). A larger the number implies the better use of environmental technologies.

The expected sign for *env.tech* is negative, since improvements in technology are expected to reduce pollution (Jaffe et al., 2003). The expected sign for *env.stringency* is negative, since more stringent regulations are expected to reduce the pollution. The expected sign for *production* is positive, since pollution is the by-product of production. The result of linear estimations is summarized as follows:[19]

$$\sum_{t=1947}^{t} pollution_{it} = -1.9635 -2.4743 \ env.tech_t \ -0.0475 \ env.stringency_t$$
$$(-3.64) \qquad\qquad (-3.96)$$

$$+0.2763 \sum_{t=1947}^{t} production_{it}$$
$$(135.05)$$

$$R^2 = 0.9698 \qquad DW = 1.8299 \qquad \rho = 0.09608.$$

I use a linear relationship to look at a first-order linear approximation to some true non-linear relationship. All of the coefficients are statistically significant ($p < 0.0001$) and have the correct sign. My results indicate that environmental technological change plays an important role in reducing pollution in the offshore industry. Compared to the impact of *tech* on production, however, the effect of pollution reduction on technological change is smaller (around 16 per cent of production technological change impact). I speculate that this may be because there is little flexibility in command-and-control regulations.

The estimated cumulative numbers of platforms and wells generated to date are used to update cumulative oil and gas production and pollution.[20] The percentage of variation explained by the production model is $R^2 = 0.9900$ and by the pollution model is $R^2 = 0.9944$. Therefore, the model fits the data very well.

Forecasting: Policy Scenario Analysis

Various scenarios for technological change, environmental policy and depletion were constructed. I estimate the impact of changes in policy variables on technological change, estimated as a function of R&D, environmental stringency and discovery number, and oil and gas price. I then trace the effects through discovery, input usage, resource production and pollution emitted. The following sections describe the construction of scenarios, prediction capability of the model, and each forecasting result.

The Scenarios

The relevant variables for projecting future production and pollution are: (1) technological change; (2) number of new discoveries; (3) stringency of environmental regulation; and (4) the form for environmental regulations (for example, market-based versus command-and-control).

Sensitivity analyses are used to determine how the results change under higher and lower policy scenarios, with a total of 11 scenarios including the baseline scenario (see Table 9.1). The baseline scenario uses average historic rates for technological change, environmental stringency indexes and the number of new field discoveries.[21] Environmental technological change follows the environmental stringency scenario using results of the Almon lag distributional model estimation. I use the reference case oil and gas price scenario proposed by the US Energy Information Administration for the period 2002 to 2020 which uses the average rate of change to project prices to 2050 (US Department of Energy, 2006).

Next I use various sensitivity analyses to analyse the impact of alternative assumptions regarding technological change, depletion and environmental regulations, as summarized in Table 9.1. I construct two alternative scenarios for R&D expenditure: one where R&D increases linearly over time, where the annual rate of increase is +1 per cent of baseline R&D expenditure; and another where R&D decreases, where the annual rate of decrease is −1 per cent of baseline R&D (see Figure 9.3a for R&D and Figure 9.3b for technological change scenarios).

The depletion effect is modelled by varying the oil and gas prices, which induce the discoveries of the fields. Once the number of discoveries is determined, its field size is generated as a random variable based on the historical distribution of the field size at each water depth. If the generated field size is larger than estimated minimum economic field size, the data is used for further simulation process. I control the oil and gas price scenarios following EIA forecasting. I consider an optimistic case, where industry continues to find new fields at historic rates to the year 2050. Note that this scenario actually leads to an increasing number of discoveries to 2050, due to improvements in technology. I also consider less optimistic cases, where the rate of discovery declines linearly over time, and new discovery completely ceases at some time prior to 2050. My three less optimistic scenarios specify new discovery ceasing in 2015, 2030 and 2045 (Figure 9.3c). In all cases, we assume the baseline level of technological change for all of the discovery scenarios. Two scenarios are also constructed for the stringency of

Table 9.1   Summary of policy scenarios

Policy Scenario	Description
Technological change	
Baseline: Historic rates	Constant over time
High-level technological change	R&D increase linearly[1]
Low-level technological change	R&D decrease linearly
Discovery number of new fields	
Baseline	Follow the EIA reference case

Most optimistic scenario:
  Historic rate of discoveries
	Follow the EIA high oil and gas
	  price scenario

Less optimistic scenarios	
No discovery after 2015	Number of discoveries decreases until 2015
No discovery after 2030	Number of discoveries decreases until 2030
No discovery after 2045	Number of discoveries decreases until 2045
Stringency of environmental regulation	
Base case	Average historic rate
High stringency	Rate equals that for highest historic decade[2]
Low stringency	Low case equals the baseline case minus the absolute
Flexible environmental policy	
Base case	Command-and-control
Flexible regulations:	
Apply to all fields	Adopt the value from Popp (2003) for all fields
Apply to new fields only	Adopt the value from Popp (2003) for new fields

Notes:
1   Technological change index follows the relationship estimated previously. I estimate that R&D value keeps the same technological change value as the baseline case. I then construct the high and low R&D cases and estimate each technological change scenario.
2   The decade 1981–90 shows the highest increase of stringency in the history.

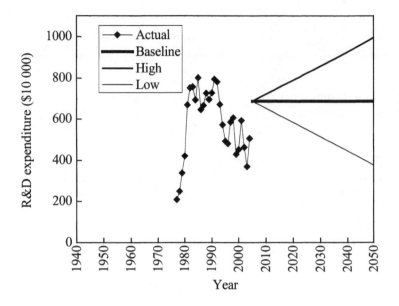

Figure 9.3a   R&D expenditure scenario

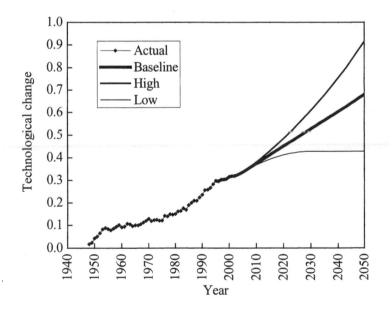

Figure 9.3b   Technological change scenario

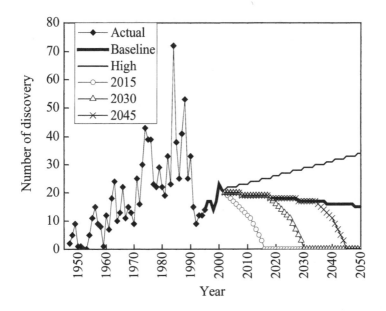

Figure 9.3c   Discovery number scenario

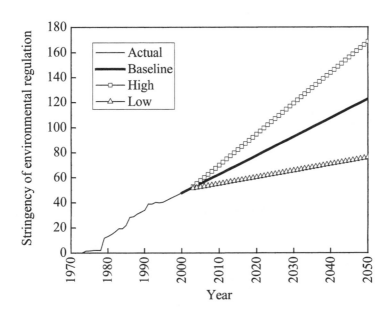

Figure 9.3d   Environmental regulation scenario

environmental regulations. The lower scenario has the stringency of environmental regulations increasing more slowly than historic rates, and the higher scenario has stringency of environmental regulation increasing more rapidly than historic rates (Figure 9.3d). The high scenario is based on the assumption that the stringency of environmental regulations grows at the rate of the decade with the fastest-growing environmental stringency in the data set (1981–90). The low scenario is based on the assumption that the stringency of environmental regulations grows at a lower rate than the baseline case. In this case, I take the rate of the baseline case minus the absolute value of the difference between the high and base cases.

The following sets of scenarios are used to identify the impact of changing the design of environmental regulations. Historically, regulation in offshore oil and gas operations has used the command-and-control approach. But there has been growing recognition in government and industry of the need for more cost-effective approaches to environmental protection. The recommendations include the development of a more flexible policy and regulatory framework, which includes more efficient recovery technologies to reduce environmental impacts. The American Petroleum Institute (API) has emphasized these concerns with a call for 'common sense' regulatory development (API, 1996). Unlike approaches that mandate specific technologies, 'common sense' approaches would give oil and gas producers more flexibility in determining how they can best meet standards, yielding the same environmental benefits at lower costs. The associated benefits (that is, increase in production by keeping the same pollution level) that can be derived from flexible approaches, such as market-based approaches for pollution controls, are estimated.[22] I consider a case where flexible environmental regulations apply to all existing fields and a case where flexible regulations apply only to new fields. None of the estimates comparing the effectiveness of flexible regulations in the oil and/or gas industry, however, is available in the literature. Therefore, I use the estimated effect of new granted patents by Popp (2003), as a proxy for technological innovation, to find the increase in removal efficiency of new scrubbers generated by a new SO_2 pollution control patent. Popp used data between 1979 and 1997 to compare command-and-control before the Clean Air Act (CAA) of 1990 and permit trading after the CAA. Popp (2003) found that permit trading is 2.217 times more efficient than the command and control method. I use this value of 2.217 to estimate the less negative impact of regulation to oil and gas production estimates.

Results

Scenario 1 in Table 9.2 (also in Figures 9.4a and 9.4b) shows the baseline forecast of annual production and pollution, respectively. The annual rate of production and pollution are calculated as the first difference of estimated successive cumulative production and pollution yields. Three-year moving averages of annual estimates are presented.[23] The highest annual production of approximately 1.6 billion barrels was attained in 2028. This is followed by a gradual decrease in production for the remainder of the forecast period. The baseline forecast of production of oil and gas shows an annual increase of 0.75 per cent until 2028, followed by a decline of approximately 2.16 per cent per year after 2028. This decline is because the depletion of old wells outweighs new discoveries. It is anticipated that in 2050, annual production will decrease to 1.1 billion barrels, 76 per cent of 2000 production. This level of production is comparable to that reported during the oil shock years of 1978 to 1979.

For comparison, Nehring (2001) used detailed data on deep-water operations in the Gulf of Mexico to forecast gas production from known and future discoveries to 2010. His work shows that production of oil and gas will continue to increase, reaching its peak in 2008, and will start to fall in 2009. The data for which production is expected to start falling is earlier than in my forecast mainly because the former ignores the importance of technological change in oil and gas production. My forecast is close to that of the US Department of Energy (2006) for the Gulf of Mexico. It forecast that oil production will increase until 2017, then begin to decrease, while the forecast for gas production would continue to increase throughout the forecast period to 2020. The summation of oil and gas production in BOE is expected to reach its maximum in year 2018. It does not forecast beyond 2020.

My model forecasts that pollution will reach its peak in 2021. At this time, the level of pollution will be the same as that experienced in the late 1980s. This peak in pollution is expected to set in somewhat earlier than the peak in oil and gas production because of improvements in environmental technology induced by more stringent environmental regulation.

Scenarios 2 and 3 in Table 9.2 (also in Figures 9.4a and 9.4b) show projections of annual production and pollution, respectively, based on technological change scenarios detailed in Table 9.1. In the high-level technological change scenario, production is expected to continue to increase and reach its maximum of 2.42 billion barrels in 2050. This level of production is twice that recorded in 2000. Under this scenario, technological change fully mitigates the depletion effects. In contrast, the low-level technological change scenario shows declining oil and gas production, with final production of only 0.2 billion barrels in 2050. This is barely 16 per cent

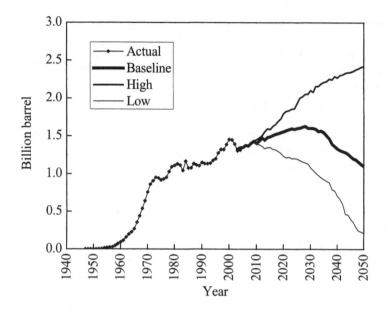

Figure 9.4a   Forecast of annual production (technological change scenario)

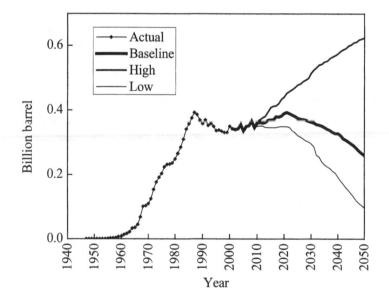

Figure 9.4b   Forecast of annual pollution (technological change scenario)

Table 9.2   Policy scenarios results (units of billion barrels)

Policy scenario	Production forecasting										
	(1)	(2)	(3)	(4)	(5)	(6)	(7)	(8)	(9)	(10)	(11)
Year											
2010	1.403	1.452	1.393	1.401	1.401	1.401	1.401	1.401	1.576	1.826	1.650
2015	1.489	1.585	1.349	1.451	1.451	1.451	1.331	1.416	1.599	2.218	1.854
2020	1.554	1.796	1.233	1.591	1.591	1.453	1.377	1.514	1.643	2.382	1.909
2025	1.596	1.926	1.197	1.638	1.638	1.368	1.201	1.522	1.687	2.458	1.665
2030	1.602	2.102	1.082	1.740	1.590	0.988	0.675	1.329	1.712	2.528	1.706
2035	1.542	2.215	0.928	1.847	1.437	0.898	0.275	1.204	1.623	2.265	1.643
2040	1.332	2.268	0.709	1.932	1.372	0.820	0.000	1.135	1.595	1.820	1.435
2045	1.232	2.345	0.397	1.903	0.841	0.635	0.000	0.929	1.533	1.642	1.347
2049	1.070	2.442	0.192	1.801	0.565	0.260	0.000	0.749	1.444	1.552	1.177

Policy scenario	Pollution forecasting								
	(1)	(2)	(3)	(4)	(5)	(6)	(7)	(8)	(9)
Year									
2010	0.359	0.364	0.349	0.331	0.331	0.331	0.331	0.316	0.366
2015	0.370	0.409	0.346	0.324	0.324	0.324	0.299	0.327	0.398
2020	0.389	0.441	0.348	0.311	0.311	0.311	0.284	0.331	0.424
2025	0.375	0.478	0.320	0.345	0.345	0.279	0.232	0.337	0.461
2030	0.363	0.515	0.295	0.418	0.418	0.260	0.206	0.303	0.456
2035	0.345	0.549	0.230	0.337	0.337	0.279	0.014	0.277	0.430
2040	0.326	0.574	0.193	0.376	0.376	0.204	0.000	0.244	0.417
2045	0.294	0.603	0.140	0.389	0.149	0.054	0.000	0.216	0.387
2049	0.260	0.625	0.095	0.321	0.119	0.024	0.000	0.182	0.364

Note: Policy Scenario (1) Baseline, (2) High-level technological change, (3) Low-level technological change, (4) High new discovery, (5) 2045, (6) 2030, (7) 2015, (8) High environmental stringency, (9) Low environmental stringency, (10) Flexible regulation for all fields, and (11) Flexible regulation for new fields.

of year 2000 production and 77 per cent lower than the baseline case for the year 2050. Pollution is forecast to increase more (241 per cent from the baseline year 2050) in the high-technology scenario than in the low-level technology scenario (63 per cent decrease from the baseline year 2050). This is expected in that high pollution is associated with high levels of production. Thus, increasing the level of technological change has a beneficial effect on oil and gas production, but a detrimental effect on pollution. Due to this pollution increase in the high-level technological change scenario, adequate environmental regulations are necessary to maintain an appropriate balance between production and pollution discharge.

Scenarios 4, 5, 6 and 7 in Table 9.2 show projections based on different scenarios for field discoveries, as detailed in Table 9.1. In the case of high rates of new discovery, production continues to increase 2.5 per cent per year, on average, until 2040 and remains relatively constant thereafter. In the case of no new discovery after 2015, production and pollution decrease, eventually ceasing in 2037. In the case of no new discoveries after 2030, production and pollution continue to decrease and produce only around 28 per cent and 15 per cent of the baseline, respectively. In the case of no new discovery after 2045, production decreases to 60 per cent of the baseline. Pollution also decreases to 77 per cent of the baseline scenario. The results show the long-term significance of new discoveries, which is determined by technological change and depletion effects.

Scenarios 8 and 9 in Table 9.2 show forecasts of annual production and pollution based on the environmental regulation scenarios detailed in Table 9.1. The differences of high and low environmental regulation scenarios are smaller than those of technological change scenarios. For the high environmental regulation case, production and pollution are less than that of the baseline environmental regulation. In 2050, both production and pollution are expected to fall by 30 per cent below the baseline. Under a low environmental regulation case scenario, production and pollution are above the baseline. In 2050, production is expected to rise 35 per cent above the baseline, while pollution will be 40 per cent points above the baseline. Environmental regulations have a significant impact on the pollution level and production.

Scenarios 10 and 11 in Table 9.2 show forecasts based on flexible regulation scenarios in Table 9.1. Given the negative impact of environmental regulation on production, further analysis of flexible regulation is investigated. If flexible regulations are applied to all existing fields, production is forecast to increase around 45 per cent, on average, compared to the baseline scenario of command-and-control. If flexible regulation is applied only to new fields, production increases by 10 per cent compared to the baseline. These two scenarios give the upper and lower bounds, respectively, of benefits using flexible environmental regulations, based on available results for benefits from improving flexibility of regulations.

Pollution per unit of production in annual value tends to fall over the entire forecast period, even though pollution does not start to decrease until 2030. In the baseline scenario, this ratio declines by 11 per cent over the forecast period and around 0.2 per cent annually. Environmental regulation can reduce

Table 9.3   Summary of policy scenarios results

Policy scenario	Size of the impacts (comparison with baseline year 2050)
Technological change	
High-level Technological Change	+189% (Production), +274% (Pollution)
Low-level Technological Change	−77% (Production), −77% (Pollution)
Discovery number of new fields*	
Most Optimistic Scenario:	
Historic Rate of Discoveries	+98% (Production), +101% (Pollution)
Less Optimistic Scenarios	
No Discovery After 2015	Production Ceases in 2037
Stringency of environmental regulation	
High Stringency	−30% (Production), −30% (Pollution)
Low Stringency	+40% (Production), +40~50% (Pollution)
Flexible environmental policy	
Flexible Regulations:	
Apply to all fields	+45% (Production)
Apply to new fields only	+10% (Production)

Note: * The two extreme cases and the other two results of no new discoveries after year 2030 and 2045 fall in between these two extreme cases.

pollution in two ways: first through its impact on production, and secondly by inducing environmental technological change. For all policy scenarios investigated, there is no significant affect on the pollution-to-production ratio, except in the flexible regulatory scenario. All other things being equal, a flexible regulatory environment is expected to reduce the existing level of pollution by 30 per cent.

9.4   Alternative Methodology and Estimation Results

I extend Walls's (1994) hybrid approach incorporating econometric and geologic-engineering models. Contrary to her predictions of declining discovery and production in the Gulf of Mexico, which are consistent with those made by other organizations, recent data show an increasing trend in production. The major reason for the forecast errors are recent technological advances, including deep-water technologies, three-dimensional (3D) seismology, horizontal drilling methods, steerable drill head techniques, and advances in computer technology. In this section, I extend Walls's model by incorporating various scenarios for technological change into the model forecasts.

I start with a discovery process of new reserves by following Walls (1994) and assuming larger reservoirs are easier to discover than smaller reservoirs: though fewer in number, larger reservoirs contain a disproportionate share of the region's oil and gas reserves. As a result, discovery rates decline as drilling proceeds given constant technology.

Therefore, the phenomenon can be described by the following equation:

$$A_t^i(W_{t-1}^i) = A_{TOT}^i[1 - e^{\theta^i W_{t-1}^i}]T_i(t)^{\beta_i} \qquad (9.9)$$

where A_t^i is the cumulative discoveries of type i (i = oil, non-associated gas) to date t, W_{t-1}^i represents cumulative successful wells of type i drilled to date $t-1$, and $T_i(t)$ is an index of technological change index at time t estimated using data envelopment analysis (DEA).[24] A_{TOT}^i, θ^i and β^i are parameters to be estimated where the expected sign of A_{TOT}^i is positive because the parameter A_{TOT}^i can be thought of as a measure of the total amount of reserves underground, including both discovered and undiscovered reserves. The parameter θ^i is a measure of the depletion effect, that is, it measures how cumulative past drilling affects the number of new discoveries in period t. The sign is expected to be negative because discovery size get smaller as cumulative drilling processes increase, given constant technology levels. The parameter β^i provides an effect of technological change. The sign is expected to be positive because new discoveries should increase as technology advances. If equation (9.9) is differentiated with respect to W_{t-1}^i:

$$\alpha_t^i = -\theta^i A_{TOT}^i e^{\theta^i W_{t-1}^i} T_i(t)^{\beta^i} \qquad (9.10)$$

where a_t^i can be seen as the discovery rate or the additional amount discovered per additional well drilled. Because θ^i is negative and A_{TOT}^i is positive, drilling more wells is expected to bring more discoveries. However, the discovery rate decreases as W_{t-1}^i increases. When β^i is positive, more advanced technology will lead to more discoveries and a higher discovery rate.

Associated gas discoveries are assumed to be proportional to oil discoveries; therefore:

$$\alpha_t^{ag} = k\alpha_t^o .$$ (9.11)

The exploration firm is assumed to choose a drilling programme in period t that consists of exploratory wells in period t and development wells in period $t+1$.[25] The drilling programme is assumed to diverge with variations in economic variables, such as the oil price and the drilling cost and the tracts leased. Specifically, more wells are drilled when the discounted net present value of profits of newly discovered fields is high. I assume that firms use current exploratory drilling and next-period development drilling in fixed proportions. This assumption makes the aggregation of the two types of wells easier. Deacon (1993) finds some empirical support for this assumption.

The equations to be estimated are (9.10) and (9.11): these model discoveries as a function of drilling. Equation (9.12) explains drilling behaviour. Taking logs of both sides of equations (9.10) and (9.11) and adding the error term yields:

$$\ln a_t^i = \gamma^i + \theta^i W_{t-1}^i + \beta^i \ln T(t)_i + \varepsilon_t^i$$ (9.12)

where

$$\gamma^i = \ln(-\theta^i A^i) \text{ and}$$

$$a_t^{ag} = k a_t^o + \varepsilon_t^{ag} .$$ (9.13)

I define a_t^i and a_t^{ag} as three-year moving averages of discoveries (new field discoveries, new reservoir discoveries and extensions) divided by the three-year moving averages of successful wells drilled (exploratory and development) lagged one period. A moving average is used because reserves found by drilling in period $t-1$ may not all be booked in the following period as the model specifies, but rather in several ensuing periods: this is allowed for by a moving average. The estimation results are as follows:

$$\ln a_t^o = 9.603 - 0.00014 W_{t-1}^o + 2.799 \ln T(t)$$
$$(9.44) \qquad (3.75) \qquad (5.25)$$

$Adj. R^2 = 0.694;$ DW $= 1.791;$ F-statistic $= 17.03$

The results for non-associated natural gas are as follows:

$$\ln a_t^{ng} = 11.202 - 0.000102 W_{t-1}^{ng} + 2.083 \ln T(t)$$
$$\quad (9.58) \quad\quad (1.94) \quad\quad\quad (2.24)$$

$Adj. R^2 = 0.402$; DW = 1.452; F-statistic = 4.038

Finally, the results for associated gas are as follows:

$$\ln a_t^{ng} = 2.042 \ln a_t^o$$
$$(18.28)$$

$R^2 = 0.874$; DW = 1.728; F-statistic = 117.945

All variables have the expected signs: the estimated θ^is are negative, γ^is are positive and the β^is are positive. This indicates that discovery rates in the Gulf of Mexico decline as cumulative drilling proceeds, given a constant level of technology. The estimated β^is are positive, indicating that discovery rates increase as technology advances. The parameter k is positive, indicating that associated gas finding rates vary positively with oil finding rates.

The following equation describes the total numbers of wells drilled in period t:[26]

$$w_t = \alpha_0 + \alpha_1 v_t + \varepsilon_t^w \, w_t \tag{9.14}$$

where v_t is the expected discounted present value of profits per well from a discovery generated by drilling in period t. The v_t consists of four important features: (1) the after-tax discounted present value of net operating profits per barrel of oil or per thousand cubic feet of gas;[27] (2) the probability of finding oil or gas measured by the success ratio, (3) the expected size of the new discovery; and (4) the after-tax average cost of drilling an exploratory or development well.

The ordinary least squares estimation of equation (9.12), known as the drilling equation, is as follows:

$$\ln w_t = 6.723 + 0.012 v_t$$
$$(11.16) \quad (1.88)$$

$R^2 = 0.84$; DW = 2.08; F-statistic = 36.91

The estimated parameters have the appropriate signs. A positive coefficient on v indicates that increases in the expected discounted net present value of profits from drilling will lead to an increase in drilling.

The net operating profit per barrel of oil produced in any period, t, is given by the following:

$$p_t^o = \overline{p}_t^o \left[1 - \tau_t(1 - \delta_t - \omega_t - \rho_t) - \omega_t - \rho_t\right] + \omega_t p_t^b - oc_t^o(1 - \tau_t) \quad (9.15)$$

where $\overline{p}_t^o$ is the wellhead price of oil in period t obtained from EIA's *Monthly Energy Review*, τ_t is the corporate income tax rate in period t, ω_t is the windfall profits tax (WPT) in period t, δ_t is the percentage depletion allowance in period t, ρ_t is the royalty rate in period t, p_t^b is the WPT base price in period t obtained from the US Department of the Treasury, Internal Revenue Service (IRS), *Statistics of Income Bulletin*, and oc_t^o is the per barrel operating cost in period t from the *Annual Survey of Oil and Gas* (ASOG) published by the American Petroleum Institute.

The net operating profit per thousand cubic feet (mcf) of gas produced in period t is given by the following equation:

$$p_t^g = \overline{p}_t^g \left[1 - \tau_t(1 - \delta_t - \rho_t) - \rho_t\right] - oc_t^o(1 - \tau_t) \quad (9.16)$$

where $\overline{p}_t^g$ is the wellhead price of natural gas in period t from EIA's *Monthly Energy Review*, and oc_t^g is the operating cost per mcf in the period from the ASOG published by the American Petroleum Institute.

Assume that we have the discounted present value of net operating profits per barrel, π_t^o, and the discounted present value of net operating profits per mcf of gas, π_t^g. In the following equations, where b and c are the respective discount rates for oil and gas:[28]

$$\pi_t^o = p_{t+j}^o (1+b)^{-j} = p_{t+j}^o e^{-bj} \quad (9.17)$$

$$\pi_t^g = p_{t+j}^g (1+c)^{-j} = p_{t+j}^g e^{-cj} \quad (9.18)$$

If I adjust the profit by the probability of finding oil or gas and the expected size of a discovery, as well as the exploration and development drilling costs, I obtain the following equation:

$$v_t = \pi_t^o s_t^o a_t^o + \pi_t^o (s_t^o a_t^{ag} + s_t^g a_t^{ng}) \\ - \left\langle dryc_t(1-\tau_t) + wetc_t \left\{1 - \tau_t \left[\exp + i(1-\exp)\right]\right\}\right\rangle \quad (9.19)$$

where s_t^o and s_t^g are the respective success ratios for oil and gas wells; that is, the probabilities of finding oil or gas. a_t^o is the additional barrels of oil discovered per successful oil well drilled, a_t^{ng} is the additional mcf of non-associated gas discovered per successful gas well drilled, and a_t^{ag} is the additional mcf of associated dissolved gas discovered per successful oil well drilled. $dryc_t$ is the exploratory and development dry hole drilling cost per total well drilled in period t obtained from ASOG, *exp* is the proportion of successful well drilling costs that can be expensed as incurred from ASOG (the 'intangible' components of drilling costs), and i is used to put depreciable drilling costs on a current value basis. Where dry hole and successful well costs are occasionally unpublished because of the possibility of revealing proprietary data, they are estimated by multiplying the total drilling costs by the ratio of dry holes to total wells drilled. From this, dry hole drilling costs are obtained, and the successful well costs are obtained by subtracting the estimated dry hole costs from the total drilling costs.

The first term in (9.19) is the discounted expected net operating profit from an oil discovery per well drilled in period t; the second term is the discounted expected net operating profit from a gas discovery per well drilled in period t; the last two terms net out the exploratory and development drilling costs per well drilled. The a_t terms, the additional barrels of oil and mcf of gas discovered per well drilled, are derived from the discovery process component in equation (9.10).

Table 9.4 shows the assumptions used as coefficients and variables to generate the forecasts. The operating costs and tax parameters are set equal to their 2004 values and combined with the predicted oil and gas operating profits. The success ratios, dry hole costs and successful well drilling costs are set equal to their averages over the sample period.

I test the reliability of the model with an out-of-sample forecast and confirm the estimated parameters. The average discovery size a^i and drilling equation are then re-estimated between 1974 and 2002 and forecasts generated after 2002. These forecasts are combined to generate the annual oil and gas discoveries. Using the reserve additions and revisions below, I generate production forecasts by estimating the relationship between production, revisions and discovery. The estimation results from the previous section are used to generate annual forecasts of drilling and average discovery sizes for the period after 2002.

Revisions are defined as measures of changes in previous estimates of reserve additions that occur due to new information, other than the extension of the reservoir. They can result from correction of a clerical error from the previous year, or they can arise from changes in prices, operating costs or anything else that materially affects the amount of oil and gas that is economically recoverable from the reservoir. Revisions can be either positive

Table 9.4 Variables and parameter values used in forecasting

exp	0.30
$dryc$	\$1.727 million/well
$wetc$	\$2.1617 million/well
i	0.921
s_t^o	0.298
s_t^g	0.265
τ_t	0.46 for 1974~86; 0.34 thereafter
δ_t	0.22 for1974; 0 thereafter
ω_t	0 for $t = 1974$~79; 30 for $t = 1980$~81; 0.275 for $t = 1982$; 25 for $t = 1983$; 0.225 for $t = 1984$; and 0 thereafter
ρ_t	0.167

or negative, but are invariably positive for oil because of enhanced recovery techniques. They are also notoriously difficult to model (MacAvoy and Pindyck, 1973; Griffin and Moroney, 1985).

The following models are specified for oil, non-associated gas and associated dissolved gas revisions:

$$r_t^o = \chi_o D_t^o + \chi_1 p_t^o + \chi_2 d_{t-1}^o + \varepsilon_t^{ro} \tag{9.20}$$

$$r_t^{ng} = v_0 D_t^{ng} + v_1 d_{t-1}^{ng} + \varepsilon_t^{rng} \tag{9.21}$$

$$r_t^{ag} = \xi_o r_t^o + \varepsilon_t^{rag} \tag{9.22}$$

where D_t^o is a dummy variable equal to one for the years 1975 and 1982 and zero otherwise, and p_t^o is the net price of oil in period t. d_{t-1}^o is the oil discoveries in period t–1. D_t^{ng} is a dummy variable equal to one for the years 1975 and 1976 and zero otherwise, and d_{t-1}^{ng} is the non-associated gas discoveries in period t–1. The error terms ε_t^{ro}, ε_t^{rng} and ε_t^{rag} are all serially uncorrelated and normally distributed with zero mean and constant variance. The reason that I include dummy variables is that I detected obvious spikes in the plot of the data. The estimation results are as follows:

$$r_t^o = -158.528 D_t^o + 4.98 p_t^o + 0.2112 d_{t-1}^o$$
$$(3.08) \qquad (1.92) \qquad (1.09)$$

$$R^2 = 0.368; \text{DW} = 1.880; \text{F-statistic} = 2.332$$

$$r_t^{ng} = 1924.296D_t^{ng} + 0.0922d_{t-1}^{ng}$$
$$(4.45) \qquad\qquad (1.88)$$

$$R^2 = 0.514; \text{DW} = 1.491; \text{F-statistic} = 6.88$$

$$r_t^{ag} = 3.054r_t^o$$
$$(3.64)$$

$$R^2 = 0.427; \text{DW} = 2.224; \text{F-statistic} = 10.451$$

From the estimation results, I find from equation (9.22) that the expected value for oil revisions declined sharply in 1975 and 1982. The coefficients for the dummy variable in equation (9.21) show that non-associated gas revisions rose sharply in 1975 and 1976. The reason I include the dummy variables is that there are obvious spikes in the plot of revisions for these years. According to the estimations, an approximately 5 million barrel increase in revision and a 10 million barrel increase in oil discoveries in period t leads to an approximately 2 million barrel increase in oil revision in period $t+1$. Similarly, a 10 mcf increase in non-associated gas discovery in period t leads to an approximately 1 mcf increase in non-associated gas revision in period $t+1$. Associated gas revisions vary positively with oil revisions: a one-barrel increase in oil revisions in period t raises associated gas revisions in the same period by 3 mcf.

Production is based on several factors, including market demand and prices, competitors' strategy, and the size of the discovery. Because I already link wells drilled with the net present value of the additional unit of discovery, I simplify the relationship between production, discovery and revision. The following models are specified for oil, non-associated gas and associated gas:

$$y_t^o = \alpha_0 d_t^o + \alpha_1 r_t^o + \varepsilon_t^{yo} \tag{9.23}$$

$$y_t^g = \beta_0 d_t^g + \beta_1 r_t^g + \varepsilon_t^{yg} \tag{9.24}$$

where

$$d_t^g = d_t^{ng} + d_t^{ag} \tag{9.25}$$

$$r_t^g = r_t^{ng} + r_t^{ag} \tag{9.26}$$

where d_t^o is the oil discovery in period t, d_{t-1}^o is the oil discovery in period $t-1$, r_t^o is the oil revision in period t, d_t^g is the gas discovery in period t, d_{t-1}^g is the gas discovery in period $t-1$, and r_t^g is the gas revision in period t. Gas discovery is the sum of non-associated gas and associated gas discoveries. Likewise, gas revision is the sum of non-associated gas and associated gas revisions. The error terms, ε_t^{yo} and ε_t^{yg}, are serially uncorrelated and normally distributed with zero mean and constant variance. The estimated results are as follows:

$$y_t^o = 1.149d_t^o + 0.051r_t^o$$
$$(6.53) \quad (1.27)$$

$$R^2 = 0.59; \text{DW} = 2.012$$

$$y_t^g = 1.029d_t^g + 0.384r_t^g$$
$$(11.50) \quad (1.53)$$

$$R^2 = 0.736; \text{DW} = 1.55$$

A recursive forecasting method is used. First, average discovery sizes are forecasted for the first year in the forecast period 2003. Because I have the data of cumulative wells drilled until 2002 and a technological change index, I can easily forecast the discovery size in 2003. I then obtain the discounted net present value per well. If I multiply the average discovery per well by the total number of wells, I obtain total oil and gas discoveries. This process continues for all forecast periods. A stochastic simulation of the model is performed using the Gauss–Seidel algorithm. The results are shown below. Different results are presented for the three different technological change assumptions used in the previous section.

9.5 Results

The results of the model are consistent with theory. Drilling corresponds positively with the net present value of the profits; discovery rates correspond negatively with cumulative drilling and positively with technological change. The amount of drilling that takes place is determined by expected discoveries, and discoveries are determined by cumulative past drilling and the level of technology. Three scenarios of base, high-level technological change, and low-level technological change are provided. Under a baseline scenario, the Gulf of Mexico will generate steady oil production until 2008. Production will then increase constantly at a rate of 1.05 per cent per year until it reaches

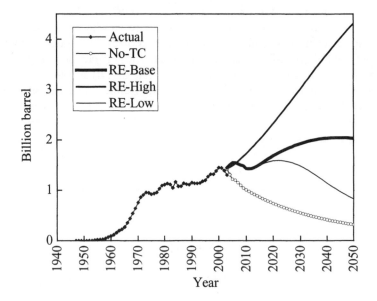

*Figure 9.5   Forecasting results of oil and gas production in the aggregated
model*

a peak in 2031 of 769 million barrels of oil. Between 2032 and 2050,
production will decline at a rate of 0.51 per cent per year. Gas production
follows a similar trend. Production will remain at about 5400 bcf. After 2005,
gas production will increase constantly at a rate of 1.02 per cent per year until
it peaks at 7719 bcf in the year 2039. It will then decline at a rate of 0.19 per
cent per year until 2050.

If a low-level technological change is assumed, the depletion effect mainly
determines the trends in oil and gas production. Because of the cumulative
drilling effect, the discovery process model leads to declining discovery rates
as the drilling process and the average discovery size decrease over the
forecast period. Because drilling is positively related to the discounted net
present value, v, and v falls over the forecast period due to a decreasing
average discovery size and constant net prices and success ratios, the number
of wells drilled also falls over the forecast period. This also contributes to the
decline in discoveries. Forecasts of oil and gas production are obtained by
combining discovery forecasts with revision forecasts.

The results are shown in Figure 9.5. Because production is positively
related to both discovery and revision, we expect a similar trend is expected.
Once I add both oil and gas production, it is possible to compare the number
with the disaggregated model. The forecasted result in 2050 is around 84 per

cent larger than that for the disaggregated model in Figure 9.4. This difference looks exceptionally large and is caused by the use of different modelling techniques, probably reflecting problems with the aggregated data.

Under a high-level technological change scenario, oil production remains at about 500 million barrels and increases at a rate of 2.41 per cent per year continuously after 2008. In the case of gas production, it remains at about 3900 bcf and increases continuously at a rate of 2.37 per cent per year after 2006. The predictions do not approach peak points during the forecast period. The forecasted result for 2050 is around 78 per cent larger than the disaggregated model in Figure 9.4. In a similar manner, the forecasted result for 2050 with this low-level technological change is around 148 per cent larger than that for the disaggregated model in Figure 9.4. Finally, the case where a constant level of technological change in 2002 is assumed and forecasted until 2050 is presented in Figure 9.5 (labelled NO-TC). In 2050, 0.31 billion barrels of oil and gas are produced. This is close to the low-level technological change case in the disaggregated model. In all three cases, the aggregated model tends to overvalue the effects of technological change on production. One reason may be the simplification of the modelling. This underscores the importance of the factors not included in this model.

9.6   Conclusion

In this study, I describe a model for analysing long-term production and pollution in the offshore oil and gas industry in the Gulf of Mexico. Reliable baseline forecasts of production and pollution and the response to different policy actions are critical in assessing long-term energy and environmental policies. An improved understanding of the potential role of technology and environmental policy provides policy-relevant information for designing and implementing sound environmental policies. Forecasts of production and pollution to 2050 are generated from a model using disaggregated field-level data: the disaggregated model generally supports better estimates than the aggregated model. In the baseline scenario, oil and gas production increase by approximately 1.5 per cent per year until 2020; a declining trend then sets in. Pollution levels remain relatively constant until 2014 and start to decrease gradually thereafter. Sensitivity analysis of the results demonstrates the importance of measuring technological progress accurately if reliable forecasts of production and pollution levels are to be made.

I have used different scenarios to explore the significance of various factors in determining forecasts. Alternative scenarios are used to explore how the results may vary with alternative assumptions. These include: (1) research and development (R&D) expenditure; (2) depletion of reserves; (3)

environmental regulations; and (4) flexible regulations in the Gulf of Mexico. As shown in Table 9.3, technological change has the greatest effect by increasing production by 189 per cent, while stringency in environmental regulations has the smallest impact. The number of new discoveries has a significant impact on the maintenance of long-term production. The scenario of no new discoveries after 2015 shows that production decreases and is expected to cease by 2037. If flexible regulations are applied, production is forecast to increase by 10–45 per cent on average compared with the baseline command-and-control scenario.

The model developed in this analysis provides an approach for measuring and analysing the impact of production and pollution from technological change and measures the impact of different policy scenarios. This is important in the sense that environmental regulations promulgated by the Environmental Protection Agency (EPA) entail a compromise and trade-off for different stakeholders: the regulatory agency, the oil and gas industry and public interest groups. Quantitative measures of the potential impacts of technological change and environmental regulations can contribute to the public debate and yield more informed policy decisions. In using environmental standards, it is important that the regulator gives industry sufficient time to develop solutions that protect the environment while still meeting important user requirements. Time may also be needed to examine whether a solution may pose yet other hazards. One way of dealing with the problem of compliance time is with phased implementation: that is, granting firms innovation waivers that initially exempt them from regulations. Another strategy is the setting of long-term standards that require the development of new technologies.

It would be an interesting topic for future work to determine the impact of environmental regulations applied to drilling (see US Environmental Protection Agency, 1999, for recent proposed guidelines regarding drilling fluids). Because the regulations for drilling fluids incur costs to the industry, and thus reduce the number of wells drilled, my forecasting of production and pollution (as a by-product of production) may be an overestimate. One of the major limitations of this study is the lack of extraction and drilling cost data: our model is therefore not based on formal theory. If cost data were available, theoretically consistent econometric modelling by Deacon (1993) could be used.[29] For example, the *Joint Association Survey on Drilling Costs* (JAS) published by the American Petroleum Institute may be used (see the previous chapter for cost estimates). The JAS data are, however, grouped into nine depth intervals for each of the offshore areas in the Gulf of Mexico (for example, offshore Louisiana and offshore Texas). Thus, some regional aggregation is required as the price for theoretical consistent modelling. Other important aspects to consider are the institutional changes (for example, fiscal regimes, acreage auctions and leasing conditions) in the US Gulf of Mexico (Boué, 2002). These factors affect production and pollution levels significantly over the long term, and econometric modelling needs to be considered for future research.

NOTES

1. Walls (1992) presented a comprehensive survey of studies on modelling and forecasting the petroleum supply. Her survey covers various geologic-engineering and econometric models that describe the relationship between exploratory drilling and discovery.
2. I treat investment in R&D as exogenous since my model simulates only the Gulf of Mexico, whereas the profitability of R&D reflects all sources worldwide.
3. The data are available from http://www.eia.doe.gov/emeu/finance/frsdata.html. The unit of R&D is $10 000.
4. I employed the linear form. End point restriction is used in the specification, and the coefficient of seven year's lag (t–7) is set to zero. t statistics are in parentheses. The coefficients are significant at 5 per cent. Since I use the linear form with one-side end point restriction, all of the t statistics in lagged R&D are same (Almon, 1965). The variable *tech* is multiplied by 100.
5. Note the problem of the Almon lag method. It assumes that lagged effects follow a polynomial, and therefore the results might overestimate the significance of lagged effects. Thus, the reliability of this model heavily depends on the assumption of polynomial form. DEA is a data-driven technique, and annual change of the index tends to fluctuate (Färe and Grosskopf, 1996). However, the fluctuation is not so large that the trend of the cumulative index, which is the multiplication of past annual change, is smooth over time. I add the lagged technological change variable to control this fluctuation.
6. It is difficult to control resource size in a conventional econometric framework and it is not suitable for forecasting. Thus, I utilize the method developed in Eckbo et al. (1978) and assume discovery is generated as a random variable.
7. Technology, depletion and water depth are statistically insignificant in this specification.
8. t statistics are in parentheses. The time period analysed is 1946–2002.
9. New discoveries larger than this threshold value are assumed to be developed immediately. Thus, analysis of asset management and delayed development is not considered in this model.
10. t statistics are in parentheses.
11. If $\mu = 0$, the density function is a half-normal density function.
12. The sensitivity of water depth is larger than that of price. However, both of them are much smaller compared to technology indexes. The one-sided error term captures the possibilities that actual minimum economic field size might be larger than frontier estimates. Note, however, my estimates might still underestimate compared to the industry estimates as appeared in the *Oil and Gas Journal*. Alternative methods of minimum economic size include Eckbo et al. (1978), though the analysis requires the cost data, which I am not able to obtain.
13. Pindyck (1978b) studies non-renewable resource production using an optimal control model. He assumes that production cost is only the function of the proved reserve base. If I also consider the platform, as well as additional production cost variables, I am able to derive the production function as a function of these variables.
14. See Baltagi (2001) for econometric methods for panel data.
15. t statistics are in parentheses. All of the coefficients are significant at 1 per cent. The time period analysed is 1946–2002. The unit of *field size* is MMbbl.
16. Note that the technological change index and the stringency of environmental regulations are time-series data instead of cross-sectional time-series data. This is because I do not

forecast these variables in a cross-sectional time-series base (that is, field level). Therefore, I assume both of the indexes remain the same over the fields in each year (that is, the industry in each field can utilize the same technology and face the same regulation stringency level in the same year).

17. t statistics are in parentheses. All of the coefficients are significant at 1 per cent. Time period analysed is 1946–95. ρ is the coefficient of serial correlation.

18. The drilling fluids, drill cuttings, deck drainage, well treatment fluids, proposal sand, and sanitary and domestic wastes are also important factors in the regulations in addition to the environmental regulations applied to production. Considering the data availability, however, I assume the regulations only applied to production. See US EPA (1976, 1985, 1993, 1999) for a detailed history of the regulations.

19. t statistics are in parentheses. All of the coefficients are significant at 1 per cent. Time period analysed is 1946–95.

20. It is assumed that: (1) new technologies are applied to all existing fields, instead of only newly discovered fields; (2) new environmental regulation is only implemented in new fields; that is, all existing fields follow old regulations.

21. The time periods of historical rate of technological change in this book are 1946–2002; 1969–2002 for environmental stringency; and 1963–2001 for discovery number.

22. In the literature, there is an ongoing discussion to which different environmental policy instruments provide firms with incentives to invest in environmental R&D. Many works have been carried out under the assumption of perfect competition (Magat, 1978; Milliman and Prince, 1989; Jung et al., 1996; Parry, 1998). These authors support the viewpoint that market-based regulations are likely to be more effective in stimulating innovation than those that mandate fixed technological or performance standards. Less consistent with the above findings are the works of Magat (1978) and Malueg (1989), who show that relative incentives might vary depending on the firm's specific technologies and elements of instrument design. Montero (2002) shows that the command-and-control method may offer greater R&D incentives for technological innovation than do market-based instruments when strategic interactions in the permits and output markets are not perfectly competitive markets.

23. Hereafter, three-year moving averages of annual estimates are used to draw annual production and pollution.

24. I specify $T_i(t) = \ln T_i$, where T_i is the technological change index.

25. Part of the reason for this aggregation is practical. Since there is a lag between exploratory and development wells, I could define total wells as above to simplify the case. It is better to wait to see what happens to the exploratory wells in period t and decide the number of development wells in period $t+1$. However, in that case, total wells in period $t+1$ will be determined jointly by current exploratory wells and development wells (hence, the results of exploratory wells in the previous period). Note that although I also attempted estimation at the aggregate level, this did not provide statistically satisfactory results.

26. I assume that depletion and technology change effects only apply to the average discovery size, which influences v, the discounted net present value per well. They will finally have an effect on the total wells drilled in period t. I tried to include these effects in the drilling equation. However, that would mean I would need to solve systems of equations before forecasting. The resulting estimation results were unsatisfactory.

27. This assumption is made since I only have access to aggregate data. I do not assume scale economies because of some practical reasons, including data set limitation.

28. We assume that $b = c = 0.05$.

29. The model requires estimates of three functions: reserve additions, drilling costs and production costs (Deacon, 1993). Other theoretically justified models include those in Pesaran (1990), which estimate an econometric model of offshore oil production in the UK.

10. Conclusion

Technological change is central to maintaining standards of living in modern economies with finite resources and increasingly stringent environmental goals. Successful environmental policies can contribute to efficiency by encouraging, rather than inhibiting, technological innovation.

Over time, economists have greatly improved our understanding of the role of technological change in economic growth and of the constituents of technological change. We have progressed from 'confessions of ignorance' based on mere observations that productivity increases over time to an increasingly sophisticated understanding of the mechanisms that drive technological change and empirical measures of the various components of technological change.

However, little research to date has focused on the design and implementation of environmental regulations that encourage technological progress, or in insuring productivity improvements in the face of the depletion of natural resources and the increasing stringency of environmental regulations.

This book contributes to the literature in several ways. First, the research provides a comprehensive analysis of these issues within the context of offshore oil and gas operations in the Gulf of Mexico. It identifies and measures the impact of technological change, both in market and environmental output sectors, in the offshore oil and gas industry, and takes steps to identify the key causal relationships.

The book's eight chapters address key issues regarding technological progress in the context of offshore oil and gas operations in the Gulf of Mexico. Chapter 2 examines the relative sizes of technological change and depletion in offshore oil and gas production, and finds that technological change has outpaced depletion over the 55-year study period. However, these results differ from conventional wisdom. I found that over the first 30 years, depletion outpaced technological change, but more recently, technological change outpaced depletion. Productivity was also found to have increased over the entire time horizon. I also develop an index for decomposing total factor productivity (TFP) into technological innovation, learning-by-doing and diffusion. The results indicate that both learning-by-doing and the diffusion of technological innovation have had a significantly larger impact on TFP than technological innovation. This implies that although technological innovation is crucial for improvements in TFP, there are even larger productivity gains from learning-by-doing (that is, the experience of engineers and managers) and the adoption of new technology in the offshore oil and gas industry. This demonstrates the importance of policies that focus on allowing flexibility in operations and that are not overly restrictive concerning the diffusion of new technologies to other companies.

Chapter 3 extends the work of Chapter 2 to examine the discovery of new fields. This chapter finds a similar pattern of productivity change as in Chapter 2, with initially decreasing productivity followed by increasing productivity in more recent years. However, the results in Chapter 3 suggest that overall productivity in the discovery phase is lower at the end of the study period than it was at the beginning.

The chapter also provides statistical measures that confirm the results found in the other parts of this book. The findings from a stochastic frontier model suggest that the effect of technological change on the industry at the field level is substantial. Because of technological progress, the negative effect of resource depletion on the field-level production frontier has been declining over time. Similarly, the negative impact of water depth on the production frontier has been falling. The results reveal that environmental regulation has had a significantly negative impact on offshore production, although such impacts have been diminishing over time due to technological change and improved management practices.

Chapter 4 extends the work of Chapter 2 to include the joint production of market and environmental outputs, and tests the Porter hypothesis. The Porter hypothesis states that well-designed environmental regulations can potentially contribute to productive efficiency in the long run by encouraging innovation. The Porter hypothesis was recast to include market and non-market outputs. I find evidence to support the restated version of the Porter hypothesis, but no support for the standard Porter hypothesis.

Advancing technologies are expected to play an important role in meeting the challenges to improve effectively and productively the discovery, production and processing of new reserves of oil and gas while complying with environmental regulations at acceptable expenses. I am not able to tell a priori, however, which effects of innovations in each sector of exploration, development and production processes most contribute to the increase in TFP. Chapter 5 concludes that the effects of exploratory innovations contribute to the increase in TFP continuously, indicating larger effects from diffusion. In contrast to the results for market technologies, I find that the production sector plays an important role in increasing environmental productivity. Clearly, the production sector engages with the environment most directly, and therefore the significance of its contribution is the greatest.

Theory has played a limited role in the development of the environmental Kuznets curve (EKC) literature (Copeland and Taylor, 2004). This has created difficulties in interpreting the empirical inverted U-shaped curve. Andreoni and Levinson (2001) provide a simple explanation for the EKC: pollution abatement efficiency may increase as abatement effort rises. Chapter 6 tests the increasing returns to pollution abatement in an EKC framework and supports this hypothesis.

Chapter 7 examines the nature of technological progress for pollution reduction. A pollution function augmented to include measures of both cost-saving technological progress in end-of-pipe treatments and pollution-saving technological progress in the production process is estimated using a generalized method of moments (GMM) approach. With respect to the effects of technological change, the chapter provides evidence in support of the existence of cost-saving technological progress in end-of-pipe treatments and pollution-saving technological progress in the production process. The results indicate that cost-saving technological progress is more significant than pollution-saving technological progress in the industry.

Chapter 8 examines the performance of various proxies for technological change used in the literature. These proxies include patent counts, weighted patent counts, innovation counts, weighted innovation counts and a simple time trend. Previously, there has been no attempt to compare the relative performance of these proxies. I find that there is no clear superiority of any of the measures.

Finally, Chapter 9 uses the results to provide forecasts under alternative scenarios for resource scarcity, research and development (R&D) expenditure and government regulations. Forecasts of production and pollution until 2050 are generated from the model. Detailed policy scenarios provide quantitative assessments that indicate the significance of potential benefits of technological change and well-designed environmental policy.

A thorough understanding of the nature and role of technological change is essential for developing well-conceived policies that contribute to the long-term well-being of society. This book illustrates the importance of understanding the process of technological change, as well as the challenges that are faced in measuring, and particularly in forecasting, technological change. In forecasting, we are explicitly dealing with the realm of uncertainty, and none can expect to formulate long-term predictions with a high degree of accuracy. Yet despite these challenges, the development of sound policy requires an improved understanding of the nature and the role of technological change in shaping future living standards.

Bibliography

Adelman, M.A. 1975. Population Growth and Oil Resources. *Quarterly Journal of Economics* 89 (2): 271–5.

Adelman, M.A., H.D. Silva and M.F. Koehn. 1991. User Cost in Oil Production. *Resources and Energy* 13 (3): 217–40.

Aghion, Philippe and Peter Howitt. 1992. A Model of Growth through Creative Destruction. *Econometrica* 60 (2): 323–51.

Aghion, P. and P.Howitt. 1998. *Endogenous Growth Theory*. Cambridge, MA: MIT Press.

Agras, J.M. and D. Chapman. 1999. A Dynamic Approach to the Environmental Kuznets Curve Hypothesis. *Ecological Economics* 28: 267–77.

Aigner, D.J., C.A.K. Lovell and P. Schmidt. 1977. Formulation and Estimation of Stochastic Frontier Production Function Models. *Journal of Econometrics* 6: 21–37.

Alchain, A. 1963. Reliability of Progress Curves in Airframe Production. *Econometrica* 31: 679–93.

Almon, Shirley. 1965. The Distributed Lag Between Capital Appropriations and Expenditures. *Econometrica* 33: 178–96.

Alpay, Ebru, Steven Buccola and Joe Kerkvliet. 2002. Productivity Growth and Environmental Regulation in Mexican and U.S. Food Manufacturing. *American Journal of Agricultural Economics* 84 (4): 887–901.

American Petroleum Institute. 1995. *Potential Impact of Environmental Regulations on the Oil and Gas Exploration and Production Industry*. March. Washington, DC: American Petroleum Institute.

American Petroleum Institute. 1996. *Achieving Common Sense Environmental Regulation: Oil and Gas Exploration and Production*. Washington, DC: American Petroleum Institute.

American Petroleum Institute. 2001. *US Petroleum Industry's Environmental Expenditures 1990–1999*. Washington, DC: American Petroleum Institute.

American Petroleum Institute, Independent Petroleum Association of America and Mid-Continent Oil & Gas Association. Various years. Joint Association Survey on Drilling Costs. Washington, DC: American Petroleum Institute.

Andreoni, J. and A. Levinson. 2001. The Simple Analytics of the Environmental Kuznets Curve. *Journal of Public Economics* 80: 269–86.

Antle, John M. and Susan M. Capalbo. 1988. An Introduction to Recent Developments in Production Theory and Productivity Measurement. In Susan M. Capalbo and John M. Antle (eds), *Agricultural Productivity: Measurement and Explanation*. Washington, DC: Resources for the Future; distributed by the Johns Hopkins University Press.

Arelleno, G. and S. Bond. 1991. Some Tests of Specifications for Panel Data: Monte Carlo Evidence and Application to Employment Equations. *Review of Economic Studies* 58: 277–97.

Arps, J.J. and T.G. Roberts. 1958. Economics of Drilling for Cretaceous Oil on East Flank of Denver-Julesberg Basin. *Bulletin of the American Association of Petroleum Geologists* 42 (11): 2240–566.

Arrow, Kenneth J. 1962. The Economic Implications of Learning by Doing. *Review of Economic Studies* 29: 155–73.

Asheim, G.B., W. Buchholz and B. Tungodden. 2001. Justifying Sustainability. *Journal of Environmental Economics and Management* 41: 252–68.

Attanasi, E.D. 1979. The Nature of Firm Expectations in Petroleum Exploration. *Land Economics* 55 (3): 299–312.

Ayres, R.C., Jr., T.C. Sauer, Jr., D.O. Stuebner and R.P. Meek. 1980. An Environmental Study to Assess the Effects of Drilling Fluids on Water Quality Parameters during High Rate, High Volume Discharges to the Ocean. In *Proceedings of a Symposium on Research on Environmental Fate and Effects of Drilling Fluids and Cuttings*, Washington, DC: American Petroleum Institute.

Baltagi, B.H. 2001. *Econometric Analysis of Panel Data*. Washington, DC: John Wiley & Sons.

Banker, R.D. 1984. Estimating Most Productive Scale Size Using Data Envelopment Analysis. *European Journal of Operational Research* 17 (1): 35–44.

Banker R.D., H.H. Chang and S.K. Majumdar. 1996. A Framework for Analyzing Changes in Strategic Performance. *Strategic Management Journal* 17: 693–712.

Barbera, A.J. and V.D. McConnell. 1990. The Impact of Environmental Regulations on Industry Productivity: Direct and Indirect Effects. *Journal of Environmental Economics and Management* 18 (1): 50–65.

Barbier, Edward B. 1999. Endogenous Growth and Natural Resource Scarcity. *Environmental and Resource Economics* 14 (1): 51–74.

Barnett, Harold and Chandler Morse. 1963. *Scarcity and Growth*. Baltimore, MD: Johns Hopkins Press.

Barro, R.J. and X. Sala-i-Martin. 1995. *Economic Growth*. New York: McGraw-Hill.

Battese, G.E. and T.J. Coelli. 1992. Frontier Production Functions, Technical Efficiency and Panel Data: With Application to Paddy Farmers in India. *Journal of Productivity Analysis* 3: 153–69.

Baumol, W.J. and W.E. Oates. 1988. *The Theory of Environmental Policy*, 2nd edn. Cambridge: Cambridge University Press.

Berck, Peter and Michael Roberts. 1996. Natural Resource Prices: Will They Ever Turn Up? *Journal of Environmental Economics and Management* 31 (1): 65–78.

Berg, S.A., F.R. Førsund and E.S. Jansen. 1992. Malmquist Indexes of Productivity Growth During the Deregulation of Norwegian Banking, 1980–89. *Scandinavian Journal of Economics* 94: S 211 – S 228.

Berman, Eli and Linda T.M. Bui. 2001. Environmental Regulation and Productivity: Evidence from Oil Refineries. *Review of Economics and Statistics* 83 (3): 498–510.

Bjurek, Hans. 1996. The Malmquist Total Factor Productivity Index. *Scandinavian Journal of Economics* 98 (2): 303–13.

Bjurek, Hans, F.R. Førsund and Lennart Hjalmarsson. 1998. Malmquist Productivity Indexes: An Empirical Comparsion. In Rolf Färe, Shawna Grosskopf and R.R. Russell (eds), *Index Numbers: Essays in Honor of Sten Malmquist*. Boston MA: Kluwer-Academic Publishers.

Blundell, R. and S. Bond. 1998. Initial Conditions and Moment Restrictions in Dynamic Panel Data Models. *Journal of Econometrics* 87, 115–43.

Blundell, R., S. Bond and F. Windmeijer. 2000. Estimation in Dynamic Panel Data Models: Improving on the Performance of the Standard GMM Estimators. IFS Working paper 00/12. Institute for Fiscal Studies.

Bohi, D.R. 1997. Changing Productivity of Petroleum Exploration and Development in the US. Resources for the Future Discussion Paper. Washington, DC.

Bohi, Douglas R. 1998. Changing Productivity in US Petroleum Exploration and Development. Resources for the Future, Discussion Paper 98-38. Washington, DC.

Boué, J.C. 2002. US Gulf Offshore Oil: Petroleum Leasing and Taxation and Their Impact on Industry Structure, Competition, Production and Fiscal Revenues. Oxford: Oxford Institute for Energy Studies. Oxford.

Boulding, Kenneth E. 1966. The Economics of the Coming Spaceship Earth. In H. Jarrett (ed.), *Environmental Quality in a Growing Economy*. Baltimore, MD: Resources for the Future/Johns Hopkins University Press.

Boussemart, J.P., W. Briec, K. Kerstens and J.C. Poutineau. 2003. Luenberger and Malmquist Productivity Indices: Theoretical Comparisons and Empirical Illustration. *Bulletin of Economic Research* 55 (4): 391–405.

Bovenberg, A. Lans and Sjak A. Smulders. 1996. Transitional Impacts of Environmental Policy in an Endogenous Growth Model. *International Economic Review* 37 (4): 861–93.

Boyd, Gale A. and John D. McClelland. 1999. The Impact of Environmental Constraints on Productivity Improvement in Integrated Paper Plants. *Journal of Environmental Economics and Management* 38 (2): 121–42.

Brock, W. and M.S. Taylor. 2006. Economic Growth and the Environment: A Review of Theory and Empirics. In S. Durlauf and P. Aghion (eds), *The Handbook of Economic Growth*. Amsterdam: North-Holland.

Caves, Douglas W., Laurits R. Christensen and W. Erwin Diewert. 1982a. Multilateral Comparisons of Output, Input and Productivity Using Superlative Index Numbers. *Economic Journal* 92 (365): 73–86.

Caves, Douglas W., Laurits R. Christensen and W. Erwin Diewert. 1982b. The Economic Theory of Index Numbers and the Measurement of Input, Output and Productivity. *Econometrica* 50 (6): 1393–414.

Chambers, R.G. 1996. A New Look at Input, Output, Technical Change and Productivity Measurement. Working Paper, University of Maryland, 96–03.

Chambers, R.G., Y. Chung and R. Färe. 1998. Profit, Directional Distance Functions, and Nerlovian Efficiency. *Journal of Optimization Theory and Applications* 98: 351–64.

Chambers, R.G. and R.D. Pope. 1996. Aggregate Productivity Measures. *American Journal of Agricultural Economics* 78: 1360–65.

Charnes, A., W.W. Cooper and E. Rhodes. 1978. Measuring the Efficiency of Decision Making Units. *European Journal of Operational Research* 2 (6): 429–44.

Chermak J.M. and R.H. Patrick. 2001. Microeconometric Test of the Theory of Exhaustible Resources. *Journal of Environmental Economics and Management* 42: 82–103.

Christensen, L.R. and D.W. Jorgenson. 1995. Measuring Economic Performance in the Private Sector. In D.W. Jorgenson (ed.), *Productivity Volume 1: Postwar US Economic Growth*. Cambridge, MA: MIT Press.

Chung, Y., Rolf Färe and Shawna Grosskopf. 1997. Productivity and Undesirable Outputs: A Directional Function Approach. *Journal of Environmental Management* 51: 229–40.

Cleveland, C.J. 1992. Yield Per Effort for Additions to Crude Oil Reserves in the Lower 48 States, 1946–1989. *American Association of Petroleum Geologists Bulletin* 76: 948–58.

Cleveland, C.J. and R. Kaufmann. 1991. Forecasting Ultimate Oil Recovery and Its Rate of Production: Incorporating Economic Forces Into the Models of M. King Hubbert. *Energy Journal* 12 (1): 17–46.

Cleveland, Cutler J. and Robert K. Kaufmann. 1997. Natural Gas in the US: How Far Can Technology Stretch the Resource Base? *Energy Journal* 18 (2): 89–108.

Coast Guard. 2000. Pollution Incidents In and Around US Waters. A Spill/Release Compendium: 1969–1999. Office of Investigations and Analysis, US Coast Guard, Department of Transportation.

Coelli, T.J. 1994. *A Guide to FRONTIER Version 4.1: A Computer Program for Stochastic Frontier and Cost Function Estimation*, Department of Econometrics, University of New England, Armidale.

Cole, H.S.D, Christopher Freeman, Marle Jahoda and K.L.R. Pavitt. 1975. *Models of Doom: A Critique of the Limits to Growth*. New York: University Books.

Coggins, Jay S. and John R. Swinton. 1996. The Price of Pollution: A Dual Approach to Valuing SO_2 Allowances. *Journal of Environmental Economics and Management* 30 (1): 58–72.

Copeland, B. and S. Taylor. 2004. Trade, Growth and the Environment. *Journal of Economic Literature* 42 (1): 7–71.

Creusen, Harold and Bert Minne. 2000. Falling R&D but Stable Investments by Oil Companies: Why? CPB Research Memorandum No. 164. The Hague, The Netherlands.

Cropper, Maureen L. and Wallace E. Oates. 1992. Environmental Economics: A Survey. *Journal of Economic Literature* 30 (2): 675–740.

Cuddington, J.T. and D.L. Moss. 2001. Technical Change, Depletion and the US Petroleum Industry: A New Approach to Measurement and Estimation. *American Economic Review* 91 (4): 1135–48.

Daly, Herman E. 1991. *Steady-State Economics*. Washington, DC: Island Press.

Deacon, R. 1993. Taxation, Depletion, and Welfare: A Simulation Study of the US Petroleum Resource. *Journal of Environmental Economics and Management* 24 (2): 159–87.

De Borger, Bruno and Kristiaan Kerstens. 2000. The Malmquist Productivity Index and Plant Capacity Utilization. *Scandinavian Journal of Economics* 102 (2): 303–10.

de Bruyn, S.M., J.C.J.M. van den Bergh and J.B. Opschoor. 1998. Economic growth and emissions: reconsidering the empirical basis of environmental Kuznets curves. Ecological Economics 25 (2): 161–75.

Debreu, G. 1951. The Coefficient of Resource Utilization. *Econometrica* 19: 273–92.

Deffeyes, Kenneth S. 2001. *Hubbert's Peak: The Impending World Oil Shortage*. Princeton, NJ: Princeton University Press.

Denison, D., T. Crocker and G. Briand. 1995. The Impact of Environmental Controls on Petroleum Exploration, Development, and Extraction. In S.

Shojai (ed.), *The New Global Oil Market: Understanding Energy Issues in the World Economy*. Westport, CT and London: Praeger Publishers.

Denison, Edward F. 1979. Accounting for Slower Economic Growth: The United States in the 1970s. Washington, DC: Brookings Institution.

Denny, M., M. Fuss and L. Waverman. 1981. The Measurement and Interpretation of Total Factor Productivity in Regulated Industries, with an Application to Canadian Telecommunications. In T.G. Cowing and R.E. Stevenson (eds), *Productivity Measurement in Regulated Industries*. New York: Academic Press.

Dietz, J. and P. Michaelis. 2004. Incentives for Innovation in Pollution Control: Emission Standards Revisited. University of Augsburg, Department of Economics Discussion Paper, Beitrag Nr. 263. Augsburg, Germany.

Diewert, W.E. 1976. Exact and Superlative Index Numbers. *Journal of Econometrics* 4: 115–45.

Diewert, W.E. 1978. Superlative Index Numbers and Consistency in Aggregation. *Econometrica* 46 (4): 883–900.

Diewert, W.E. 1992. The Measurement of Productivity. *Bulletin of Economic Research* 44 (3): 163–98.

Diewert, W.E. 2005. Diewert on Index Number Theory. *American Journal of Economics and Sociology* 64 (1): 311–60.

Downing, P. and L. White. 1986. Innovation in Pollution Control. *Journal of Environmental Economics and Management* 13, 18–29.

Drew, L.J., J.H. Schuenemeyer and W.J. Bawiec. 1982. Estimation of the Future Rates of Oil and Gas Discoveries in the Western Gulf of Mexico. USGS Professional Paper 1252, Washington, DC: US Government Printing Office.

Eckbo, Paul L., Henry D. Jacoby and James L. Smith. 1978. Oil Supply Forecasting: A Disaggregated Process Approach. *Bell Journal of Economics* 9 (1): 218–35.

Eddy, W.F. and J.B. Kadane. 1982. The Cost of Drilling for Oil and Gas: An Application of Constrained Robust Regression. *Journal of the American Statistical Association* 77 (378): 262–9.

Energy Modeling Forum. 1991. *International Oil Supplies and Demands*. EMF Report 11 Vol. I. Standard University.

Engineering News Record (ENR). 2000. *ENR Market Trends*. ENR Index Review. Construction Cost Index. Engineering News Record. New York.

Epple, Dennis. 1985. The Econometrics of Exhaustible Resource Supply: A Theory and an Application. In T.J. Sargent (ed.), *Energy, Foresight, and Strategy*. Washington, DC: Resources for the Future.

Erickson, E.W. and R.M. Spann. 1971. Supply Response in a Regulated Industry: The Case of Natural Gas. *Bell Journal of Economics* 2 (1): 94–121.

Fagan, Marie N. 1997. Resource Depletion and Technical Change: Effects on US Crude Oil Finding Costs from 1977 to 1994. *Energy Journal* 18 (4): 91–105.

Färe, Rolf and Shawna Grosskopf. 1996. *Intertemporal Production Frontiers.* Boston, MA: Kluwer-Nijhoff Publishing.

Färe, Rolf and D. Primont. 1995. *Multi-Output and Duality: Theory and Application.* Boston, MA: Kluwer-Nijhoff Publishing.

Färe, Rolf, E. Grifell-Tatjé, Shawna Grosskopf and C.A.K. Lovell. 1997a. Biased Technical Change and the Malmquist Productivity Index. *Scandinavian Journal of Economics* 99 (1): 119–27.

Färe, Rolf, Shawna Grosskopf and C.A. Knox Lovell. 1985. *The Measurement of Efficiency of Production.* Boston, MA: Kluwer-Nijhoff.

Färe, Rolf, Shawna Grosskopf and Edward C. Kokkelenberg. 1989. Measuring Plant Capacity, Utilization and Technical Change: A Nonparametric Approach. *International Economic Review* 30 (3): 655–66.

Färe, R., S. Grosskopf, C.A.K. Lovell and C. Pasurka. 1989. Multilateral Productivity Comparisons When Some Outputs are Undesirable: a Nonparametric Approach. *Review of Economics and Statistics* 71 (1): 90–98.

Färe, R., S. Grosskopf, C.A.K. Lovell and S. Yaisawarng. 1993. Derivation of Shadow Prices for Undesirable Outputs: a Distance Function Approach. *Review of Economics and Statistics* 75 (2): 374–80.

Färe, Rolf, Shawna Grosskopf and C.A.K. Lovell. 1994a. *Production Frontiers.* Cambridge: Cambridge University Press.

Färe, R., S. Grosskopf, M. Norris and Z. Zhang. 1994b. Productivity Growth, Technical Progress, and Efficiency Change in Industrialized Countries. *American Economic Review* 84 (1): 66–83.

Färe, Rolf, Shawna Grosskopf and Mary Norris. 1997b. Productivity Growth, Technical Progress, and Efficiency Change in Industrialized Countries: Reply. *American Economic Review* 87 (5): 1040–43.

Färe, Rolf, Shawna Grosskopf and Pontus Roos. 1998. Malmquist Productivity Indexes: A Survey of Theory and Practice. In Rolf Färe, Shawna Grosskopf and R.R. Russell (eds), *Index Numbers: Essays in Honor of Sten Malmquist.* Boston, MA: Kluwer-Academic Publishers.

Farrel, M.J. 1957. The Measurement of Productive Efficiency. *Journal of the Royal Statistical Society* Series A, 120: 253–81.

Farrow, R.S., J.M. Broadus, T.A. Grigalunas, P. Hoagland and J.J. Opaluch. 1990. *Managing the Outer Continental Shelf Lands: Ocean of Controversy.* New York: Taylor and Francis.

Federal Register (FR). 1973. Oil Pollution Prevention; Non-Transportation Related Onshore and Offshore Facilities; Proposal. Environmental Protection Agency. *Federal Register* 38 (237): 34164–170, Washington, DC.

Federal Register. 1974. Oil Pollution Prevention; Miscellaneous Amendment. Environmental Protection Agency. *Federal Register* 39 (169): 31602–13, Washington, DC.

Federal Register. 1975a. Offshore Segment of the Oil and Gas Extraction Point Source Category; Notice of Limitation Final Rulemaking. Environmental Protection Agency. *Federal Register* 40 (179): 42543–53, Washington, DC.

Federal Register. 1975b. Offshore Segment of the Oil and Gas Extraction Point Source Category; Proposed Effluent Limitations for Existing Sources, Standards of Performance and Pretreatment Standards. Environmental Protection Agency. *Federal Register* 40 (179): 42572–77, Washington, DC.

Federal Register. 1976. State and Area wide Clearinghouse Region VI Arkansas, Louisiana, New Mexico, Oklahoma, Texas. Environmental Protection Agency. *Federal Register* 41 (150): 12567–82, Washington, DC.

Federal Register. 1979. Effluent Guidelines and Standards, Oil and Gas Extraction Point Source Category. the Environmental Protection Agency. *Federal Register* 44 (73): 22069, Washington, DC.

Federal Register. 1980. Water Programs; Oil Pollution Prevention; Non-Transportation Related Onshore and Offshore Facilities; Proposed Revision to Existing Rules. Environmental Protection Agency. *Federal Register* 45 (99): 33814, Washington, DC.

Federal Register. 1985. Oil and Gas Extraction Point Source Category, Offshore Subcategory; Effluent Limitations Guidelines and New Source Performance Standards. Environmental Protection Agency. *Federal Register* 53 (204): 34592–636, Washington, DC.

Federal Register. 1986. Final NPDES General Permit for the Outer Continental Shelf (OCS) of the Gulf of Mexico. Environmental Protection Agency. *Federal Register* 51 (131): 24897–927, Washington, DC.

Federal Register. 1988a. Oil and Gas Extraction Point Source Category, Offshore Subcategory; Effluent Limitations Guidelines and New Source Performance Standards; New Information and Request for Comments. Environmental Protection Agency. *Federal Register* 53 (204): 41354, Washington, DC.

Federal Register. 1988b. Oil and Gas Extraction Point Source Category, Offshore Subcategory; Effluent Limitations Guidelines and New Source Performance Standards; New Information and Request for Comments. Environmental Protection Agency. *Federal Register* 53 (204): 41356–90, Washington, DC.

Federal Register. 1989. Oil and Gas Extraction Point Source Category, Offshore Subcategory; Effluent Limitations Guidelines and New Source Performance Standards; Collection. Environmental Protection Agency. *Federal Register* 54 (5): 634–42, Washington, DC.

Federal Register. 1990. Oil and Gas Extraction Point Source Category, Offshore Subcategory; Effluent Limitations Guidelines and New Source Performance Standards; Proposed Rules. Environmental Protection Agency. *Federal Register* 55 (227): 49094–6, Washington, DC.

Federal Register. 1991. Oil Pollution Prevention; Non-Transportation Related Onshore and Offshore Facilities; Proposed Rules. Environmental Protection Agency. *Federal Register* 56 (204): 54612, Washington, DC.

Federal Register. 1993. Oil and Gas Extraction Point Source Category; Offshore Subcategory Effluent Guidelines and New Source Performance Standards. Environmental Protection. *Federal Register* 58 (204): 12454, Washington, DC.

Fisher, Franklin. 1964. *Supply and Costs in the United States Petroleum.* Washington, DC: Resources for the Future.

Fisher, I. 1922. *The Making of Index Numbers.* Boston, MA: Houghton Mifflin Company.

Forbes, K.F. and E.M. Zampelli. 2000. Technology and the Exploratory Success Rate in the US Offshore. *Energy Journal* 21 (1): 109–20.

Forbes, K.F. and E.M. Zampelli. 2002. Technology and the Exploratory Success Rate in the US Onshore. *Quarterly Review of Economics and Finance* 42 (2): 319–34.

Fuentes, H.J., E. Grifell-Tatje and S. Perelman. 2001. A Parametric Distance Function Approach for Malmquist Productivity Index Estimation. *Journal of Productivity Analysis* 15 (2): 79–94.

Fuss, M. and D. McFadden. 1978. *Production Economics: A Dual Approach to Theory and Applications.* Amsterdam, North-Holland: North Holland Publishing Company.

Gallini, Nancy T. 2002. The Economics of Patents: Lessons from Recent US Patent Reform. *Journal of Economic Perspectives.* 16 (2): 131–54.

German Council of Environmental Advisors. 1994. *Für eine dauerhaft-umweltgerechte Entwicklung – Umweltgutachten.* Stuttgart: Metzler-Poeschel.

Giles, J.A. and S. Mirza. 1999. Some Pretesting Issues on Testing for Granger Noncausality. Department of Economics, University of Victoria. Working Paper.

Giuliano, F.A. 1981. *Introduction to Oil and Gas Technology.* Second Edition. Boston, MA: International Human Resources Development Corporation.

Gollop, F.M. and M.J. Roberts. 1983. Environmental Regulations and Productivity Growth: The Case of Fossil-fueled Electric Power Generation. *Journal of Political Economy* 91 (4): 654–74.

Goulder, L.H. and S.H. Schneider. 1999. Induced Technological Change and the Attractiveness of CO_2 Abatement Policies. *Resource and Energy Economics* 21 (3–4): 211–53.

Granger, C.W.J. 1969. Investigating Causal Relations by Econometric Models and Cross-Spectral Methods. *Econometrica* 37 (3): 424–38.

Greene, William. 1981. Sample Selection Bias as a Specification Error: Comment. *Econometrica* 49 (3): 795–98.

Grifell-Tatjé, E. and C.A.K. Lovell. 1995. A Note on the Malmquist Productivity Index. *Economics Letters* 47: 169–75.

Grifell-Tatjé, E. and C.A.K. Lovell. 1996. Deregulation and Productivity Decline: The Case of Spanish Saving Banks. *European Economic Review* 40: 1281–303.

Griffin, J.M. and J.R. Moroney. 1985. The Economic Impact of Severance Taxes: Results from an Econometric Model of the Texas Oil and Gas Industry. Report of the Texas Mid-Continent. Oil and Gas Association, Washington, DC.

Griliches, Zvi (ed.). 1984. *R&D, Patents, and Productivity*. NBER Conference Report. Chicago and London: University of Chicago Press.

Griliches, Zvi. 1994. Productivity, R&D and the Data Constraint. *American Economic Review* 84 (1): 1–23.

Grimston, M.C., V. Karakoussis, R. Fouquet, R. van der Vorst, P. Pearson and M. Leach. 2001. The European and Global Potential of Carbon Dioxide Sequestration in Tackling Climate Change. *Climate Policy* 1: 155–71.

Grossman, G.M. and A.B. Krueger. 1993. Environmental Impacts of a North American Free Trade Agreement. In P. Garber (eds), *The Mexico–US Free Trade Agreement*. Cambridge, MA: MIT Press.

Grossman, G.M. and A.B. Krueger. 1995. Economic Growth and the Environment. *Quarterly Journal of Economics* 110: 353–77.

Hailu, A. and T.S. Veeman. 2000. Environmentally Sensitive Productivity Analysis of the Canadian Pulp and Paper Industry, 1959–1994: An Input Distance Function Approach. *Journal of Environmental Economics and Management* 40 (3): 251–74.

Hall, Bronwyn H., Adam B. Jaffe and Manuel Trajtenberg. 2000. Market Value and Patent Citations: A First Look. NBER Working Paper No. W7741.

Hall, Bronwyn H., Adam B. Jaffe and Manuel Trajtenberg. 2001. The NBER Patent Citations Data File: Lessons, Insights and Methodological Tools. NBER Working Paper No. W8498.

Hall, M. and C. Winsten. 1959. The Ambiguous Notion of Efficiency. *Economic Journal* 69: 71–86.

Hansen, L.P. 1982. Large Sample Properties of Generalized Method of Moments Estimators. *Econometrica* 50: 1029–54.

Harrington, Winston, Richard D. Morgenstern and Peter Nelson. 2000. On the Accuracy of Regulatory Cost Estimates. *Journal of Policy Analysis and Management* 19 (2): 297–322.

Harvey, A.C. 1990. *The Economics Analysis of Time Series*. New York, London: Philip Allan.

Heal, Geoffrey. 2001. Optimality or Sustainability? Plenary address to the 2001 conference of the European Association of Environmental and Resource Economists, Southampton.

Heckman, James. 1979. Sample Selection Bias as a Specification Error. *Econometrica* 47 (1): 153–61.

Hicks, J. 1932. *The Theory of Wages*. London: Macmillan.

Hicks, J. 1961. Measurement of Capital in Relation to the Measurement of Economic Affregates. In F.A. Luts and D.C. Hague (eds), *The Theory of Capital*. London: Macmillan.

Hilton, H. and A. Levinson. 1998. Factoring the Environmental Kuznets Curve: Evidence from Automotive Lead Emissions. *Journal of Environmental Economics and Management* 35: 126–41.

Hjalmarsson, Lennart, Subal C. Kumbhakar and Almas Heshmati. 1996. DEA, DFA and SFA: A Comparison. *Journal of Productivity Analysis* 7 (2–3): 303–27.

Hubbert, M.K. 1967. Degree of Advancement of Petroleum Exploration in United States. *American Association of Petroleum Geologists Bulletin* 51: 2207.

Hulten, C.R. 1986. Productivity Change, Capital Utilization, and the Sources of Efficiency Growth. *Journal of Econometrics* 33: 31–50.

Iledare, O.O. and A.G. Pulsipher. 1995. Effects of an Increasing Role for Independents on Petroleum Resource Development in the Gulf of Mexico OCS Region. *Energy Journal* 16 (2): 59–76.

Iledare, O.O. and A.G. Pulsipher. 1999. Sources of Change in Petroleum Drilling Productivity in Onshore Louisiana in the US, 1977–1994. *Energy Economics* 21(3): 261–7.

Israel, D. and A. Levinson. 2004. Willingness to Pay for Environmental Quality: Testable Empirical Implications of the Growth and Environment Literature. *Contributions to Economic Analysis and Policy* (Berkeley Electronic Press) 3 (1): article 2.

Jaffe, Adam B. and Karen Palmer. 1997. Environmental Regulation and Innovation: A Panel Data Study. *Review of Economics and Statistics* 79 (4): 610–19.

Jaffe, Adam and Trajtenberg. Manuel. 2002. *Patents, Citations, and Innovations: A Window on the Knowledge Economy*. Cambridge, MA: MIT Press.

Jaffe, A.B., R.G. Newell and R.N. Stavins. 2003. Technological Change and the Environment. In Karl-Göran Mäler and Jeffrey Vincent (eds), *Handbook of Environmental Economics*. Elsevier Science, Amsterdam: North-Holland.

Jaffe, Adam, Steven Peterson, Paul Portney and Robert Stavins. 1995. Environmental Regulation and the Competitiveness of US Manufacturing: What Does the Evidence Tell Us? *Journal of Economic Literature* 33: 132–63.

Jin, Di and Thomas A. Grigalunas. 1993a. Environmental Compliance and Optimal Oil and Gas Exploitation. *Natural Resource Modeling* 7 (4): 331–52.

Jin, Di and Thomas A. Grigalunas. 1993b. Environmental Compliance and Energy Exploration and Production: Application to Offshore Oil and Gas. *Land Economics* 69 (1): 82–97.

Jin, Di, H. Kite-Powell and M. Schumacher. 1998. Total Factor Productivity Change in the Offshore Oil and Gas Industry. Woods Hole Oceanographic Institution Working Paper. Woods Hole, MA.

Johansen, L. 1968. Production Functions and the Concept of Capacity. Recherches Recentes sur le Fonction de Production. *Collection Economie Mathematique et Econometrie* no.2, Namur; also in F.R. Førsund (ed.), 1987. *Collected Works of Leif Johansen*. Vol. 1, Amsterdam: North-Holland.

Johansen, Soren. 1988. Statistical Analysis of Cointegration Vectors. *Journal of Economic Dynamics and Control* 12 (2/3): 231–54.

Johansen, Soren and Katarina Juselius. 1990. Maximum Likelihood Estimation and Inference on Cointegration: With Applications to the Demand for Money. *Oxford Bulletin of Economics and Statistics* 52 (2): 169–210.

Johnson, D. 1999. 150 years of American Inventions: Methodology and a First Geographical Application. Wellesley College Department of Economics Working Paper 99–01.

Johnson, R.A. and D.W. Wichern. 2002. *Applied Multivariate Statistical Analysis*. Cambridge, MA: Prentice Hall.

Jones, Larry E. and Rodolfo E. Manuelli. 2001. Endogenous Policy Choice: The Case of Pollution and Growth. *Review of Economic Dynamics* 4: 369–405.

Jorgenson, D.W. and Z. Griliches. 1967. The Explanation of Productivity Change. *Review of Economic Studies* 34 (3): 249–80.

Jorgenson, Dale W. and Peter J. Wilcoxen. 1990. Environmental Regulation and US Economic Growth. *RAND Journal of Economics* 21 (2): 314–40.

Jung, C., Krutilla and R.K. Boyd. 1996. Incentives for Advanced Pollution Abatement Technology at the Industry Level: An Evaluation of Policy Alternatives. *Journal of Environmental Economics and Management* 30 (1): 95–111

Kemp, R. 1997. *Environmental Policy and Technical Change: A Comparison of the Technological Impact of Policy Instruments.* Cheltenham, UK, and Northernpton, MA, USA: Edward Elgar.

Khazzoom. 1971. The FPC Staff's Econometric Model of Natural Gas Supply in the United States. *Bell Journal of Economics The RAND Corporation* 2 (1): 51–93.

Kneese, A.V. and C.L. Schultze. 1978. *Pollution, Prices and Public Policy.* Washington, DC: Brookings Institution.

Krautkreamer, J.A. 1998. Nonrenewable Resource Scarcity. *Journal of Economic Literature* 36: 2065–107.

Kumbhakar, S.C. and C.A.K. Lovell. 2000. *Stochastic Frontier Analysis.* Cambridge, MA: Cambridge University Press.

Kunce M., S. Gerking and W. Morgan. 2004. Environmental and Land Use Regulation in Nonrenewable Resource Industries: Implications from the Wyoming Checkerboard. *Land Economics* 80 (1): 76–94.

Lach, Saul. 1995. Patents and Productivity Growth at the Industry Level: A First Look. *Economics Letters* 49: 101–8.

Lanjouw, J.O. and Ashoka Mody. 1996. Innovation and the International Diffusion of Environmentally Responsive Technology. *Research Policy* 25: 549–71.

Lanjouw, J.O. and Mark Schankerman. 1999. The Quality of Ideas: Measuring Innovation with Multiple Indicators. NBER Working Paper No. 7345.

Lewin and Associates. 1985. *Replacement Costs of Domestic Crude Oil.* Vols. 1–2. DOE/FE30014–1. Prepared for US Department of Energy, Lewin and Associates, Inc., Washington, DC.

Liss, R.G., F. Knox, D. Wayne and T.R. Gilbert. 1980. Availability of Trace Elements in Drilling Fluids to the Marine Environment. In *Proceedings of a Symposium on Research on Environmental Fate and Effects of Drilling Fluids and Cuttings.* Washington, DC: American Petroleum Institute.

Livernois, J.R. and R.S. Uhler. 1987. Extraction Costs and the Economics of Nonrenewable Resources. *Journal of Political Economy* 95 (1): 195–203.

Lohrenz, J. 1991. Horizontal Oil and Gas Wells: The Engineering and Economic Nexus. *Energy Journal* 12 (3): 35–53.

Löthgren, Mickael. 1997. Generalized Stochastic Frontier Production Models. *Economics Letters* 57 (3): 255–9.

Lucas, R.E. 1988. On the Mechanics of Economic Development. *Journal of Monetary Economics* 22: 3–42.

Luenberger, D.G. 1992a. Benefit Functions and Duality. *Journal of Mathematical Economics* 21: 461–81.

Luenberger, D.G. 1992b. New Optimality Principles for Economic Efficiency and Equilibrium. *Journal of Optimization Theory and Applications* 75: 221–64.

Lynch, M.C. 2002. Forecasting Oil Supply: Theory and Practice. *Quarterly Review of Economics and Finance* 42 (2): 373–89.

MacAvoy, P.W. and R.S. Pindyck. 1973. Alternative Regulatory Policies for Dealing with the Natural Gas Shortage. *Bell Journal of Economics* 4 (2): 454–98.

Magat, W.A. 1978. Pollution Control and Technological Advance: A Dynamic Model of the Firm. *Journal of Environmental Economics and Management* 5 (1): 1–25.

Malmquist, S. 1953. Index Numbers and Indifference Curves. *Trabajos de Estatistica*, 4 (1): 209–42.

Malthus, Thomas. 1826. *An Essay on Population*. London: Ward, Lock & Company.

Malueg, D.A. 1989. Emission Credit Trading and the Incentive to Adopt New Pollution Abatement Technology. *Journal of Environmental Economics and Management* 16 (1): 52–7.

Massachusetts Institute of Technology. 1973. *The Georges Bank Petroleum Study: Summary*. Vols. 1–2. Offshore Oil Task Group, Cambridge, MA: Massachusetts Institute of Technology.

Mátyás, L. 1999. *Generalized Method of Moments Estimation*. Washington, DC: Cambridge University Press.

McCulloch, W.L., J.M. Neff and R.S. Carr. 1980. Bioavailability of Heavy Metals from Used Offshore Drilling Fluids to the Clam Rangia Cuneata and the Oyster Crassostrea Gigas. In: *Proceedings of a Symposium on Research on Environmental Fate and Effects of Drilling Fluids and Cuttings,* American Petroleum Institute Washington, DC.

Meadows, Donella H., Dennis L. Meadows, Jorgen Randers and William W. Behrens III. 1972. *The Limits to Growth*. New York: Potomac Associates.

Meeusen, W. and J. van den Broeck. 1977. Efficiency Estimation from Cobb-Douglas Production Functions with Composed Error. *International Economic Review* 18: 435–44.

Meyer, Stephen M. 1993. *Environmentalism and Economic Prosperity: Testing the Environmental Impact Hypothesis.* MIT Project on Environmental Politics and Policy, Harvard University, Cambridge, MA.

Milliman, S.R. and R. Prince. 1989. Firm Incentives to Promote Technological Change in Pollution Control. *Journal of Environmental Economics and Management* 17(3): 247–65.

Mineral Management Service. 1998. *Federal Offshore Statistics.* US Department of Interior, Mineral Management Service.

Mohr, Robert. 2002. Technical Change, External Economies, and the Porter Hypothesis. *Journal of Environmental Economics and Management* 43 (1): 158–68.

Montero, J.P. 2002. Permits, Standards, and Technology Innovation. *Journal of Environmental Economics and Management* 44 (1): 23–44.

Moorsteen, R.H. 1961. On Measuring Productive Potential and Relative Efficiency. *Quarterly Journal of Economics* 75: 451–67.

Moroney, J.R. and M.D. Berg. 1999. An Integrated Model of Oil Production. *Energy Journal* 20: 105–24.

Moss, D.L. 1993. Measuring Technical Change in the Petroleum Industry: A New Approach to Assessing its Effect on Exploration and Development. National Economic Research Associations, Working Paper Number 20.

Nehring, R. 2001. Reservoir Temperatures, Low Thermal Gradient Limit US Gulf's Deepwater Gas Potential Offshore. January, 2001, New York: PennWell Publishing Company.

Norgaard, R.B. and G.J. Leu. 1986. Petroleum Accessibility and Drilling Technology: An Analysis of US Development Costs from 1959 to 1978. *Land Economics* 62 (1): 14–25.

NPC (National Petroleum Council). 1967. *Impact of New Technology on the US Petroleum Industry: 1946–1965,* National Petroleum Council, Washington, DC.

NPC (National Petroleum Council). 1983. *Drilling Discharges in the Marine Environment.* Washington, DC: National Academy Press.

NPC (National Petroleum Council). 1995. *Research Development and Demonstration Needs of the Oil and Gas Industry.* Washington, DC: National Petroleum Council.

Opschoor, J.B. 1990. Ecologische Duurzame Economische Ontwikkeling: Een theoretisch idee en een weerbarstige praktijk. In: P. Nijkamp, H. Verbruggen (eds), *Het Nederlands Milieu in de Europese Ruimte: Preadviezen van de Koninklijke Vereniging voor Staathuishoudkunde.* Leiden: Stenfert Kroese.

Page, D.S., B.T. Page, J.R. Hotham, E.S. Gilfillan and R.P. Gerber. 1980. Bioavailability of Toxic Constituents of Used Drilling Fluids. In: *Proceedings of a Symposium on Research on Environmental Fate and Effects of Drilling Fluids and Cuttings,* Washington, DC: American Petroleum Institute.

Palmer, Karen, Wallace E. Oates and Paul R. Portney. 1995. Tightening Environmental Standards: The Benefit–Cost or the No-Cost Paradigm? *Journal of Economic Perspectives* 9 (4): 119–32.

Parry, I.W.H. 1998. Pollution Regulation and the Efficiency Gains from Technological Innovation. *Journal of Regulatory Economics* 14 (3): 229–54.

Pearson, Frank A. and Kenneth R. Bennett. 1942. *Statistical Methods: Applied to Agricultural Economics.* New York: John Wiley & Sons.

Pesaran, M.H. 1990. An Econometric Analysis of Exploration and Extraction of Oil in the U.K. Continental Shelf. *Economic Journal* 100 (401): 367–90.

Pesaran, M. Hashem and Hossein Samiei. 1995. Forecasting Ultimate Resource Recovery. *International Journal of Forecasting* 11 (4): 543–55.

Pezzey, J. 1989. Economic Analysis of Sustainable Growth and Sustainable Development. Environment Department Working Paper No. 15, World Bank.

Pezzey, J. 1992. Sustainability: An Interdisciplinary Guide. *Environmental Values* 1: 321–62.

Pezzey, J. 1997. Sustainability Constraints versus 'Optimality' versus Intertemporal Concern, and Axioms versus Data. *Land Economics* 73: 448–66.

Pindyck, R.S. 1974. The Regulatory Implications of Three Alternative Econometric Supply Models of Natural Gas. *Bell Journal of Economics* 5 (2): 633–45.

Pindyck, R.S. 1978a. Higher Energy Prices and the Supply of Natural Gas. *Energy Systems and Policy* 2 (2): 177–207.

Pindyck, R.S. 1978b. The Optimal Exploration and Production of Nonrenewable Resources. *Journal of Political Economy* 86 (5): 841–61.

Popp, David. 2001. Pollution Control Innovations and the Clean Air Act of 1990. NBER Working Paper No. 8593.

Popp, David. 2002. Induced Innovation and Energy Prices. *American Economic Review* 92 (1): 160–80.

Popp, D. 2003. Pollution Control Innovations and the Clean Air Act of 1990. *Journal of Policy Analysis and Management* 22 (4): 641–60.

Porter, E. 1990. Non-OPEC Supply and World Petroleum Markets: Past Forecasts, Recent Experience, and Future Prospects. Research Study Number 054. Washington, DC: American Petroleum Institute.

Porter, Michael E. 1991. America's Greening Strategy. *Scientific American* 264: 168.

Porter, Michael E. and C. van der Linde. 1995. Toward a New Conception of the Environment–Competitiveness Relationship. *Journal of Economic Perspectives* 9 (4): 97–118.

Portney, P.R. 1994. Does Environmental Policy Conflict with Economic Growth? *Resources* 115: 21–23.

Ray, S.C. and E. Desli. 1997. Productivity Growth, Technical Progress, and Efficiency Change in Industrialized Countries: Comment. *American Economic Review* 87 (5): 1033–9.

Ray, S.C. and K. Segerson. 1990. A Profit Function Approach to Measuring Productivity Growth: The Case of US Manufacturing. *Journal of Productivity Analysis* 2 (1): 39–52.

Ray, Subhash C. and Kankana Mukherjee. 1996. Decomposition of the Fisher Ideal Index of Productivity: A Nonparametric Dual Analysis of US Airlines Data. *Economic Journal* 106 (439): 1659–78.

Repetto, Robert. 1996. *Has Environmental Protection Really Reduced Productivity Growth: We Need Unbiased Measures.* Washington, DC: World Resources Institute.

Romer, Paul M. 1990. Endogenous Technological Change. *Journal of Political Economy* 98 (5, pt. 2): S71–S102.

Rose, A., T. Witt and W.C. Labys. 1986. The West Virginia Natural Gas Industry Model. *Modeling and Simulation* 16 (4): 1345–51.

Schmookler, Jacob. 1954. The Level of Inventive Activity, *Review of Economics and Statistics* 36 (2): 183–90.

Selley, R. 1998. *Elements of Petroleum Geology*, 2nd ed. Toronto: Academic Press.

Shephard, Ronald W. 1970. *Theory of Cost and Production Functions.* Princeton, NJ: Princeton University Press.

Simar, Leopold and Paul W. Wilson. 2000. Statistical Inference in Nonparametric Frontier Models: The State of the Art. *Journal of Productivity Analysis* 13 (1): 49–78.

Simpson, D.R. and R.L. Bradford, III. 1996. Taxing Variable Cost: Environmental Regulation as Industrial Policy. *Journal of Environmental Economics and Management* 30: 282–300.

Slade, M. 1982. Trends in Natural-Resource Commodity Prices: An Analysis of the Time Domain. *Journal of Environmental Economics and Management* 9 (2): 122–37.

Slade, M. 1988. Grade Selection Under Uncertainty: Least Cost Last and Other Anomalies. *Journal of Environmental Economics and Management* 15 (2): 189–205.

Smith, Adam. 1776. *The Wealth of Nations.* New York: Prometheus Books.

Smith, James L. and James L. Paddock. 1984. Regional Modelling of Oil Discovery and Production. *Energy Economics* 6 (1): 5–13.

Smulders, S. 2000. Economic Growth and Environmental Quality. In H. Folmer and L. Gabel (eds), *Principles of Environmental Economics*, Cheltenham, UK and Northampton, MA, USA: Edward Elgar.

Solow, R.M. 1957. Technical Progress and the Aggregate Production Function. *Review of Economics and Statistics* 39: 312–20.

Stern, D.I. 1998. Progress on the Environmental Kuznets Curve? *Environment and Development Economics* 3: 175–98.

Stern, D.I. 2004. The Rise and Fall of the Environmental Kuznets Curve. *World Development* 32: 1419–39.

Stiglitz, Joseph E. 1974. Growth with Exhaustible Natural Resources: Efficient and Optimal Growth Paths. *Review of Economic Studies:* 123–37.

Stijn, R., C.A.K. Lovell and G. Thijssen. 2002. Analysis of Environmental Efficiency Variation. *American Journal of Agricultural Economics* 84 (4): 1054–65.

Stokey, N.L. 1998. Are there Limits to Growth? *International Economic Review* 39: 1–31.

Stollery, K. 1985. Environmental Controls in Extractive Industries. *Land Economics* 61: 136–44.

Tisdell, Clem. 2001. Globalisation and Sustainability: Environmental Kuznets Curve and the WTO. *Ecological Economics* 39 (2): 185–96.

Tornqvist, L. 1936. The Bank of Finland's Consumption Price Index. *Bank of Finland Monthly Bulletin* 10: 1–8.

Trajtenberg, Manuel. 1990. A Penny for Your Quotes: Patent Citations and the Value of Innovations. *Rand Journal of Economics* 21 (1): 172–87.

Trefry, J.H., R.P. Trocine and D.B. Meyer. 1981. Tracing the Fate of Petroleum Drilling Fluids in the Northwest Gulf of Mexico. Oceans '81. 732–6. Available from Marine Technology Society, Washington, DC.

Tyteca, D. 1997. Linear Programming Models for the Measurement of Environmental Performance of Firms: Concepts and Empirical Results. *Journal of Productivity Analysis* 8 (2): 183–98.

Uhler, R.S. 1976. Costs and Supply in Petroleum Exploration: The Case of Alberta. *Canadian Journal of Economics* 19 (1): 72–90.

Ulph, Alistair. 1996. Environmental Policy and International Trade When Governments and Producers Act Strategically. *Journal of Environmental Economics and Management* 30 (3): 265–81.

US Department of Energy. Various years. *Cost and Indices for Domestic Oil and Gas Field Equipment and Production Operations.* Washington, DC: Energy Information Administration.

US Department of Energy. 1982. *Outer Continental Shelf Oil and Gas Supply Model.* Vols. 1–3, DOE/EIA-0372/1-3. Washington, DC: Energy Information Administration.

US Department of Energy. 1993. *Drilling Sideways: A Review of Horizontal Well Technology and Its Domestic Application.* DOE/EIA/TR-0565. Washington, DC: Energy Information Administration.

US Department of Energy. 1996. Environmental Benefits of Advanced Oil and Gas Exploration and Production Technology. Washington, DC.

US Department of Energy. 2002. Financial Reporting System (FRS) Database http://www.eia.doe.gov/emeu/finance/frsdata.html. US Department of Energy.

US Department of Energy. 2006. *Annual Energy Outlook 2006 with Projections to 2030*. DOE/EIA/0383. Washington, DC: Energy Information Administration.

US Department of the Interior. 1996. *Offshore Statistics*. Second Quarter. Minerals Management Services, Operations and Safety Management, Herndon, VA.

US Department of the Interior. 2006. *Technical Information Management System (TIMS) Database*, US Mineral Management Service. Washington, DC: US Department of Interior.

US Environmental Protection Agency. 1976. *Development Document for Interim Final Effluent Limitations Guidelines and New Source Performance Standards for the Oil and Gas Extraction Point Source Category*. Washington, DC: Environmental Protection Agency.

US Environmental Protection Agency. 1985. *Economic Impact Analysis of Proposed Effluent Limitations and Standards for the Offshore Oil and Gas Industry*. Washington, DC: Environmental Protection Agency.

US Environmental Protection Agency. 1993. *Economic Impact Analysis of Final Effluent Limitations Guidelines and Standards for the Offshore Oil and Gas Industry*. Washington, DC: Environmental Protection Agency.

US Environmental Protection Agency. 1999. *Environmental Assessment of Proposed Effluent Limitations Guidelines and Standards for Synthetic-Based Drilling Fluids and other Non-Aqueous Fluids in the Oil and Gas Extraction Point Source Category*. Washington, DC: Environmental Protection Agency.

US Minerals Management Service. 1999. http://www.gomr.mms.gov. Washington, DC: US Minerals Management Service.

US Minerals Management Service. 2002. Estimated Oil and Gas Reserves, Gulf of Mexico, December 31, 1999. OCS Report MMS 2002-007. Washington, DC.

US Minerals Management Service, 2000a. *Deepwater Gulf of Mexico: America's Emerging Frontier*. OCS Report 2000-022, Washington, DC.

US Minerals Management Service, 2000b. *Mineral Revenue Collections*. Washington, DC: U.S. Department of Interior.

US Minerals Management Service. 1996. Summary of the 1995 Assessment of Conventionally Recoverable Hydrocarbon Resources of the Gulf of Mexico and Atlantic Outer Continental Shelf. OCS Report, MMS 96-0047, Washington, DC.

van Biema, Michael. 1995. Studies in Technology and Productivity in the Service Sector, Columbia University Business School.

Walls, M.A. 1992. Modeling and Forecasting the Supply of Oil and Gas. *Resources and Energy* 14 (3): 287–309.

Walls, M.A. 1994. Using a 'Hybrid' Approach to Model Oil and Gas Supply: A Case Study of the Gulf of Mexico Outer Continental Shelf. *Land Economics* 70 (1): 1–19.

Wenders, T. 1975. Methods of Pollution Control and the Rate of Change in Pollution Abatement Technology. *Water Resources Research* 11, 393–6.

Windmeijer, F. 2005. A Finite Sample Correction for the Variance of Linear Efficient Two-Step GMM Estimators. *Journal of Econometrics* 126: 25–51.

World Commission on Environment and Development (WCED). 1987. *Our Common Future*. New York: Oxford University Press.

Xepapadeas, A. 2003. Economic Growth and Environment. In K.-G. Mäler and J. Vincent (eds), *Handbook of Environmental Economics*, Vol. 3. Amsterdam: North-Holland.

Xepapadeas, A. and A. de Zeeuw. 1999. Environmental Policy and Competitiveness: The Porter Hypothesis and the Composition of Capital. *Journal of Environmental Economics and Management* 37: 165–82.

Young, Alwyn. 1993. Invention and Bounded Learning by Doing. *Journal of Political Economy* 101 (3): 443–72

Zaim, O. and F. Taskin. 2000. A Kuznets Curve in Environmental Efficiency: An Application on OECD Countries. *Environmental and Resource Economics* 17: 21–36.

Zar, J.H. 1999. *Biostatistical Analysis*, 4th edn. New York: Prentice Hall.

Zerbe, R. 1970. Theoretical Efficiency in Pollution Control. *Western Economic Journal* 18: 364–76.

Zimmerman, Martin B. 1982. Learning Effects and the Commercialization of New Energy Technologies: The Case of Nuclear Power. *Bell Journal of Economics* 13 (2): 297–310.

Index